Women in Sports

Women in Sports

Breaking Barriers, Facing Obstacles

Volume 1: Sportswomen and Teams

Adrienne N. Milner and
Jomills Henry Braddock II, Editors

PRAEGER™

An Imprint of ABC-CLIO, LLC
Santa Barbara, California • Denver, Colorado

Library of Congress Cataloging-in-Publication Data

Names: Milner, Adrienne N., editor. | Braddock, Jomills H., editor.
Title: Women in Sports : Breaking Barriers, Facing Obstacles / Adrienne N. Milner and Jomills Henry Braddock II, Editors.
Description: Santa Barbara, California : Praeger, an imprint of ABC-CLIO, LLC, 2017. | Includes bibliographical references and index.
Identifiers: LCCN 2016058150 (print) | LCCN 2017000391 (ebook) | ISBN 9781440851247 (set : alk. paper) | ISBN 9781440851261 (volume 1) | ISBN 9781440851278 (volume 2) | ISBN 9781440851254 (ebook)
Subjects: LCSH: Sports for women—History. | Sports for women—Social aspects. | Sports—Sex differences. | Sexism in sports. | Women athletes—Social conditions.
Classification: LCC GV709 .W5745 2017 (print) | LCC GV709 (ebook) | DDC 796.082—dc23
LC record available at https://lccn.loc.gov/2016058150

ISBN: 978-1-4408-5124-7 (set)
978-1-4408-5126-1 (vol. 1)
978-1-4408-5127-8 (vol. 2)
EISBN: 978-1-4408-5125-4

21 20 19 18 17 1 2 3 4 5

This book is also available as an eBook.

Praeger
An Imprint of ABC-CLIO, LLC

ABC-CLIO, LLC
130 Cremona Drive, P.O. Box 1911
Santa Barbara, California 93116-1911
www.abc-clio.com

This book is printed on acid-free paper ∞
Manufactured in the United States of America

Contents

Introduction

While sports have traditionally been viewed as "male turf," with their growing participation and significant accomplishments, women have been breaking barriers in sports for decades. Each year women continue to surpass previously held expectations about their athletic capabilities and their potential to achieve greatness in sports. For instance, at the 2016 Rio Olympic Games, Katy Ledecky shattered her own world records to become the woman with the most individual swimming titles ever (four Olympic and seven World Aquatics Championships),[1] and Simone Biles set a new American record for Olympic gymnastics gold medals at a single Games and was chosen as the Team USA flag bearer for the closing ceremonies.[2] Also within the past year: Serena Williams's win at Wimbledon marked her record-tying 22nd Grand Slam singles title and 9th title since reaching the age of 30 (no other woman has won more than 3 since turning 30);[3] Lindsey Vonn recorded her 25th super giant slalom (Super G) downhill skiing victory, surpassing the record for most Super G wins for women or men;[4] the University of Connecticut women's basketball team earned their 4th straight and 11th total national championship, becoming the college basketball team (men's or women's) with the most undefeated seasons and most consecutive wins;[5] and Jessie Graff became the first woman to scale the 14.5-foot wall in the sex-integrated American Ninja Warrior competition, finishing 2nd in the Los Angeles City finals and 8th out of 90 competitors in the national finals Stage 1 competition and as one of only 17 who completed the full course.[6]

These accomplishments and other instances of women breaking barriers contribute to changing ideology about women's ability and place in sports. For instance, in 2014, Mo'ne Davis became the first African American girl to participate and the first girl to pitch a shutout in the Little League World Series.[7] Because of this achievement, sportswriter Nick Martin tributes Davis with changing the conversation surrounding women's capability to compete with men in Major League Baseball (MLB) and at the highest levels of sport from a question of "if" to "when."[8] MLB has not only recognized but capitalized on the inevitability of female athletes in the league through their partnership with Fox to develop the television show *Pitch*, which premiered in September 2016. *Pitch* stars Kylie Bunbury as Ginny Baker, a rookie pitcher and the first woman to play MLB, with writer/producer Dan Fogelman crediting Davis as part of his inspiration for Baker.[9] It can be argued that not only might the television program never have been created without Davis first breaking Little League barriers, but that the show would not have been as successful as it currently is (Rotten Tomatoes critic score 93 percent and audience score 83 percent)[10] without Davis to convince viewers that a black woman playing MLB is a realistic premise for a television drama rather than a ridiculous comedy.

Yet despite tangible and ideological progress, today, as in the past, women continue to face both systemic and individual access and treatment challenges as they pursue not only greatness but fairness and full inclusion in sports. Barriers to women's inclusion and equitable treatment in sports have large-scale social, legal, health, and economic consequences. For instance, sex segregation in sports prevents women from receiving financial compensation, media coverage, and decision-making power in athletic contexts on par with that of men. Furthermore, women in sports continue to be subjected to sex testing, critiqued on their physical appearance rather than their athletic performance, and perceived as biologically and athletically inferior to men.

This two-volume collection addresses women's sport involvement in contemporary society with a focus on issues of equity that women currently face. Through empirical and conceptual analyses of women's current experiences in a diverse array of sports roles—from recreational through professional levels as athletes, coaches, referees, and administrators—this collection provides a comprehensive overview of the "the state of women in sports." The volumes' overarching framework is sociological and examines the state of women in sports by questioning dominant ideology surrounding biological notions of athletic inferiority and interrogates social constructs that affect women's experiences in sports, such as race, socioeconomic status, sexual orientation, nationality, religion, and physical size. However, the contributions in this collection are also multidisciplinary and include research grounded in sociology, psychology, communications, gender studies, education, cultural studies, anthropology, and history to explore the diversity, challenges, and achievements of women in sports. The volumes' broad international scope also contextualizes women's experiences in sports within culturally diverse patriarchal societies. In addition, the collection highlights specific areas in need of social change on both the individual and structural levels in order to achieve significant progress toward gender equity and fairness in sports.

VOLUME I

The first volume of this book focuses on sportswomen and teams. Chapters 1 and 2 examine two different women's football leagues. In Chapter 1, Andrew Young argues for an alternative feminist reading of the Legends (formerly, Lingerie) Football League, similar to that of feminist pornography, as a space for disrupting, complicating, and challenging notions of hegemonic femininity rather than confirming them. In Chapter 2, J. A. Carter frames her own experience as a member of the Cincinnati Sizzle full-contact tackle football team (Women's Football Alliance) within the larger context of women's sports to show how women's participation is often limited through boundaries associated with spatial and material resources, cultural capital, and invisibility.

Chapters 3, 4, and 5 examine challenges that face several high-profile female athletes because of intersecting characteristics associated with sex, gender, race, socioeconomic status, and citizenship. In Chapter 3, Roxane Coche examines the case of elite French skater Sandrine Rangeon and her inability to secure an American visa because of the lack of opportunity for professional female athletes in the United States. In Chapter 4, Rachel Laws Myers, scholar, former National Collegiate Athletic Association (NCAA) basketball player, and 2016 Binghamton University Athletics Hall of Fame inductee, analyzes how gymnastic superstars Gabby Douglas and Simone Biles were portrayed within the context of this predominantly white sport by the media and public leading up to, during, and after the 2016 Rio de Janeiro Olympic Games. Examining the framework of another predominantly white sport, tennis, in Chapter 5, Scott Brooks argues that as a dominant black female athlete, Serena Williams is uniquely situated and both pays a price and maximizes her media marketability.

In connection with the marketability of women's sports, using interview data from recent sports competitions, Chapters 6 and 7 highlight sexist sports media coverage. In Chapter 6, Cheryl MacDonald, Courtney Szto, and Johnathon Edwards examine the 2015 Inaugural Women's Winter Classic Outdoor Ice Hockey Game in terms of how the event was perceived and (de)legitimized by athletes and the media. In Chapter 7, Kenneth Robinson analyzes the travails associated with the lack of media coverage of women's sports, using the history-making University of Connecticut women's basketball team as a case study.

In addition to sexism in the sports media, Chapters 8 and 9 emphasize issues of sexism in professional women's sports reflected in unequal rules and pay. In Chapter 8, NCAA soccer player Meredith Schertzinger examines the controversy surrounding the use of artificial turf at the 2015 Fédération Internationale de Football Association (FIFA) Women's World Cup as well as pay inequality in women's professional soccer. In Chapter 9, Diana Cohen analyzes interview data from athletes, coaches, race and team directors, and others involved in elite cycling to argue that women in the sport straddle a professional–amateur margin because of governing bodies, sponsors, and media that delegitimize female athletes through sexist rules and allocation of resources.

Chapters 10 and 11 examine issues of real and symbolic violence in sports. In Chapter 10, Helen Owton and Jacquelyn Allen-Collinson analyze the experience of one female athlete who was abused in childhood by her male coach and how their continued relationship developed into adulthood as athlete domestic violence. In Chapter 11, Angie Henderson, Christine Ingoldsby, and Mark Shuey use interview data to examine how women on different sports teams at the same university participated in symbolic, horizontal violence, where they acted aggressively toward their peers rather than their oppressors.

The final chapter of the first volume also examines women's participation on different sports teams competing for the same institution. In Chapter 12, Christina Sanchez Volatier et al. use quantitative data to show that gender diversity of U.S. Olympic teams between 1932 and 2012 was positively and significantly associated with success over time.

VOLUME 2

The second volume of this collection focuses on general social trends for women in sports. Chapters 1 and 2 highlight some of the correlates of women's participation and exclusion in certain sports. In Chapter 1, Ashley Mikulyuk and book editors Jomills Braddock and Adrienne Milner quantitatively examine the relationship between the gender-typed sports that girls play and relevant individual, interpersonal, and contextual factors that may be associated with their sport choices. In Chapter 2, Alicia Smith-Tran uses an intersectional approach to examine potential barriers that may prevent black girls and women from becoming recreational runners.

Chapters 3, 4, and 5 highlight challenges to women's participation in traditionally masculine sports. In Chapter 3, Heidi Nordstrom analyzes women's experiences as football officials using interview data from current and former female football referees. In Chapter 4, Vanessa Kauffman explores how women surfers employ both strategies of sexlessness and hyperfemininity to negotiate the gender order in surfing. In Chapter 5, scholar and current Norwegian boxing champion (women's lightweight) Anne Tjønndal examines how gender is related to boxers' and coaches' perceptions and expectations of coach leadership and coach–athlete relationships.

The ways in which gender expectations impact sport outcomes are also examined in Chapters 6 and 7 in terms of how stereotypes are associated with perceived size and strength of women and men. In Chapter 6, Brittany Harder and Felecia Theune use a sociohistorical perspective and apply theories of the body to explain how a gendered culture of sports has been produced through beliefs regarding bodily capabilities. In Chapter 7, weightlifter Nicola Medlin-Silver and colleagues Tanya Bunsell and Pete Lampard examine women's experiences in United Kingdom university strength and conditioning coaching courses that emphasize traditionally masculine traits, such as strength, muscularity, and power over others.

While Chapter 7 evaluates women's experiences in mixed-sex university scholastic courses, Chapters 8 and 9 examine how differently integrated university athletic programs relate to diverse outcomes for female athletes. In Chapter 8, Kristina Navarro, Michael Salm, and Jennifer Scherer analyze how female athletes may be disadvantaged by career-development programs that are not fully integrated into campus-wide initiatives. In Chapter 9, former rower and two-time NCAA national champion Kirsten Hextrum uses an intersectional approach to understand how sex-segregated and sex-integrated college athletic teams both preserve and disrupt patriarchy and racism in sports.

Chapters 10 and 11 also explore how patriarchy is preserved in sports contexts through examination of media coverage of women's professional soccer and basketball. In Chapter 10, Yann Descamps analyzes the announcing of soccer and basketball games on French television from 2011 to 2016 to investigate the evolving media construct of female athletes. In Chapter 11, Olesya Venger studies media reactions to the Qatari women's basketball team's and the Iranian women's soccer team's recent controversies involving the freedom to wear or refuse to wear headscarves during competition.

The final chapter of the volume also focuses on challenges that women face in legitimizing their place in sports by reducing emphasis on their appearance and gaining decision-making power. In Chapter 12, Robin Hardin et al. examine the experiences of early-career women working in collegiate athletics to gain an understanding of the obstacles women face in nonathlete roles in sports organizations.

NOTES

1. S. L. Price, "Iron Butterfly: Katie Ledecky Fulfills Her Fate with Five Medals at Rio Olympics," *Sports Illustrated*, last modified August 17, 2016, http://www.si.com/olympics/2016/08/17/katie-ledecky-rio-olympics-gold-medals-bruce-gemmell.

2. Jo-Ann Barnas, "Biles Becomes Most Decorated U.S. Gymnast with Olympic Vault Gold," *USA Gymnastics*, last modified August 14, 2016, https://usagym.org/pages/post.html?PostID=19143&prog=.

3. Carl Bialik, "Serena Williams Ties Graf's Majors Record Thanks to a Remarkable Run in Her 30s," *FiveThirtyEight*, last modified July 9, 2016, http://fivethirtyeight.com/features/serena-williams-wins-wimbledon-ties-grafs-majors-record-thanks-to-a-remarkable-run-in-her-30s/.

4. Nick Zaccardi, "Lindsey Vonn Grabs 70th World Cup Win with Weekend Sweep," *NBC*, last modified December 6, 2015, http://olympics.nbcsports.com/2015/12/06/lindsey-vonn-wins-lake-louise-super-g-mikaela-shiffrin-alpine-skiing-world-cup/.

5. Adam Berry, "Mo'ne Takes Home Breakthrough Athlete ESPY Award," *MLB*, last modified July 15, 2016, http://m.mlb.com/news/article/136879232/mone-davis-won-the-breakthrough-athlete-espy/.

6. Des Bieler, "Stunt Woman Jessie Graff Makes 'American Ninja' History," *The Washington Post*, last modified August 30, 2016, https://www.washingtonpost.com/news/early-lead/wp/2016/08/30/stunt-woman-jessie-graff-makes-american-ninja-history/.

7. John Altravilla, "UConn Women Ring Up 11th National Title; Defeat Syracuse, 82–51," *Hartford Courant*, last modified April 6, 2016, http://www.courant.com/sports/uconn-womens-basketball/hc-uconn-women-syracuse-0406-20160405-story.html.

8. Nick Martin, "In 'Pitch,' Fox Shows What It Would Be Like for Mo'ne Davis-Like Female to Play in MLB," *The Washington Post*, last modified May 20, 2016, https://www.washingtonpost.com/news/early-lead/wp/2016/05/17/in-pitch-fox-shows-what-it-would-be-like-for-mone-davis-like-female-to-play-in-mlb.

9. Kate Feldman, "See It: Fox Releases Promo Trailer for 'Pitch,' TV Show about First Female in MLB," *NY Daily News*, last modified May 17, 2016, http://www.nydailynews.com/entertainment/tv/fox-releases-promo-trailer-pitch-female-mlb-article-1.2639937.

10. "Pitch (2016–)," *Rotten Tomatoes*, last modified October 28, 2016, https://www.rottentomatoes.com/tv/pitch/.

1

Action, Impact, and Beauty: The Lingerie Football League and the Pornography of Sport

Andrew J. Young

The Lingerie Football League has become the Ultimate Fan-Driven Live Sports Phenomenon—Blending Action, Impact and Beauty.

—Lingerie Football League Mission Statement[1]

The Lingerie Football League (LFL) is one of the most controversial sports leagues in the United States. The LFL debuted in a single-game format in 2004 as an alternative to the National Football League's (NFL) Super Bowl halftime show and began full-season play in 2009. The league grew quickly between 2009 and 2012, with the 2011–2012 season featuring 12 teams from across the United States and one Canadian team. In 2012, the LFL announced it was delaying its upcoming season to focus on international expansion and to shift the U.S. season to the spring and summer months (initially, the league's championship game was played the same day as the NFL's Super Bowl in early February). In lieu of the U.S. 2012 season, the league scheduled three international All-Star games. The first, in Mexico City on Cinco de Mayo, hosted a live crowd of approximately 20,000 people, with many more tuning in to the pay-per-view broadcast online.[2] The LFL's growth has leveled off since 2012. Now called the Legends Football League after a 2013 rebranding, the LFL is still widely known by its former moniker. The 2016 season featured eight teams in the U.S. league as well as four- and five-team leagues in Canada and Australia, respectively.

Teams currently play a four-game season with additional conference and league championship games. While the games are quite different from traditional gridiron football, the field and game rules are similar to the (men's) Arena Football League (AFL). LFL women play full-contact football, though there is a significant difference in the uniforms when compared to men's professional leagues. Initially, the uniforms consisted of a bra and panties, a garter, helmet, and pads (shoulder, knee, and elbow). Since the 2013 rebranding, players no longer wear "lingerie"; they now wear "performance wear." However, with the exception of removing the garter, choker necklace, and frilly trimming from the uniforms, little seems to have changed besides the name.

The LFL has faced criticism from feminists and sports enthusiasts alike for exploiting women and being more "sexual entertainment" than serious sport. Critics cite the skimpy, lingerie-inspired uniforms players wear as evidence of the LFL's triviality, but concerns over player treatment and the LFL's limited allure also surface frequently. Though initially provided with a small stipend, players are no longer paid for their participation in the league, which many cite as evidence of the league's questionable status. Since its inception, the LFL has also courted and capitalized on a primary audience of (presumably heterosexual) men ages 18 and older by actively highlighting players' looks and physique in addition to their football skills. A cornerstone of LFL criticism has been the overt comparison to pornography, arguing that the LFL values women more for their sexy, feminine appearance than their athletic talents.

LFL players have mixed responses to the LFL's uniform requirements and the mix of sexualization and athleticism. "I came out here to pursue semipro athletics at all costs," said Rachel Carroccio, who was drafted to the San Diego Seduction. "I don't care if it's in lingerie. That's how much I would love to be able to make a living playing sports."[3] The league's founder and commissioner, Mitchell Mortaza, has been largely upfront about his intentions and the league's target audience—college-aged and older men. The LFL's initial tagline, "True Fantasy Football," does speak quite clearly to the sexualized nature of the game, yet it merits mentioning that the LFL attracts significantly more fans than any of the other professional women's football leagues and is arguably doing better in terms of male audience than many other women's leagues, regardless of sport.

Despite extensive criticism from outside the league, the LFL is certainly the most well-known and followed women's tackle football league in the United States. While admittedly an imperfect metric, a quick look at the Facebook pages of the most prominent nonlingerie women's football leagues puts the LFL's media dominance into perspective. The Women's Football Alliance, with teams that appear to be made up mostly of high school and college women and that play many of their games in high school football stadiums, had 10,409 "likes" in September 2016.[4] The Independent Women's Football League (IWFL), which also plays many of its games in high school stadiums, had 9,419 "likes," and the small-market U.S. Women's Football League had 1,333.[5] In contrast, the Legends Football League's page had 727,049 "likes" in September 2016. Though it is difficult to say what, if anything, to make of the difference of 1,000 "likes" between the Independent Women's Football

League and the Women's Football Alliance, the more than 700,000 "likes" that separate the LFL from the other leagues says much about the relative visibility and popularity of the LFL in mainstream popular culture. Game videos posted to YouTube by the LFL and the IWFL tell a similar story. The 2015 IWFL Championship game video (one of the most popular posted by the group) has been viewed 15,259 times as of September 2016.[6] In comparison, a video of the first quarter of the 2015 Legends Cup game has 27,402 views and is one of the least popular posted of the league.

LFL promotional materials and spokespeople have consistently highlighted the focus on quality football in addition to the physical appearance of the players. Writing about the 2012 All-Star game in Mexico City, LFL staff writer Patrick Murphy claimed in 2012:

> Interest in the LFL has never been higher. The same goes with the level of play. As the game has grown over the last few years, so has the talent, athleticism, commitment, football IQ and skill. This group of athletes will put on what may be the greatest display of women's football to date. Read that last line again. Who could have possibly thought this would be the case? LFL Commissioner and founder Mitchell Mortaza has built a spectacular brand of football. League staff, coaches and especially players have combined to create a fantastic game that has turned the pithy judgments into tired conversation. It is too insulting NOT to talk about the skills of the players and the work that goes into what the world will see tonight. Even Mortaza may be surprised at the beast he created.[7]

LFL may have initially been marketed (and perhaps still is in league owner Mortaza's mind) to heterosexual men, but more and more women are watching televised sports. In 2014, 45 percent of National Football League viewers were women,[8] and straight men are not the only fans of lingerie football.

What is going on here? How is it that the premier women's football league in the country is the same league that rates potential players on how good they look in their underwear as well as whether or not they can catch a football? Sports journalism and academic scholarship alike has largely dismissed the Lingerie Football League as "just porn" despite the transgressive potential of women playing football.[9] Recently, however, sports journalists (and a small handful of academics) have been taking the LFL and its players more seriously. In this paper, I argue that all professional sports, but especially women's sports and the Lingerie Football League, function as desire industries[10] in mainstream U.S. culture. This positions women's sport alongside pornography and other sex work as spaces where women's bodies are evaluated on their attractiveness, (hetero)sexual availability, and femininity, and, subsequently, valued based on their adherence to normative expectations in these areas. By taking seriously the agency of LFL players, their motivations for playing, and their experiences in the league, I contend that the LFL opens up possibilities similar to those of feminist pornography to disrupt, complicate, and challenge notions of hegemonic femininity, even while the Lingerie Football League appears to reproduce these tropes. Ultimately, I argue here *for* a feminist reading of the Lingerie Football League and a reevaluation of its potential as a space to expose an often difficult-to-reach audience to feminist ideals.

Rather than trying to determine whether or not the LFL or women's sport is "really" porn, I believe it is more productive to think of both sport and porn as "desire industries." Siobhan Brooks defines "desire industries" as "venues that produce sexual images and erotic fantasies for consumption, and are influenced by movies, television, and magazines regarding the creation of notions of attractiveness."[11] By conceptualizing sport and porn—and by extension the Lingerie Football League—as desire industries, we can simultaneously engage with the sexualized gaze that structures both while allowing for differences between them.

Desire and eroticism have a long history in sports, dating back to the ancient Greeks and their adoration of the athletic body.[12] Erotic elements in sport were feared and denounced in the Victorian era and "critics of sports have deplored their sensuality and their ability to entice, excite, and sexually arouse participants and spectators alike."[13] The use of athletes in advertisements and the growing trend of fit bodies as sexy bodies[14] showcases the erotic element of sport. Furthermore, though Brooks's original definition of a desire industry cites specifically *erotic* fantasies, we cannot ignore the concerted attempt of professional sports organizations to sell their fans on a more general fantasy—a place where the normal rules of the world don't apply, where gladiators do battle and seek honor and glory—a reality removed from the day-to-day alienation and misery of our contemporary world.

WATCHING SPORTS: PLEASURE IN THE LOOKING

It is true that the erotic element in sport is not always as obvious or central as the erotic element of pornography, where eroticism is always front and center. But this difference is a matter of degree rather than of kind. In his chapter "Why We Watch and Enjoy Mediated [Televised] Sports," Arthur Raney discusses "factors that motivate the use and viewing of mediated sports,"[15] drawing on numerous studies in psychology and sociology around sport spectatorship and fandom. Raney suggests three broad motivations for watching sports: emotional, behavioral, and social. Most important here are the emotional motivations, which Raney sees as the most prominent of the three. He argues that "people view mediated sports because they expect positive emotional impacts from their viewing,"[16] and multiple "studies have demonstrated that sports can lead to increased arousal."[17] Though the arousal of sports is not necessarily sexual, it certainly stems from desire—a desire for your team to win, a desire to be entertained, a desire to feel part of something larger than oneself. The physical embodiment of this arousal is not so different from the sexual arousal of pornography. When I watch a close game, especially if one of my favorite teams is involved and the stakes are high, my heart races, my palms sweat, and my skin feels electrified. If I am physically present in the stands or watching with a large group of people (as opposed to watching alone on my couch), the physical excitement is even more heightened, drawing off the collective arousal of the crowd around me. These feelings are not so different from the feeling of a racing heart, heavy breathing, and the heightened sensitivity of my skin when I watch porn or a steamy sex scene in a film. Commentators and women's sports leagues often capitalize on this similarity to draw in viewers who may be otherwise reticent to watch women's sports. The Women's Tennis Association launched the Strong Is Beautiful campaign in 2012, featuring many of the association's top stars playing tennis in formal gowns and full makeup amid swaths of glitter and colored fog. And, of course, the LFL provides its fans with full-contact tackle football and skimpy "performance wear" uniforms.

The relationship between sports and sex is not limited to women's sport. Nick Trujillo's analysis of the 1993–1994 *Monday Night Football* season found significant evidence of sexualized pleasure in NFL broadcasters' commentary and the audiovisual production of the men's games.[18] Additionally, athletes from various men's professional leagues also utilize sex, or at least sensuality, to market and celebrate their athleticism. *ESPN Magazine*'s Body Issue consistently photographs top athletes (men and women) naked while they play and labels them with clear double entendre as "bodies we want." While the focus is on their athletic accomplishments and hard work, these are funneled through striking visuals of muscular, sexually attractive bodies. Male athletes also consistently grace the covers of popular men's magazines, such as *GQ*, *Esquire*, and *Men's Health*, complete with workout tips for "sexy abs" and "glutes that will make her want to reach out and touch." Soccer player David Beckham was even crowned *People* magazine's "Sexiest Man Alive" in 2015. Finally, the link between watching sports and sexual arousal was made explicit with a 2016 Super Bowl commercial featuring "Super Bowl babies," people conceived the night of the NFL's annual championship game in the winning city. While it is true that men are less actively sexualized by color commentators than women during athletic play (something that we should not lose sight of), the suggestion that men who play sports are not sexualized by spectators on and off the field relies on outdated ideas of who watches sports. Sports fandom is no longer the exclusive domain of heterosexual men (if it ever was). Increasingly, straight women and lesbian, gay, bisexual, and transgender (LGBT) people of all genders are being recognized by professional leagues as important fan bases.

As we have seen, watching sporting events has long been considered pleasurable for the spectator, and there is a considerable body of literature in the sociology of sport dedicated to understanding why watching sports is so enjoyable. Much of this research builds on the understandings of scopophilia, or the pleasure of looking, as taken up in film theory and cinema studies. Building on the work of psychoanalyst Jacques Lacan and feminist film theorist Laura Mulvey, sport sociologists have focused on the two categories of scopophilia: voyeurism and fetishism. For both voyeurism and fetishism, the viewer derives pleasure from the object being looked at. Voyeurism is a particularly illicit form of looking, with pleasure coming from not only the object being looked at but also the fact that one is looking without permission. Fetishism, in contrast, is the pleasure in looking at a spectacle, "an object of frank, even invited, viewing pleasure."[19] Sports spectating draws strongly on both fetishism and voyeurism.

According to Margaret Carlisle Duncan and Barry Brummett, "televised sport creates fetishes by commodifying athletes and their actions, that is, by treating the material of sports as goods to be closely examined, appraised, and assessed."[20] Athletes are looked at intently as the "objects" of the game. Their performance is broken down into statistics, looked at again through instant replays, and literally turned into commodities by printing their likenesses on everything from T-shirts to cereal boxes to posters. Fetishizing is most evident in televised or recorded sports, but live spectating retains this fetishistic aspect as well. Arena and stadium technology now provides spectators with many of the same experiences as watching at home—instant replay, close-up views of particular athletes and plays—with the added experience of having the live athletes present in front of you. Trujillo's analysis of *Monday Night Football* cites multiple examples of fetishism as broadcasters described players as "big hunks of men" and described arm and leg muscles in detail.[21] Since spectators are explicitly invited to look at athletes, most of the pleasure of looking in sport is fetishistic in nature. However, there is still ample opportunity for voyeurism.

Since televised sports are "live" programs without scripts, there are a number of "unexpected opportunities for uninvited, illicit, and therefore voyeuristic looking."[22] When unexpected events occur—such as injuries, coaches yelling curse words on camera, and uniform mishaps (such as a swimmer losing his swim trunks in the pool)—there is a break in the fetishistic looking that opens up a space for voyeurism. For me, televised sports seem most voyeuristic when athletes are injured, with close-ups of athletes' faces contorted in pain and battered by emotions of fear, anger, and frustration. Duncan and

Brummett argue that sexually explicit voyeurism in sport is avoided due to FCC regulations but is always possible "and may be seen in camera angles and shots that are aimed at women's cleavages and buttocks,"[23] though any time "looking at sports is sexual, it is always illicit and therefore voyeuristic."[24] Since Duncan and Brummett are concerned largely with mainstream sports viewing, I will concede that they are mostly correct in their assertion that sexual looking in sports is largely discouraged when we are talking about men's sports, though Trujillo argues that sexual voyeurism is indeed present. He makes note of broadcasters' frequent use of sexualized language, such as "tight end," "penetration," and "scoring"[25]—all words linked in our cultural lexicon to sexual activity. Voyeurism is also present for audiences attracted to whichever sex is playing. Gay sports bars offer the usual array of football, basketball, baseball, rugby, and others depending on the season along with liberal commentary on players' looks, musculature, and sexual appeal. Ultimate Fighting Championship/Mixed Martial Arts matches are popular in many gay bars (sport focused or otherwise) for their not-so-subtle homoeroticism of sweaty, half-naked men rolling around a ring clutching one another. Voyeurism, by definition, is based on the looker taking an uninvited look, so even when sports are not necessarily marketed in explicitly sexual terms, the possibility of sexualization is always present.

Fetishism and voyeurism, while clearly present in sport, are more commonly associated with pornography and the sexual. There are entire genres of porn devoted to voyeurism (or at least simulated voyeurism) as well as a variety of fetishistic genres focused on the spectacle of invited looking. Feminist critiques of pornography have often centered on the objectification of women by the male gaze that takes place through fetishistic and voyeuristic looking.[26] Feminist critiques of women's sport have also followed similar lines, arguing that the way female athletes are sexualized in sport invites the male gaze similarly to porn.[27] Although there are many ways sport and pornography are different, the basic scopophilic form of sport shares a number of key features with pornography, particularly when we look at women's sports. The Lingerie Football League is much more explicit about its fetishistic and voyeuristic aspects than most other women's sporting events, which is perhaps why it has drawn such outrage from feminists and sports writers alike. However, it is *because* the Lingerie Football League sits at the crossroads between sport and pornography that it is an important cultural site for us to take seriously to better understand how the sexualization of female bodies is engaged and resisted.

Judith Butler argues for the subversive power of parody as a form of resistance to binary gender divisions that arise from heteronormativity.[28] Butler contends that the reiteration of dominant gender norms in non-normative spaces can become a site for resistance to such norms. She argues that "the replication of heterosexual constructs in non-heterosexual frames brings into relief the utterly constructed status of the so-called heterosexual original. Thus, gay is to straight *not* as copy is to original, but, rather, as copy is to copy. The parodic repetition of 'the original,' . . . reveals the original to be nothing other than a parody of the *idea* of the natural and the original."[29] For example, by mapping heterosexual gender norms onto gay relationships, the incongruence produces a possibility to see not only the gay relationship as imitative but also the contingency of straight relationships that are often seen as "natural." For Butler, drag performance is the quintessential example of gender parody and performance. In drag "we see sex and gender denaturalized by means of a performance which avows their distinctness and dramatizes the cultural mechanism of their fabricated unity. The notion of gender parody defended here does not assume there is an original which such parodic identities imitate. Indeed, the parody is *of* the very notion of an original."[30] Because the sex and performed gender of a drag queen or king are distinctly disconnected from one another, it becomes easier to see how sex and gender are contingently connected to one another "in real life"—that gender is a performance at all times for everyone, not just in the context of drag.

Because desire industries are necessarily built on fantasy and the performance of fantasy, they provide an entry point into exploring the performativity of desire and of the "originals" that they copy. The Lingerie Football League, with its unique position at the intersection of sport and porn, allows us to see the contingency of both cultural forms. The mismatches that occur as we map porn on to sport and sport on to porn in the Lingerie Football League push us to see not only the artifice at work in the LFL but also the constructed fantasy of both pornography and sport as cultural objects. Most importantly, by laying bare the performative, contingent structures of sport and pornography, we open up the possibility to imagine these structures differently, thus creating space for resistance to hegemonic understandings of female attractiveness, (hetero)sexuality, and femininity at work in the LFL.

FEMINISM AND PORNOGRAPHY

The initial feminist response to pornography as a cultural phenomenon was almost exclusively negative and focused on the exploitation of women by male producers and viewers. "By the late 1970s slogans like 'pornography is the theory, rape is the practice', had become articles of radical feminist faith."[31] The 1980s saw a diversification of feminist reactions to porn, resulting in the so-called "sex wars" of the 1980s, which pitted the antiporn feminists against more "sex-positive" feminists who attempted to celebrate female sexual desire and accept that women, not just men, may find sexual gratification in pornography.[32] The often extreme views of antiporn feminists caused them to quickly lose standing in the eyes of many, women and men, and by the late 1980s such views were largely dismissed as out of touch and limiting to women's sexuality. Porn was officially "in" "insofar as talking about, referring to or borrowing from its codes and conventions had lost much of its transgressive, taboo quality and became acceptable, even fashionable."[33] The 1990s saw the rise of a new feminist rhetoric to reflect this. Liking pornography was now seen by many prominent feminist writers as sexually empowering for women.

The intrusion of pornography into the larger culture is part of what Brian McNair calls the "pornographication of the mainstream"[34] and Feona Attwood refers to as the "mainstreaming of sex."[35] The rise in "porno-chic" has resulted in what Ariel Levy has derided as "raunch culture"[36] and includes "the representation of porn in non-pornographic art and culture; the pastiche and parody of, the homage to and investigation of porn; the postmodern transformation of porn into mainstream cultural artifact for a variety of purposes including . . . advertising, art, comedy, and education."[37] Recently, the sexualization of culture has become a hot topic within feminism and cultural studies and has prompted a rethinking of the 1990s glorification of porno-chic as female empowerment. "Rosalind Gill has developed this argument, noting that the contemporary sexing up of culture involves a 'deliberate *re-sexualisation and re-commodification* of bodies' which, though incorporating depictions of women as knowing, active and desiring', only works to instate a feminine 'self-policing, narcissistic gaze.'"[38] In other works, Gill has strongly criticized scholars working on the sexualization of culture for ignoring the unequal ways in which different identities are sexualized in culture. In "so much of the discussion about 'sexualization,'" Gill writes, "there is scant consideration of power,"[39] or the ways in which histories of power and social inequality have been reinscribed in contemporary discourses of sexualization.

Bobbi Knapp, in her analysis of "messages about femininity" in media coverage of the Lingerie Football League, identifies five major themes: "(1) just another form of soft porn, (2) real women play lingerie football, (3) men take care of business, (4) promoting white-defined beauty, and (5) narratives of empowerment" and argues that "dominant notions of gender were supported through each of these themes."[40] In her article, Knapp spends nearly three whole pages with multiple subheadings on the LFL as "just another form of soft porn" while each of the other four themes is covered in a page or less, each in a single block. Having explicitly identified the "LFL as soft-core porn" as the dominant theme in mainstream media coverage, she uses this as evidence to conclude that any possible subversion of traditional femininity is lost in the overall sexualization of the players by the league.[41] Earlier in the article, Knapp cites Jane Caputi's definition of pornography as "material developed around exploitation, objectification, and a denigration of women"[42] and adds that pornography thus "works to reinforce the current gender hierarchy."[43] Working with an understanding of pornography by definition as exploitive, objectifying, and denigrating to women preemptively closes off any potential for transgression or resistance. By subsequently linking the LFL to pornography as defined by Caputi, Knapp also forecloses any possibility for resistance to traditional notions of femininity in the LFL. Working under such definitional constraints, how could Knapp *not* find the LFL lacking in feminist possibilities?

All too often the word "pornography" is used as an epithet to categorize something as beyond the pale, irredeemably immoral, and obscene.[44] Calling something pornographic is used as a moral trump card that shuts down debate and places the other side irrevocably in the wrong, much like calling someone a racist or a fascist. "As George Ritzer . . . puts it, pornography stands for the obscenity of a consumption that lacks substantive content. In other words, pornography represents the wasteful, greedy, and immoral consumption of 'nothing.'"[45] Linda Williams, however, disagrees with the blanket disregard of pornography as both a social product and as a theoretical tool. She responds to Ritzer's criticism, stating, "while there is a pornograph*ic* nature of American consumption practices, pornography—as in moving images of explicit sex—is not in itself pornograph*ic*. Pornography deserves a better, more precise, critique than that leveled against the generic, uprooted, dehumanized, immoral, nothingness of McDonald's or McMansions."[46] So, I argue, does the Lingerie Football League.

We must acknowledge, though, that the possibilities for resistance are always mitigated or complicated by the women's intersecting identities, particularly players' race and sexuality. In her exploration of racism in strip clubs, another desire industry, Siobhan Brooks puts forth the concept of erotic capital as a way of understanding how power and privilege is distributed in desire industries. She defines erotic capital as "a form of capital that is related across bodies, and what gives bodies value based on a socially constructed ideal model of beauty/attractiveness held by the dominant culture, that is recognized and accepted by the general public."[47] In her study of strip clubs, Brooks found that "low erotic value [due to low erotic capital] is tied to structural racism, sexism, and classism,"[48] putting women of color and low-income women at a disadvantage when negotiating employment terms as well as curtailing possibilities for resistance to existing structures of power in the industry. We could expect to find similar devaluation of women of color compared to white women in the LFL tied to similar distributions of erotic capital, since the LFL and these other desire industries are drawing on the same ideal models of beauty and attractiveness.

The LFL's position as sexualized sport also pulls on cultural narratives about raced bodies and a history of sport as racist, further complicating the ability of women of color to participate in, much less resist dominant notions of, femininity and beauty. Though all athletic bodies in televised sports are commodified and consumed to some extent, black athletic bodies have a long history of being discursively colonized by white team owners, coaches, and viewers.[49] This history of racism in sport intersects with and is compounded by historical narratives about black female bodies, particularly narratives that paint black women as "overly aggressive" and "unfeminine" women who "emasculate their lovers and husbands."[50] Narratives of aggression and unfeminine behavior are then compounded by black women playing football, a particularly masculine sport, which exacerbates tropes of black women as masculine and emasculating. At the same time, however, the sexualized trappings of Lingerie Football tap into cultural narratives about black female bodies being sexually available, a narrative that has been used frequently to justify the sexual assault and rape of black women for centuries.[51] While white women may be sexualized, their whiteness protects them by allowing them to retain the privilege of consent, which black women are not granted because their blackness is perceived as indicating a constant, undiscerning sexual availability.[52] The confluence of all of these conflicting cultural narratives about black women, and specifically black female athletes, heightened by the Lingerie Football League's positioning as a desire industry at the crossroads of sport and pornography, produces a sexual field littered with land mines for black women to traverse. Having to manage and navigate so many strongly contradictory narratives about the self does not preclude black women in the LFL from resisting these narratives or performing their role in the league as a parody of these narratives, but it does considerably complicate their ability to perform parody and have it be recognized as such. At this point, not enough systematic empirical evidence has been gathered to fully support this reading of women of color in the LFL. However, Anastasiya Khomutova and Alexander Channon, in their analysis of the 2013 LFL season, did find evidence of racial stacking, similar to other football leagues, which suggests that the LFL is not immune to racialized understandings of athleticism.[53]

Heterosexuality serves as a central characteristic of hegemonic femininity, which complicates the ability of lesbian and queer women to engage in acts of resistance. The LFL draws on the cultural imperative in various ways. Sexual availability is evident in many of the promotional images for the league. Not only are the players shown almost exclusively in their uniforms of lingerie/performance wear bras and briefs, they are often posed in ways reminiscent of soft-core pornography and "lad mags," such as *Maxim* and *FHM*. Oftentimes players are pictured in small groups, either facing one another or touching one another on the shoulders, arms, or waist in poses that evoke the "hot lesbian" aesthetic currently popular in mainstream advertising. Though posing the women in ways that invoke lesbianism may be a counterintuitive way of reinforcing the supposed heterosexuality of their players, it makes sense in the prevailing cultural narratives at work in advertisements where "male fantasy lesbians" are pictured using conventional forms of female beauty, rather than the more masculine butch stylings often associated with lesbians. "The packaging of 'lesbians' within conventional norms of heterosexual female attractiveness is one way in which the figure appears to be constructed primarily for the straight male gaze. Commercial Closet [an organization that monitors gay-themed advertisements] lists an entire category of ads centered on 'male fantasy lesbians,'" or 'lesbians' that have less to do with women who are attracted to other women than with male-constructed images of girl-on-girl actions for male sexual arousal.[54]

The LFL's use of allusion to other cultural examples of "male fantasy lesbians" is an excellent example of what Diamond has called "hetero flexibility" to denote heterosexual women "experimenting" sexually with other women.[55] It presents girl-on-girl action as exciting, fun, but, crucially, as entirely unthreatening to heterosexuality.[56] Through linkage to wider cultural discourses of women's sexual empowerment (and subsequent ability to "experiment" with lesbianism without fear of marginalization), the influence of porno-chic and pornographic narratives, and other indicators of heterosexuality (large breasts, lingerie, long hair, and makeup), the Lingerie Football League effectively uses hints of female homosexuality to more strongly reinscribe the women's bodies with heterosexual availability.

In addition to signaling sexual availability to (male) spectators and fans, the use of overt heterosexuality represents an attempt to downplay the cultural association between women athletes and lesbianism. In contemporary Western culture, overt femininity is equated with heterosexuality. As Molly George notes, "an emphasis on a female athlete's appearance is a not so subtle way of critiquing her sexual orientation."[57] The overemphasis on heteronormative sexual desirability may be understood as minimizing lesbian associations in women's sport. By marginalizing, or simply erasing or ignoring, lesbian identities, the league makes it more difficult for lesbian and queer women to remain visible and perform their gender and sexuality in ways that invoke parodic resistance.

THE LINGERIE FOOTBALL LEAGUE: NOT QUITE FEMINIST PORN

Of course, the LFL, like any entity in an unequal system, has its flaws. Though these flaws do not foreclose the possibility of resistance in the LFL any more than in pornography, sport, or any other desire industry, such issues must be addressed. LFL owner Mitch Mortaza consistently acknowledges the explicit sexualized marketing of players and the league and "apologizes for none of this. 'We're never going to lose the marketable athlete,' Mortaza told [*Grantland* writer Conn]. 'That's not going to change. The Danica Patrick, the

Anna Kournikova, the Gabby Reece—that's our brand.'"[58] Sports journalists initially dismissed the LFL for just this reason, assuming it would simply be models in lingerie running around with footballs, as have academics. To date, only three articles have been published in academic journals about the LFL,[59] and all three are highly critical of the sexualized portrayal of the players. Knapp[60] and Weaving[61] see little to no value in the league and actively call for its dissolution, refusing to see any feminist potential in women playing football in lingerie. Weaving argues, the LFL "makes a mockery out of women playing football by regulating that players wear skimpy uniforms,"[62] and a "false sense of sexual empowerment entangles women LFL players who may believe they are 'doing it for themselves', but in actuality are playing into stereotypical heterosexual male sexual fantasies."[63] Knapp, as mentioned earlier, equates the league to pornography and thereby places it outside the realm of redemption or resistance.[64] Knapp argues, "Although women on the gridiron have the potential to push the boundaries of traditional femininity, the Lingerie Football League and its representations thwart any such subversion."[65] Empirical evidence from the 2013 LFL season supports feminist claims of sexualization. Khomutova and Channon analyzed the full 2013 LFL season and found "the visual content clearly and overtly foregrounded sexual imagery in a number of ways, such that our [qualitative] findings here principally indicated an overt sexualization of the players."[66] However, unlike Knapp and Weaving, Khomutova and Channon argue that sexualization does not preclude resistance. They conclude, "Our analysis of the 2013 LFL US season produced findings which can be interpreted as evidence of the continuation of heteronormative gender construction and the centering of male privilege in sport, yet also of the partial disruption of how such privileges are typically constructed,"[67] and I am inclined to agree with them.

As Judith Butler argues, drawing on Foucault, the possibility of resistance is present wherever there is power. This potential for resistance is certainly present in the Legends, *née* Lingerie, Football League. While much remains the same in the league, changing the league's tagline from "True Fantasy Football" to "Women of the Gridiron" and removing the word "lingerie" from the league name provides just enough difference in this reiteration of the league to provide a space for powerful resistance and critique. However, the league's rebranding is complicated and not simply a straightforward move away from sexualization. League founder and commissioner Mortaza has commented on the rebranding, saying, "While the Lingerie Football League name has drawn great media attention allowing us to showcase the sport to millions, we have now reached a crossroad of gaining credibility as a sport or continuing to be viewed as a gimmick . . . In order to reach the next milestone, we feel the focus has to be the sport and our amazing athletes."[68] Mortaza acknowledges criticisms of the LFL as simply "soft porn" and questions about the LFL as a legitimate sports league. Implicit in his comments about "legitimacy" and "amazing athletes," as well as in the conspicuous dropping of the overtly sexualizing language of "lingerie" and "true fantasy football" is a move away from the sexualization of players toward a more enlightened, sport-focused form of women's tackle football.

However, tied up with all of this is the frank recognition of rebranding as a necessary step to continue to grow the league as a business, to expand to other markets, to build revenue, and, ultimately, to increase the profitability of the league. It seems fairly clear that the impetus behind the rebranding was economic in nature, rather than out of concern for players' subjectivities. Indeed, from the beginning, the LFL faced criticism from journalists that players were being treated unethically, concerns that far outweighed qualms about lingerie uniforms. Writing for ESPN.com's *Page 2*, Mary Buckheit argued, "To me eight months on the job without a contract undermines the league's straight-faced plea for legitimacy more than lacy garters."[69] Grantland.com writer Jordan Ritter Conn seconds this, noting, "Few [players] complain about the lingerie. They're bothered by what their uniforms seem to represent: that they are replaceable bodies, each no more valuable than the last."[70] This disposability is most evident when looking at play compensation, or lack thereof. Initially, LFL players were paid based on revenue and profit,[71] similarly to other professional women's leagues.[72] However, after the 2012 season, player remuneration was eliminated and the LFL was reorganized into an "amateur" league.[73] Owner Mortaza has repeatedly stated that paying players would mean the end of the league itself due to financial instability,[74] though it remains unclear how accurate this claim is. Currently, LFL players receive neither compensation nor health insurance and pay a $45 registration fee at the beginning of each season.[75]

Rebranding also moves the sexualization of players under the radar to some extent. Instead of lingerie, uniforms are now "performance wear," though little has changed in the cut or styles of the clothing. Safety equipment has not changed, and the style of merchandise available in the league's online shop remains the same. From this perspective, only the league's name has changed, and there may be serious implications for the resistance possible under the new brand. "True fantasy football" is much easier to peg as outrageous and sexualizing than "women of the gridiron." To an extent, "true fantasy football" is a visible parody of itself, much easier to mark as a "copy of a copy," while "women of the gridiron" is relatively neutral and might even be considered empowering for women. And perhaps it is. But the new tagline is merely a stand-in for the entire rebranded league, "performance wear" and all, which may have changed just enough to be seen as legitimate, so that resistance becomes more difficult to enact. It remains to be seen what the effect of the rebranding will be on the league long term, both financially and in terms of how players are perceived, but regardless of the future outcome, there is always the possibility of resistance.

LINGERIE FOOTBALL: TRULY TRANSGRESSIVE OR MORE OF THE SAME?

So where does all this leave us? Is the Lingerie Football League a site for the transgression of dominant notions of gender and sexuality, or does it simply compound the worst aspects of sexism, racism, and heterosexism found in both sport and pornography? One answer might be found in pornography. Feminist-minded pornographers are addressing similar questions in pornography and have turned to a standard of "ethical pornography." "The real issue for feminists should not be trying to determine whether porn is degrading to women, because as sex educator and film director Tristan Taormino says, 'there is no monolithic one thing called porn with a capital P.' The more important issue, she says, is whether pornography is made ethically."[76] A number of feminist-identified women in pornography have moved away from trying to answer, definitively, the question of whether porn is a site of gender resistance for women or a site of gender oppression. What matters, they argue, is whether porn has been produced ethically—Are the actors given a say in what acts will be performed? Are there safe working conditions? Do the actors and production staff have health care? and so on. This discussion of ethical pornography has surfaced as similar conversations about ethics are beginning to gain steam in the sports world around player safety (NFL and the National Hockey League [NHL]), doping and drug testing (Major League Baseball [MLB], the Olympics, and cycling), and fines and other penalties for possible hate speech, such as using the word "fag" (National Basketball Association [NBA]). To be sure, part of a conversation about ethics and ethical treatment of players in the Lingerie Football League should concern the ability of the players to represent themselves as they choose to some extent, which would open additional opportunities to resist hegemonic ideals of gender and sexuality while still playing lingerie football.

"Scholars examining women's experiences in sport have noted that contact sports such as ice hockey, rugby, and football have the potential to transgress dominant notions of femininity . . . [Knapp] would argue that the transgressive potential of women playing football is undermined when said women play in next to nothing with severely modified field, rules, and equipment."[77] As I have argued throughout, it is not wise to simply dismiss the Lingerie Football League on the basis that women are playing football in underwear-like uniforms. The 2016 Summer Olympics fans saw many women athletes in beach volleyball, track and field, and gymnastics wearing tight and/or skimpy uniforms with little to no public outcry that such uniforms undermine the athleticism or transgressive potential of female athletes. To summarily dismiss the LFL is to also deny the women who play in the league any agency over their actions and understanding of what they do with and to gender when they play. Many players have spoken about their choice to play in the LFL despite less than ideal conditions in uniforms or labor relations. Nikki Johnson, a former player with the Las Vegas Sin, says, "Sometimes, when you're a female athlete, you have to suck it up. . . .To me it felt like this [the LFL] is the highest level of competition if you're a female football player. So if I want to keep playing, this is where I need to do it."[78] Tiffani Hardin agrees; she played for the Orlando Fantasy, saying of her experience, "I thought I was one in a million being pretty and athletic. The first time I played with the LFL, I got knocked on my ass. You can say what you want about the uniforms, but these women are real athletes and they're fierce."[79] Many women in the LFL are former National Collegiate Athletic Association (NCAA) Division I athletes. They are smart and used to a high level of competition. They are also accustomed to playing in front of crowds larger than those drawn by the more traditional women's professional football leagues.[80] Contrary to assumptions made by Weaving and others, these women take their sport seriously, spending multiple days a week at practice and watching game film.[81] Many women drive hours to practices and games[82] and do so "for the love of the game," since they aren't paid for their time. Players also don't simply accept everything the league tells them. There are currently two lawsuits pending against the LFL arguing that players are employees rather than independent contractors and so should be paid in accordance with minimum wage laws and provided health insurance.[83] These suits are similar to others brought against the NCAA and the NFL in recent years and may force the LFL to compensate players in the future and for back wages.

There is also evidence that the LFL as an organization does not see its players simply as sexy bodies but as legitimate, high-level athletes. Khomutova and Channon's analysis of the 2013 season "revealed that commentary heavily favored an overt construction of LFL as 'real' sport, and broadly represented LFL players as tough, skillful athletes."[84] Game analyst commentary contained an average of 125 comments per game that focused on LFL as a "real sport" with competent athletes, compared to only 28.9 comments per game on average that "trivialized" the athletes and the game.[85] This overwhelming focus in the official commentary on athleticism, game strategy, and leadership suggests LFL is more than just simple sexualization. Although the visuals of the LFL may suggest hyperfemininity and sexual availability, the action on the field and the analysis from the media booth suggests a serious commitment to the sport. And while we cannot ignore the visual focus on sexuality, we should not discount the serious athleticism of these women. To focus on one but not the other tells only one side of a complex story. As Leslie

Heywood and Shari Dworkin note in their analysis of the female athlete as a cultural icon, "in the culture of images, we are always dealing with a mixed bag, both/and, not either/or."[86]

To refuse the LFL any possibility for gender transgression or resistance to hegemonic gender norms ignores the very real possibility for parody that arises when we map sport and pornography onto one another. However, we must also remember that "parody by itself is not subversive, and there must be a way to understand what makes certain kinds of parodic repetitions effectively disruptive, truly troubling, and which repetitions become domesticated and recirculated as instruments of cultural hegemony."[87] Taking feminist pornography as the model, we must ask ourselves not just whether the LFL sexualizes players but how much agency players have in that process. At this point in time, while players are still unpaid, without health insurance, and without a say in what uniforms they wear, I am hard pressed to say that the LFL is meeting the standards set by feminist porn. However, given players' commitment to the league and their current fight for better working conditions, I am unwilling to simply dismiss the LFL and write off the players as dupes of the patriarchy.

CONCLUDING REMARKS

Sex may sell, and women's sports may still be inextricably tied to eroticism and appearance (which we should not overlook or discount), but we must also ask to whom sex is being sold. More work needs to be done exploring who the LFL's actual audience is, not simply who we assume it is. And even if sex is the most prominent aspect of the LFL's marketing (though as we have seen, it is certainly not the only aspect of the game), is that what is most important to players and fans? Why do women choose to play in the LFL knowing that they will be playing wearing next to nothing and with no compensation? When women and girls—straight or otherwise—watch the LFL, what do they see? Empirical analysis of LFL games and television coverage is needed to answer these questions, as well as interviews with current and former players, coaches, and management. Ethnographic work studying the LFL fan experience would also shed light on many of these questions. LFL players, and by extension their fans, would benefit significantly from stronger employee protection and oversight from regional and national bodies concerned with worker compensation, safety, and employment nondiscrimination.

Let us not return to the follies of the sex wars, accusing all women who capitalize on their appearance of false consciousness or of selling out to the patriarchy. With a larger audience than any other women's football league, the LFL has proven time and again that women can play high-quality football—a major milestone even in a post-Title IX world. Let us not simply write off the LFL as sexist misogyny and pat ourselves on the back for a feminist job well done. We would do better to take the Legends Football League seriously, holding it to account for not adequately paying its employees, for not providing adequate health insurance, and for not hiring and promoting women into coaching and administrative positions—all claims, I might add, that have also been brought against the NFL. The LFL is not perfect—not by a long shot—but let's not further undermine these women, these athletes, with feminist arrogance and hubris. Instead, let's reach out in solidarity and ask them, What support do you need? What do you want out of your time in the LFL?, and work to create more spaces for strong female athletes to draw crowds, to demonstrate their skills, and to do so with dignity.

NOTES

1. "Mission Statement," *Lingerie Football League*, accessed June 12, 2016, https://www.facebook.com/Lingerie-Football-League-384923778187526/info/?entry_point=page_nav_about_item&tab=page_info.
2. Patrick Murphy, "LFL Reaches New Heights in All-Fantasy Game," *LFL360.com*, last modified 2012, http://www.lfl360.com/articles/world-afg-mexico-city-lfl-reaches-new-heights/.
3. Quoted in Mary Buckheit, "Can We Take Lingerie Football Seriously?" *ESPN.com Page 2*, last updated June 12, 2009, http://sports.espn.go.com/espn/page2/story?page=buckheit/090612.
4. All Facebook data was retrieved on September 19, 2016.
5. The organizational viability of these leagues and their impact on women's professional sports has been covered elsewhere in the academic literature. It is beyond the scope of this chapter to fully analyze and assess these leagues and how they challenge or resist gender norms.
6. All Youtube.com data was retrieved on September 19, 2016.
7. Murphy, "LFL Reaches New Heights."
8. Emily Kaplan, "We're Not Going to Show You These Women Playing Football in Their Bikinis," *Sports Illustrated Monday Morning Quarterback*, last updated September 23, 2015, http://mmqb.si.com/mmqb/2015/09/23/legends-football-league-lingerie-football-lfl-dakota-hughes-atlanta-steam.
9. Bobbi A. Knapp, "Garters on the Gridiron: A Critical Reading of the Lingerie Football League," *International Review for the Sociology of Sport* (2013): 1–20.
10. Siobhan Brooks, *Unequal Desires: Race and Erotic Capital in the Stripping Industry* (Albany: State University of New York Press, 2010).
11. Ibid., 6.
12. Allen Guttman, *The Erotic in Sports* (New York: Columbia University Press, 1996).
13. Ibid., 1.
14. Susan Bordo, *Unbearable Weight: Feminism, Western Culture, and the Body* (Berkeley: University of California Press, 1995).

15. Arthur A. Raney, "Why We Watch and Enjoy Mediated Sports," in *Handbook of Sports and Media*, eds. Arthur A. Raney and Jennings Bryant (New York: Routledge, 2006), 339.

16. Ibid., 341.

17. Ibid., 343.

18. Nick Trujillo, "Machines, Missiles, and Men: Images of the Male Body on ABC's *Monday Night Football*," *Sociology of Sport Journal* 12 (1995): 403–23.

19. Margaret Carlisle Duncan and Barry Brummett, "Types and Sources of Spectating Pleasure in Televised Sports," *Sociology of Sport Journal* 6, no. 3 (1989): 198.

20. Ibid., 199.

21. Trujillo, "Machines, Missiles, and Men," 415.

22. Duncan and Brummett, "Spectating Pleasure," 203.

23. Ibid.

24. Ibid., 204.

25. Trujillo, "Machines, Missiles, and Men," 416.

26. For example, Andrea Dworkin, *Pornography: Men Possessing Women* (London: The Women's Press, [1979] 1999).

27. Marie Hardin, Susan Lynn, and Kristie Walsdorf, "Challenge and Conformity on 'Contested Terrain': Images of Women in Four Women's Sport/Fitness Magazines," *Sex Roles* 53, no. 1 (2005): 105–17; and Michael A. Messner, Margaret Carlisle Duncan, and Kerry Jensen, "Separating the Men from the Girls: The Gendered Language of Televised Sports," *Gender & Society* 7, no. 1 (1993): 121–37.

28. Judith Butler, *Gender Trouble* (New York: Routledge, 1990).

29. Ibid., 43.

30. Ibid., 188.

31. Brian McNair, *Striptease Culture: Sex, Media, and the Democratisation of Desire* (New York: Routledge, 2002), 23.

32. Ibid., 24–26.

33. Ibid., 55.

34. McNair, *Striptease Culture*.

35. Feona Attwood, "Sexed Up: Theorizing the Sexualization of Culture," *Sexualities* 9, no. 1 (2006): 77–94.

36. Ariel Levy, *Female Chauvinist Pigs: Women and the Rise of Raunch Culture* (New York: Free Press, 2005).

37. McNair, *Striptease Culture*, 61.

38. Rosalind Gill, quoted in Attwood, "Sexed Up," 83, emphasis in original.

39. Rosalind Gill, "Media, Empowerment and the 'Sexualization of Culture' Debates," *Sex Roles* 66 (2012): 741.

40. Knapp, "Garters on the Gridiron," 8.

41. Ibid., 15.

42. Jane Caputi, "Everyday Pornography," in *Gender, Race, and Class in Media: A Text Reader*, eds. G. Dines and J. M. Humez (Thousand Oaks, CA: SAGE, 2003), 434.

43. Knapp, "Garters on the Gridiron," 6.

44. Whitney Strub, *Perversion for Profit: The Politics of Pornography and the Rise of the New Right* (New York: Columbia University Press, 2011).

45. Linda Williams, "The Pornography of Consumption/the Consumption of Pornography," in *21st Century Sexualities: Contemporary Issues in Health, Education, and Rights*, eds. Gilbert Herdt and Cymene Howe (New York: Routledge, 2007), 74.

46. Ibid., 75.

47. Brooks, *Unequal Desires*, 6.

48. Ibid., 45.

49. Brendan Hokowhitu, "Race Tactics: The Racialized Athletic Body," *Junctures: The Journal for Thematic Dialogue* (2003).

50. Patricia Hill Collins, *Black Feminist Thought* (New York: Routledge, 1991), 74.

51. Collins, *Black Feminist Thought*.

52. Kevin J. Mumford, *Interzones: Black/White Sex Districts in Chicago and New York in the Early Twentieth Century* (New York: Columbia University Press, 1997).

53. Anastasiya Khomutova and Alexander Channon, "'Legends' in 'Lingerie': Sexuality and Athleticism in the 2013 Legends Football League US Season," *Sociology of Sport Journal* 32, no. 2 (2015): 173.

54. Rosalind Gill, "Beyond the 'Sexualization of Culture' Thesis: An Intersectional Analysis of 'Sixpacks,' 'Midriffs' and 'Hot Lesbians' in Advertising," *Sexualities* 12, no. 2 (2009): 152.

55. Lisa M. Diamond, "'I'm Straight, but I Kissed a Girl': The Trouble with American Media Representations of Female-Female Sexuality," *Feminism & Psychology* 15, no. 1 (2005): 104–10.

56. Gill, "Beyond 'Sexualization of Culture,'" 153.

57. Molly George, "Making Sense of Muscle: The Body Experiences of Collegiate Women Athletes," *Sociological Inquiry* 75, no 3 (2005): 326.

58. Jordan Ritter Conn, "The Lingerie Football Trap," *Grantland.com*, last updated July 23, 2015, http://grantland.com/features/legends-football-league-womens-lingerie-football-league-mitchell-mortaza/.

59. Knapp, "Garters on the Gridiron"; Charlene Weaving, "It Is Okay to Play as Long as You Wear Lingerie (or Skimpy Bikinis): A Moral Evaluation of the Lingerie Football League and Its Rebranding," *Sport in Society* 17, no. 6 (2014): 757–72; Khomutova and Channon, "'Legends' in 'Lingerie.'"

60. Knapp, "Garters on the Gridiron."

61. Weaving, "It Is Okay to Play."

62. Ibid., 762.

63. Ibid., 764.

64. Knapp, "Garters on the Gridiron."

65. Ibid., 15.

66. Khomutova and Channon, "'Legends' in 'Lingerie,'" 172.

67. Ibid., 175.

68. John Beattle, "Lingerie Football League Changes Name to Legends Football League, Removes Lingerie Aspects of Uniform," *NESN Newswire*, last modified January 10, 2013, http://nesn.com/2013/01/lingerie-football-league-changes-name-to-legends-football-league-removes-lingerie-aspects-of-uniform/.

69. Buckheit, "Can We Take Lingerie Football Seriously?"

70. Conn, "The Lingerie Football Trap."

71. Jason Lisk, "Lingerie Football Players Stopped Getting Paid Because One Dared Ask for Check After Title Game Four Years Ago," *Thebiglead.com*, last modified September 23, 2015, http://thebiglead.com/2015/09/23/lingerie-football-players-stopped-getting-paid-because-one-dared-ask-for-check-after-title-game-four-years-ago/.

72. Ellen C. Berg, Todd A. Migliaccio, and Rosemary Anzini-Varesio, "Female Football Players, the Sport Ethic and the Masculinity-Sport Nexus," *Sport in Society* 17, no. 2 (2014): 176–89.

73. Lisk, "Players Stopped Getting Paid."

74. Conn, "The Lingerie Football Trap."

75. Current player compensation and playing fee.

76. Tina Vasquez "Ethical Pornography," *Herizons*, last modified Spring 2012, http://www.herizons.ca/node/517.

77. Knapp, "Garters on the Gridiron," 15.

78. Conn, "The Lingerie Football Trap."

79. "The New Skins Game," *Bloomberg.com*, last modified November 24, 2010, http://www.bloomberg.com/news/articles/2010-11-24/the-new-skins-game.

80. Kaplan, "Not Going to Show You."

81. Ibid.

82. Ibid.; Alex Hall, "Cruz Travels Far for Football Dream," *New Hampshire Union Leader*, last modified June 25, 2016, http://www.unionleader.com/article/20160626/SPORTS04/160629489&template=mobileart.

83. Kaplan, "Not Going to Show You."

84. Khomutova and Channon, "'Legends' in 'Lingerie,'" 171.

85. Ibid.

86. Leslie Heywood and Shari L. Dworkin, *Built to Win: The Female Athlete as Cultural Icon* (Minneapolis: University of Minnesota Press, 2003), 99.

87. Butler, *Gender Trouble*, 189.

2

"Dude, Those Are Girls": Boundary Maintenance in Women's Full-Contact Tackle Football

J. A. Carter

So far it had been a pretty typical Cincinnati Sizzle football practice. We had done our usual warm-ups of stretching and sprinting, jogged about 250 yards, and completed separate offensive and defensive drills. We only had 15 players, so we lined up for a seven-on-seven drill, with the offense challenging the defense. I headed to the defensive side. I had been learning to play safety, but now I was back at my typical cornerback spot. We ran a few plays, but some confusion within the offense caused a short delay. As we were waiting, I noticed the large crowd of people starting to cross the field from the baseball diamond that sat behind the football field. Since we played at a high school, we were often witness to the exodus of baseball fans once the home team finished their games. We lined back up and the offense ran a play. Once again, they huddled together to work out some issues. On defense, we watched as groups of high school students wandered past parents and grandparents, and little kids sprinted past everyone, all proudly displaying school colors—red and white for the home team and blue and white for the visitors. Several of the players wandered past, hauling their bat bags and eating snacks, having shed their cleats for sandals. "Dude, those are girls!" one of the visiting fans proclaimed, the heightening pitch of his voice indicating his shock. His friends turned to look at the field, laughter filling the air, while Sizzle players turned to meet their gaze. "Why does everyone always seem so shocked to see women playing football? They look at us like we're crazy," Audrey stated in response. Other players remarked about the "ignorance" of people who do not think women can play football. One veteran proclaimed, "We're here every week; it's not like it's the first time they've seen us out here."

Encountering people who are surprised to see or hear of women playing full-contact tackle football is quite common. However, its frequency does not make it less frustrating for the players; they believe the invisibility of women's football serves to devalue the team and the sport. And it does. The invisibility of women's football serves as a form of "boundary maintenance"[1] that establishes barriers to women's full participation in football. However, it is not the only boundary. This research will show, first, that spatial and material resources are restricted for women's football teams. Women's teams experience difficulty in gaining access to game facilities, locker rooms, and football equipment. Additionally, societal boundaries impact women's access to football cultural capital. By restricting young girls' access to organized football, the sporting structure discourages girls and women from gaining important knowledge and skills that can be translated into capital within the sport. Finally, this research will show that visibility of the sport is limited by local and national media, which challenges the ability of teams and leagues to gain fan and financial support. In what is a circular relationship, this lack of visibility can impact access to material resources and the acquisition of cultural capital. Consequently, these boundaries do not exist independently but instead serve to reify one another. Michael Schwalbe and coauthors have argued that by "maintaining boundaries between dominant and subordinate groups," and limiting the subordinate group's access to valuable resources, "boundary maintenance" is one of four generic processes that reifies gender inequality in society.[2] Thus, this article will end with a discussion of how breaking down boundaries within women's football has the potential to reshape ideological expectations about women and female bodies and alter barriers that exist in other facets of society, such as the workforce.

THE CINCINNATI SIZZLE

This article draws on more than 300 hours of participant observation with the Cincinnati Sizzle women's tackle football team during 2011 and 2012. Autoethnographic data was also collected through my full participation with the team. In autoethnography, the life of the researcher becomes a site of research; thus, my direct experience of playing for this team was also recorded as data. The inclusion of this data necessitates the use of first person in some areas of this article.

The Sizzle franchise, located in Cincinnati, Ohio, formed in 2003 and began full league play in 2005. During the period of research, the Sizzle was a member of the Women's Football Alliance (WFA), the largest of the women's football leagues in the United States. The team is owned by former Cincinnati Bengal player Elbert "Ickey" Woods. He served as the head coach with a small volunteer staff of two to three coaches during the 2011 and 2012 seasons. The roster varied in size from season to season, and even week to week, with around 45 players on the official roster for the two seasons and 35 players required by the league. Participants in this study were given the choice of using a pseudonym, thus some names have been changed; all coaches are simply identified as "Coach." Other identifying information, such as positions and numbers, has been omitted in some cases to maintain anonymity. A total of 37 players, coaches, and support staff gave their consent to participate and were consulted over the two-year study. Sizzle players came from diverse backgrounds. Ages on the team ranged from 18 to 53. Racially, Sizzle players were nearly equally divided between those who identified as white and black, with one player each identifying as Hispanic, Native American, and white/Native American. The players also spanned several income classes from the unemployed to six-figure earners. Players were employed in varying jobs, with nurses, high school administrators, construction workers, engineers, pharmaceutical representatives, factory line workers, personal trainers, cooks, social workers, military members, and high school and college students all sharing the same field. Education levels also varied, with most respondents having completed at least some college.

The Cincinnati Sizzle and its league more generally are often described as "professional," but players are not commonly paid to play. Sizzle players must cover their own expenses, paying a league registration fee and team travel fee each year and a uniform fee as a rookie. Players incur additional expenses for equipment (e.g., helmets, shoulder pads, practice jerseys, etc.) and health care, including health insurance coverage, a requirement of the league. In my own experience, purchasing the needed equipment and paying team fees cost more than $500 in my first year of research. In total, I spent more than $2,000 on football-related expenses during my two seasons, including travel and medical costs. Unlike my teammates, I was able to cover some of my expenses through a research grant from a university Graduate Student Governance Association. Like other women's teams, the Sizzle experiences many difficulties in gaining and retaining players. The time and monetary commitment required, in addition to the physical challenges, makes recruitment difficult. Additionally, women must overcome other boundaries, including challenges in gaining access to spatial and material resources and football cultural capital, and the consistent invisibility of the sport in the mainstream.

RESTRICTING MATERIAL RESOURCES

Perhaps the easiest boundaries to "see" in women's football are those that restrict access to spatial and material resources, including fields for practice and play, locker rooms in those facilities, and football equipment. Finding facilities willing to house women's football can be a challenge. The Sizzle was lucky in that it had access to two indoor practice facilities and a stable home field during the two seasons I was a participant observer. However, this did not preclude the team from experiencing difficulty when accessing these facilities.

Most off-season conditioning sessions were held at an indoor D1 Sports Training facility. D1 has training facilities throughout the country, specializing in training athletes at all levels. The team was able to use their weight room and 50-yard indoor practice field, but the Sizzle often had to wait for other teams to complete practices and/or share the field. Several times the Sizzle practice was overtaken by a men's semiprofessional team also on the field. During a January practice session, the team was limited to 10 yards at the end of the field. Most off-season conditioning took place without coaches, so Lindsey, a veteran player and team captain, ran the practice. She set up several work stations, including cone drills. As we worked out in our small section of the field, we were nearly hit by players from the other team several times as they worked on passing patterns using the majority of the field. "This is some bullshit," one of the Sizzle players commented to teammates, as a player from the other team ran into our space again. As another player pointed out, this often happens in school settings as well, with boys' teams getting gym, weight room, and field access for longer periods of time and in more convenient time slots. Girls' teams are often relegated to secondary facilities or time slots that are less desirable. She had experienced this while coaching girls' basketball at a local high school.

In addition to complications at our practice facility, there were also issues at the high school that served as our home field. Often other events at the field would interfere with our practices or even games. On several occasions, a Little League baseball team practiced at the far end of the stadium. There were times when our paths would cross, and an errant baseball would roll into our field of play or vice versa. But their presence was less invasive than larger events because they took up a very small section of the field. One practice was canceled due to a Special Olympics event being held in the stadium. No one affiliated with the team was aware of the event until we arrived for the practice session.

On another occasion, a high school track meet delayed the beginning of a home game. Coaches attempted to move the game to a different high school to avoid a conflict with the track meet, but playing at that stadium would mean no access to locker room facilities, or the press box, scoreboard, and public address system. Because we would be able to use the locker room and press box at our usual home field, it was decided that the game would not be moved. We simply would have to wait to enter the locker room facilities and field until the track meet was completely finished. The track meet ran about an hour later than expected, delaying locker room access, pregame warm-ups, and the game start. Although we had access to the press box, the school would not allow us to use the public address system due to objections from the neighbors. Those living nearby had complained about the use of the address system for the track meet all day long, prompting our inability to use the system. "We can't even play the national anthem?" Coach asked, frustrated by the restrictions.

We lacked access to other resources at the facility as well, most notably stadium lights, locker rooms, and restrooms at practices. To accommodate players' work schedules, practices were scheduled from 7 p.m. to 9:15 p.m. Darkness would begin to fall around 8 p.m., making the last hour of practice difficult to manage without lights. Although Coach had spoken with the school several times about using the lights for practices, we were only able to use the lights several times over the two-year period, usually when another event was taking place at the school. Many nights we would run our practice-ending laps in complete darkness. Having an issue with lighting was not new for the team. When the team first began, the players would park their cars where their headlights could be used to illuminate the practice field. This strategy has been used by other women's football teams as well.[3] Luckily, lighting was never an issue during games.

As players, we never knew what to expect with regards to locker room access. During practices at our home field, we never had access to locker rooms. This meant that during practice we had no bathrooms, and changing clothes before and after practice took place on the sideline. "Is it legal for us to change out here?" one player asked on a day when a couple hundred elementary school-aged children were participating in activities on the field. Since we lacked access to bathrooms, many players would stop at a gas station down the street to use the restroom before practice. Others would slip behind the away bleachers when it was a necessity.

Even when the locker room building was open, we were not necessarily guaranteed locker room space. During the 2011 season, the Sizzle used the facility weight room as a locker room on game nights, while away teams used a locker room down the hall. Players would use weight benches, stacked weights, and other exercise equipment as a place to sit and store their gear. In 2012, both teams used the same locker rooms. At away stadiums, we generally had access to locker rooms, but what was included in those locker rooms was never known in advance. During a 2011 game in Indianapolis, we used a basketball gym as a locker room until semiprofessional men's teams and Little League baseball teams finally cleared out of the space designated to us. Sizzle veterans told of times when locker rooms consisted of fold-up tables in school hallways. Several times we lacked shower facilities even when in locker rooms.

A bigger issue for Sizzle players was accessing football equipment. Most women's tackle leagues play a spring season. Sporting goods stores consider the spring to be the "off-season" for football and instead increase their stock of items for "spring sports," like baseball, softball, and track. This makes equipment difficult to find and limits size options when it is available. Limited options mean that women are often unable to try on equipment to determine proper sizes. Most rookies have never tried on football equipment before, so determining a proper size is even more important. The majority of women on the Sizzle team bought their items locally at a major retailer, such as Dick's Sporting Goods, or a resale retailer, such as Play It Again Sports. Financial limitations made it difficult for many athletes to purchase the higher-priced items that might offer a better fit, comfort level, or may be more effective at injury prevention and pain management. Players who joined the team after the fall football season ended were more likely to have difficulty finding equipment. Darcy, a rookie, indicated that she had to go to three different stores to find her equipment because none of the stores had all of the items she needed in stock. When I went to purchase my own equipment, I was taken to the stock room where the equipment was being stored for the "off-season." The store clerk and I dug through box after box, looking for each of the basic equipment items necessary to play: a helmet; chinstrap; mouthguard; shoulder pads; practice jersey; practice pants; a belt; hip, knee, thigh, and tailbone pads; socks; and cleats. It being the "off-season," this store had no football cleats in stock, so I had to travel to a different store for cleats, finding a limited selection there, again, due to the "off-season." Stocking football equipment only during the fall serves as another boundary restricting women's access to needed material resources.

LIMITING FOOTBALL CULTURAL CAPITAL

While spatial and material limitations might be the easiest to conceptualize, limiting a group's access to important resources begins by restricting "knowledge, skills, habits, values, and tastes . . . which can be turned to one's advantage in particular social settings," or cultural capital.[4] Symbolic and ideological boundaries have been set for women before they even hit the football field. Football is seen as a symbol of manhood and masculinity, thus its association with male bodies and men. These ideological associations uphold structural boundaries in organized football and impact the socialization process through which cultural capital is largely transmitted.

Structurally, organized football is for male-bodied boys and men. For many boys growing up in the United States, the attainment of football knowledge and skills starts at a very young age. Boys as young as five are already playing organized tackle football, which allows them to learn the intricacies of the sport. Although some youth leagues have accepted girls into their organizations, school-sanctioned teams still often require girls to challenge legislation that negates their participation. For example, in 2013, Makhaela Jenkins, a 12-year-old in Ohio, was removed from the active roster of her middle school football team due to a long-standing policy in her school district that states that females cannot play contact sports. After the Ohio chapter of the American Civil Liberties Union (ACLU) became involved, the school rescinded their decision but still defended their policy. In a statement, the superintendent stated, "Our position on this issue has been made clear. However, we are also adamant that local tax dollars will not be wasted. We have no intent of competing with the deep pockets of the ACLU in any litigation situation in order to secure a favorable judgment."[5] In this case, the school district believed that their policy did not violate any federal regulations with regards to equal participation. Under Title IX this is likely true, as this legislation excludes protections for contact sports. However, the Equal Protection Clause has been used by girls to gain access to the football field in other similar cases.[6] Jenkins obtained the right to play on the football team after challenging the district, but by maintaining its policy, the district reinforced its ideological belief that football is for boys and men and ensured that other girls would still have to challenge the district's policy to play. Legislation that inhibits girls' participation in football, and that which did so in the past, ensures that most women entering the sport have never played organized football and have been denied access to football cultural capital.

Heidi, a veteran of the team who became the special teams coach in 2012, was the only Sizzle player to have played in high school. Although some women had played flag football, or nonorganized football, most were experiencing organized tackle football for the first time. This is expected in the recruiting process. Shannon acknowledged this in a television interview meant to be used as a recruiting tool. She said:

> We have people out here who have never played sports before, they just love the game, and they never thought they would have the opportunity to play. . . . You don't even need to know anything about the game because we'll teach you when you get here. I always tell people you just have to have a desire, have a hunger to play and we'll do the rest.[7]

Both coaches and veterans were tasked with teaching the game. This included everything from basic terminology to complicated offensive and defensive schemes.

For one coach, this was the biggest difference in the men's and women's games. "Coaching women is very different than coaching boys or men; [women] just don't have the background in football like men," he said. "We do spend a lot of time on fundamentals," Sizzle veteran Mary acknowledged in an interview. "The things that little kids are taught in pee wee [football] we're just now learning from scratch. There's times when Coach gets frustrated and we get frustrated, but we're all doing the very best we can." As she also acknowledges, failure on the field can sometimes be attributed to everything being "so new for everybody."[8] This was clear during my two seasons as rookies were socialized into the intricacies of tackle football.

The 2012 rookie class included 10 new players. Audrey, an avid football fan, espoused her knowledge early and often upon joining the team. She often had in-depth conversations with the coaches about the state of National Football League (NFL) football teams and their off-season decisions. But the disparity between Audrey's knowledge and that of other players was often evident. For example, Jess joined the team after learning about it from some friends. "Someone told me because of my size I should be a tight end or linebacker, so I had to watch some football on television to figure out which ones those were," Jess admitted. She was not the only rookie who had to seek out sources to learn more about positions. During one of her first practices, Alya was told she should go in and play safety. She looked around with a confused look on her face. "Hey, what does a safety do?" she quietly asked me. I was able to tell her generally what the responsibilities of a safety were, but even though I had already been playing for a year, I could not tell her specifically how to play the position. I directed her to Tahlia, a veteran player on the team.

While most avid football fans know where linebackers or offensive linemen play on the field, football positions are much more complicated. Perhaps one of the most common questions posed by players was "Where do I stand?" Both veterans and rookies asked this question. Whether it was how close to the line of scrimmage one was to stand, or how far away from another player one should be, lining up on the field often elicited this question. This question illustrates how something seemingly so simple, where a player should be standing, can be extremely complex. If you are a defender, where you line up, or stand, will depend on the defensive scheme, where the offensive players line up, the speed of the offensive players, and even the distance to a first down or the end zone. For example, if you are a cornerback your job is to cover, or defend, the wide receiver. You might line up close to the wide receiver and try to hit her when the ball is snapped to impede her progress. Or, if she is faster than you are, you might line up several yards away, so you can catch up with her when she runs her route. Ultimately the answer to the question "Where do I stand?" will be different from play to play and is dictated by a strong understanding of the situational aspects of the game that must be learned over time.

Beyond learning where specific positions played on the field, many rookies, and even veterans, were overwhelmed by the need to learn multiple positions. This was a necessity due to the small number of Sizzle players, especially during practices. Often players were expected to learn positions on both offense and defense, requiring an even broader range of vocabulary and memorization. Li, a rookie in 2012, was vocal in her confusion about responsibilities. "I understand the purpose of offense and the purpose of defense, but I don't understand all of the positioning," Li explained to a male coach. "Well, hell, I've been doing this some-odd years, and I don't understand it sometimes," the coach responded. The coach's response is indicative of the complexities involved—for all football players, regardless of sex—in learning multiple positions within various defensive schemes. Because Sizzle players play multiple positions, players often found that the breadth of knowledge necessary hinders the ability to play any one position well. Shelley, a retired player who returned to the team, had concerns: "I just feel like I don't know what I'm doing," she said. "It would be better if they let me learn something, instead of just giving me everything [every position]." I certainly understood the confusion. Although I had been pegged as a cornerback during my rookie season, over the course of my two years I played five different positions during games, one on offense and four on defense, and every position except for quarterback during practices. During a single game against West Michigan, I played cornerback, inside linebacker, outside linebacker, defensive line, safety, and was a kick returner on special teams. During this game, I got scolded by coaches for not "getting low enough" while playing on the defensive line. I had never played on the defensive line before being inserted into the game, so I had little idea of what my responsibilities were in this position, and I certainly had no conception of proper technique. I would learn on the sideline that because the women I was playing against outweighed me by about 150 pounds each, I should use my hands to make sure they did not grab my jersey and drop down low to try to trip them up. It was intricacies such as this that made raising one's football IQ more difficult.

To assist in learning the game, the team would watch game film once a week during the season to analyze upcoming opponents and examine our own play. These sessions often focused on proper technique and certainly on learning how to better execute plays. However, learning from college and professional games was also encouraged. Watching men's football games on television was a common source for learning the game. On many occasions coaches suggested watching football as a way to learn various techniques, like tackling. "Watch those smaller guys especially. Watch how they tackle. They are going to go for the legs. The other guy can't run without his legs," Coach stressed. Often during off-season workouts, players would watch football being played on the televisions in the gym. These included everything from high school games to college and professional games. Beyond watching games on television, players were encouraged by both coaches and teammates to play the Madden NFL video game. Audrey had conversations with one of the coaches about how playing the game could help with deciphering plays and especially with terminology. My own experience of playing the Madden game gave me useful information on various types of plays. For example, several rookies were confused by the coaches' use of the terms "four-three defense" and "four-four defense." In these terms, the first number indicates the number of defensive linemen the defensive scheme will include. The second number indicates the number of linebackers. The team used both of these defensive schemes in games, so it was important to differentiate between the two. These terms were used consistently with few questions openly raised, but in a more private setting, players often expressed confusion. These were terms that some were familiar with from playing the Madden game, and from watching football on television, yet not everyone was clear on their meaning. These are terms that boys are likely to learn while playing youth football, or early in school-based football programs, and serve as an example of the knowledge women are often lacking upon beginning to play organized football. Restrictive policies and ideological barriers that limit the access girls and women have to playing opportunities at a young age inhibit the achievement of football-related cultural capital.

RENDERING WOMEN'S FOOTBALL INVISIBLE

In perhaps the most impactful form of "boundary maintenance," women's football is rendered invisible to the general public. Invisibility impacts access to a strong fan base, corporate sponsorships, material resources like fields and equipment, and the ability of players to serve as role models to young girls. It also maintains the broader idea that football is solely a man's sport, which, as previously discussed, impacts the development of football-related cultural capital.

Although the Cincinnati Sizzle franchise has existed for more than a decade, its presence is not well known within the city. As illustrated in the opening vignette, the Sizzle often met people who were unaware of the team, especially during practices at the home field, which was at an all-male high school. Outside of practices and games, players had similar experiences with the public in other venues. Upon arriving at the University Hospital emergency room with Alex after she suffered a leg injury during practice, we encountered stares and confused looks from people in the waiting room. I did not enter the exam room with her, but Alex reported that many doctors and nurses came by to see her and learn more about the team. On a slow evening, learning of the women's team was exciting for those working in the ER. Alex said that none of the doctors or nurses had heard of the team, but many indicated interest in attending future games.

Other players and support staff had similar encounters. Katie, the team's athletic trainer, often spent time educating people on the existence of the

Sizzle football team. She would often get the standard "Oh, I didn't know there was a women's team" response when her patients learned she was heading to our practices or games. Audrey, a college student, had this reaction from her classmates, and many of the players indicated similar responses from coworkers. As Shannon stated in a media interview, "People's first reaction is normally, 'Oh they have a team?' or 'Wow, really?' But then we get the obligatory questions like, 'Oh, is it flag football? Oh, is it two-hand touch? Oh, it must be powder-puff,' and I reply that it is just like men's football. Yes, we do wear pads. Yes, we do wear helmets."[9] Nearly every player on the team indicated having interactions such as these with someone.

Interestingly, some players, especially those new to the sport, mentioned that they had initially reacted in this way as well. For example, Jess, a rookie during the 2012 season, indicated that she had learned about the team from some friends. "No way, girls don't play football, you're kidding," she responded. Although she did not immediately seek out the team, she was interested in the prospect of playing and a year later decided to give it a try. "I didn't realize girls had the opportunity to play 'real' football," she told me at her first practice, an off-season conditioning session. Beyond the invisibility of the team and women's football locally, I found that women's football seemed to be invisible in other areas of the country as well.

As the study was winding down, I spent much of my time speaking about my research in academic circles, in my department, at conferences, and to anyone who asked me about my dissertation work. I spoke to people from all areas of the country, from small and large universities, from sports enthusiasts to sports critics, and yet I rarely spoke to anyone who knew of women's football leagues. At conferences I did talk to sports sociologists who had heard of women's football. However, when I mentioned my research, most assumed that I was researching the Lingerie Football League (now called the Legends Football League). The LFL was fairly well known to sports sociologists, largely due to the controversy surrounding its requirement that women play in lingerie. I often found myself explaining that there are many teams, and whole leagues, in which women play in the standard football uniform.

It took more than a year for me to encounter someone outside of academia who had heard of women's football. One night I was questioned by a city utility worker while leaving my apartment building for a home game. I was dressed in my football pants and a team logo T-shirt, and I was carrying all of my equipment. When I told him that I played for the women's team, he asked if that was the team coached by Ickey Woods. Unlike other encounters, this was the first time someone indicated that they had heard of the team. The team was so invisible that it took more than a year for me to find someone who had heard of the Sizzle.

It is likely that finding someone who has heard of women's football leagues is difficult due to the limited coverage of women's football within the mainstream media. This exists on a local and national level. In the Cincinnati area, the local media rarely cover the Sizzle. TJ, a retired player and the Sizzle's statistician, provided me with news articles that had been published in the Cincinnati media since the team's inception. This included five articles from local publications. My own research through archives uncovered four additional articles. The focus of each of these articles was on the team's beginnings. I also located a short video clip from a WLWT-NBC news telecast in 2008, which focused on tryouts and the upcoming season. Subsequent local media coverage of the team could not be found.

During my time with the team, we received a fair amount of media attention. However, the main focus of much of this coverage was not on the team itself but on Ickey Woods. For example, in early May 2011, the team was on a live telecast of a local news station's morning show.[10] Woods's 16-year-old son, Jovante, had died in 2010 after an asthma attack following a high school football practice. Subsequently Woods and his ex-wife, Chandra, a Sizzle player who retired after the 2011 season, created a foundation focused on asthma education and research. On this day, the foundation was holding a 5K run-walk. All Sizzle players were required to be in attendance at the event. After the 5K was complete, the newscast went live from the event, with the Sizzle in the foreground. Although the main focus of this coverage was the foundation and Woods, the team did get some airtime.

The team received local media attention later in the 2011 season as well, but again the focus of this coverage was on Woods. ESPN was in town to feature him on their show *E:60*, offering a story of triumph over tragedy both for Woods's ability to move forward when his NFL career was cut short by injury and for overcoming the death of his young son.[11] WLWT-NBC featured the team in a short segment on the late news discussing ESPN's presence with the team. In this case, the newscast did feature some game footage.[12] This was the only time there was local television media coverage of a game over the two-year span of the study.

The team received one additional segment of media coverage on the local Time Warner cable access show *Around Town*. The mother of one of the players worked for Time Warner and helped put together an eight-minute piece that aired on Time Warner access channels throughout the state of Ohio.[13] This was an informative and in-depth piece examining the team's history, the coaches, players, how to become a player, and when and where games were played. Being that this aired on a cable access channel, it may be a stretch to include this as an example of mainstream media coverage. However, as this was the most extensive coverage the team received during my two seasons, it warrants mention.

Just as with the local media coverage, national coverage of women's football is largely nonexistent. As stated, the Sizzle did receive some airtime in the ESPN *E:60* story. Beyond the Sizzle, ESPN also featured a story on a player from the Houston Energy, of the Independent Women's Football League, during a 2012 airing of *College GameDay*, the flagship college football pregame show. This story discussed University of Nebraska defensive lineman Thad Randle, whose mother, Julia, plays for the Energy. Interestingly, the report indirectly acknowledges the invisibility of women's football in the mainstream. During the lead-in to the story, ESPN anchor Chris Fowler says Thad has "a very interesting family story involving his football bloodlines," continuing to say in an excited tone that "this is unique." This is followed by a short introduction by ESPN reporter Gene Wojciechowski, who argues that the accomplishments of Thad in his college career and academics are "nothing; just wait until [Thad's son] hears about grandma." Within the piece, even Thad admits to a lack of knowledge of women's football, at least before his mother began playing. When Julia said she wanted to play, Thad responded, "Mama, they don't do football like that for girls."[14] Each of these reactions illustrates how limited the knowledge of women's football is in the mainstream. What is not acknowledged in this is that more coverage of women's football by ESPN would assist in increasing the visibility of women's participation in the sport. It is important to note that the piece itself speaks of Julia Randle as a tough, dedicated, hardworking, All-Star player in much the same way a man playing the game would be discussed. This powerful portrayal of a woman playing football, which included a Nebraska assistant coach speaking highly of Julia's technique while watching her game film, has the potential to change stereotypes regarding women playing contact sports, not just tackle football. However, with so little coverage, the impact is not enough to change long-standing cultural ideologies regarding female bodies or participation in contact sport.

The WFA National Championship game has been aired on ESPN3 (now called WatchESPN), the network's online channel, for several years. But this coverage never makes it to the ESPN television channels. Women's teams have continuously used social media sites, like Facebook and Twitter, to request that ESPN air highlights of this and other women's games on *SportsCenter* and other ESPN programs, without success. Requests have also been made for ESPN's website focusing on women's sports, ESPNW, to include coverage of women's football. Although the website does have a section on football, all coverage in this section is of men's football at the college and professional level. Women's football is invisible even on the website that states that it "is fully dedicated to serving female athletes and fans."[15]

Women's participation in football has occasionally been seen on other mainstream networks, such as CNN and the NFL Network. In a 2013 online

CNN video, players from the Atlanta Phoenix talk about the hard-hitting action they experience while playing football. The segment also includes the story of Maddy Baxter, a teen who was fighting for the opportunity to continue playing for her football team.[16] A 2010 NFL Films segment that aired on the NFL Network and on ESPN spotlights Nikki Johnson of the Las Vegas Showgirlz. Johnson played flag football as a teen and was "recruited" by the WFA's Showgirlz team during that time. She joined the Showgirlz as soon as she turned 18, while still in high school. The segment chronicles her journey to the football field and her love of the game. The story begins and ends by directly acknowledging the invisibility of women's football, saying "on a team you've probably never heard of, in a league you likely didn't know exists."[17]

BREAKING BOUNDARIES

Since "media representations of sport are particularly powerful in naturalizing and normalizing hegemonic meanings about the body and social relations,"[18] the invisibility of women's participation in football reinforces the idea that football is a man's game. The visibility of strong, powerful women playing football at a high level would challenge the notion that women are not physically capable of playing the game and are not interested in playing. The failure to cover the game in the media on the local level contributes to the lack of coverage on the national level and vice versa. Ultimately this reifies a societal structure that constrains girls and women. Opportunities for girls and young women to play football and other contact sports are still limited in today's sports structure. Girls are still guided toward sports that are less physical in nature, many of which focus on artistic performance over physicality. It is still commonplace for girls to have to "fight the system" to gain access to opportunities within football. Withholding opportunity for girls and young women reinforces football as a masculine game meant for boys and men, or more specifically, for male bodies. This also stunts girls' acquisition of important football skills that boys often receive from the time they are in elementary school. For women just beginning their careers, this means learning nearly every aspect of the game from scratch. This translates into what is perceived to be a lower level of play for women's semiprofessional and professional teams, which challenges fandom and acceptance from the broader culture. However, girls and boys can be socialized differently. A quarterback for the Las Vegas Showgirlz shared this story about her children: "I came to a Pop Warner game to support one of my teammates' daughters who played on a boys' team, and when we pulled up in the parking lot my boys were like 'Boys play football?' because they only knew women played."[19] Offering girls the opportunity to play throughout the life course, and letting boys see that girls and women can play, can alter both the opportunities available to girls and women and the ideology surrounding the game.

Breaking down the boundaries used to maintain men's dominance in football also has the potential to impact other areas of society. Successful participation in football by female bodies can disrupt the notion that females are unfit for physical and/or aggressive spaces, such as those within the workforce. Research has shown that women still experience difficulties obtaining and holding employment in occupations that are considered too physical for female bodies. This includes occupations such as firefighters, police officers, corrections officers, military positions, and those in the building trades. Physicality is valued in each of these positions, thus it is expected that men, or at least male bodies, are better equipped to fill these roles. As with sports, changes in the view of female bodies over time has allowed for more integration of these positions; however, they are still male dominated, numerically and ideologically. Additional changes in the expectations our culture has of the physical abilities of female bodies could positively impact opportunities for females in the occupational and sporting realm. As Deutsch has explained, "resistant acts can also affect discourses about gender," and "alternative discourses can create alternative conceptions of gender."[20] Thus, the potential for altering the discourse surrounding female bodies and debunking essentialist views exists within women's football. While women still face considerable obstacles on the football field due to existing boundaries, women playing football are breaking through those barriers and are changing what it means to be a woman.

NOTES

1. Michael Schwalbe, Sandra Godwin, Daphne Holden, Douglas Schrock, Shealy Thompson, and Michelle Wolkomir, "Generic Processes in the Reproduction of Inequality: An Interactionist Analysis," *Social Forces* 79 (2000): 430.
2. Ibid., 434.
3. Jennifer Yee, *Pittsburgh Passion: Inside Women's Professional Football in the United States* (Los Angeles, CA: Back Light Productions, 2009), DVD.
4. Schwalbe et al., "Generic Processes," 430.
5. Associated Press, "Ohio School Allows Girl to Play on Football Team," *Ohio.com*, accessed August 17, 2013, http://www.ohio.com/news/ohio-school-allows-girl-to-play-on-football-team-1.421808.
6. Sarah Fields, *Female Gladiators: Gender, Law, and Contact Sport in America* (Chicago: University of Illinois Press, 2005).
7. Chelsea Gilbertson, "Cincinnati Female Football Team Ready to Kickoff," *WCPO Cincinnati*, accessed April 13, 2012, http://www.wcpo.com/news/local-news/cincinnati-female-football-team-ready-to-kickoff.

8. Terry Boehmker, "For Love of the Game: Assistant Principal Savors Time on the Field," *The Cincinnati Post*, April 22, 2006, B1.

9. Gilbertson, "Cincinnati Female Football Team."

10. WLWT, *WLWT News 5 Today Weekend* (New York: Hearst Television Inc., May 7, 2011), Television Program.

11. Jeremy Schaap, "Football, Fame, and Loss: Ickey Woods," *E:60* (Bristol, CT: ESPN, October 5, 2011), Television Program.

12. WLWT, *WLWT News 5 at 11:00* (New York: Hearst Television Inc., June 18, 2011), Television Program.

13. Khrys Styles, "Around Town," *Time Warner Cable* (Cincinnati, OH: DHProductions, 2012), OnDemand Television Program.

14. Gene Wojciechowski, "College GameDay," *ESPN* (Bristol, CT: ESPN, September 14, 2013), Television Program.

15. ESPNW, "One Letter Says a Lot," accessed July 25, 2014, http://www.espn.go.com/espnw/about.

16. CNN, "Women Hit Hard on the Football Field," YouTube Video File, 2013, accessed July 1, 2013, https://youtu.be/74hB3H5_lno.

17. NFL Films, "Nikki Johnson," *NFL Films Presents*, YouTube Video File, 2010, accessed June 15, 2013, http://youtu.be/hpN2IwyCe4U.

18. Jan Wright and Gill Clarke, "Sport, the Media, and the Construction of Compulsory Heterosexuality: A Case Study of Women's Rugby Union," *International Review for the Sociology of Sport* 34 (1999): 227.

19. NFL Films, "Nikki Johnson."

20. Francine M. Deutsch, "Undoing Gender," *Gender & Society* 21(2007): 121.

3

Sandrine Rangeon: Denied "Alien" Visa despite Out-of-This-World Abilities

Roxane Coche

Immigration laws in the United States are an ever-changing puzzle that millions around the world try to solve. What worked last year may not work today, and what works today might not have worked a few years ago. Congress has complete power under the plenary power doctrine to regulate immigration without any judicial review from another entity.[1]

Foreign individuals wishing to move to the United States are offered two major types of visas: immigrant and nonimmigrant. The former gives them permanent residency in the United States, while the latter only gives them a temporary entry—whether for a few days or a few years.[2]

With the current globalization happening throughout professional sports leagues, the number of foreign athletes in the United States has drastically increased in the past few years. Canadian Sidney Crosby was perceived as ice hockey's savior before he even played his first game for the Pittsburgh Penguins; more than a quarter of Major League Baseball (MLB) players are foreign born,[3] and more than 100 foreign-born athletes play in the National Basketball Association (NBA), up from 45 in 2000–2001.[4]

As the system stands today, athletes can usually move to the United States as nonresidents only, under either the O-1 visa or the P-1 visa. The O-1 visa is "for the individual who possesses extraordinary ability in the sciences, arts, education, business, or athletics."[5] To demonstrate "extraordinary ability," as the United States Citizenship and Immigration Services (UCSIS) defines it, one must show "sustained national or international acclaim" in one's field.

The P-1 visa, which was revised through the COMPETE Act of 2006,[6] is reserved for the "internationally recognized athlete" or members of an "internationally recognized entertainment group."[7] To qualify for a P-1 visa, one must show "a degree of skill and recognition substantially above that ordinarily encountered so that the achievement is renowned, leading or well known in more than one country." Although sports and athletes were given their own separate due with the COMPETE Act of 2006, it is noteworthy that neither the O-1 visa nor the P-1 visa allows for self-petition, which means that one must be sponsored by a United States–based entity in order to apply for these visas.

In the case of professional sports, a team can sponsor an athlete as long as it "is a member of an association of 6 or more professional sports teams whose total combined revenues exceed $10,000,000 per year."[8] In amateur sports, coaches and athletes can be sponsored only by teams "that are part of an international league or association of 15 or more amateur sports teams."[9] These conditions de facto exclude most national women's leagues, which limits their petitions to O-1 visas only.

Women's inclusion and exclusion in athletics is an international problem. The following case study brings light to a seldom-discussed problem caused by the lack of professional sports opportunities for women: immigration. Sandrine Rangeon has played on three national teams for her home country of France and has represented it at the highest level in two other sports, yet she still cannot make a living from sports, and more importantly, she does not even qualify for an "athlete" visa to the United States, where she wanted to live.

Rangeon was "born to skate,"[10] practicing a myriad of skating sports at the international level: from ice hockey in the early 2000s to ice cross downhill on the Red Bull Crashed Ice circuit in 2016. She has been a successful athlete for about 15 years in five different skating-based sports, but with little recognition. Because of current immigration laws and the lack of opportunities in professional sports for women, Rangeon has given up on her dream of living in the United States for now and has turned her attention down under as "Australia seems to be a lot more welcoming than the U.S."[11] Because of current immigration laws and the lack of opportunities in professional sports for women, the United States has lost perhaps one of the most complete athletes of this generation.

IMMIGRATING TO THE UNITED STATES

Immigration in the United States is regulated by the federal government, which more than a hundred years ago perceived it to be a political issue.[12] As a result, the government's political branches[13] have sole power to regulate all aspects of immigration, to the detriment of the judiciary branch. In fact, as is discussed next, courts have regularly held that immigration matters "are frequently of a character more appropriate to either the Legislature or the Executive than to the Judiciary."[14]

This plenary power doctrine, as it is called, has been widely criticized by scholars over the years,[15] but it remains at the heart of immigration laws in the United States.

The Plenary Power Doctrine

The plenary power doctrine dates back to the 19th century. It is usually traced back to a case often referred to as "The Chinese Exclusion Case," involving a Chinese immigrant, Chae Chan Ping, who was denied reentry to the United States in late 1888 upon his return from a temporary visit to China. Three years later, the first comprehensive law placing immigration under federal control was enacted. The Immigration Act of 1891 established an Office of Immigration (falling under the Department of Treasury), which had authority to exclude and/or deport individuals and which became the "Court of Last Resort" (in lieu of the Supreme Court) for aliens using the appeals process. Indeed, the head of the Office of Immigration (the superintendent of immigration) and the secretary of the treasury had jurisdiction over all immigration case appeals.[16]

Today, aliens facing charges of violating immigration laws still do not go through the traditional court systems. Instead, their cases are reviewed by the Immigration Court and, if necessary, the Board of Immigration Appeals, both of which compose the Executive Office for Immigration Review created in 1983[17] within the executive branch of the federal government. As such, the plenary power doctrine, giving the political (executive and legislative) branches full power over immigration matters, lives on, justified by years of court decisions stating that immigration is a political issue.

Foundation cases

Chae Chan Ping v. United States (1889) is considered by many to be the seed of the plenary power doctrine. Chae Chan Ping, who had been a legal resident of the United States for 15 years, was denied reentry to the country after a trip to China, during which Congress enacted the Scott Act—an expansion of the 1882 Chinese Exclusion Act, which prohibited reentry to Chinese people after leaving the United States. After reviewing the case, the Supreme Court established that the decision to allow was not a question "for judicial determination" but was solely political.[18] The verdict was primarily grounded in the principle of sovereignty of a nation, which is protected by international law:

> That the government of the United States, through the action of the legislative department, can exclude aliens from its territory is a proposition which we do not think open to controversy. Jurisdiction over its own territory to that extent is an incident of every independent nation. It is a part of its independence. If it could not exclude aliens it would be to that extent subject to the control of another power.[19]

Other foundation cases relied on this sovereignty principle,[20] including *Nishimura Ekiu v. United States* (1892), which reinforced the power of

Congress in immigration matters and laid down a stone for the Immigration Act of 1893 (which, for almost 60 years, gave "immigration inspectors" the right to decide cases related to the deportation or exclusion of foreigners[21]):

> Congress may, if it sees fit . . . authorize the courts to investigate and ascertain the facts on which the right to land depends. . . . The final determination of those facts may be entrusted by Congress to executive officers; and in such a case, as in all others, in which a statute gives a discretionary power to an officer, to be exercised by him upon his own opinion of certain facts, he is made the sole and exclusive judge of the existence of those facts, and no other tribunal, unless expressly authorized by law to do so, is at liberty to reexamine or controvert the sufficiency of the evidence on which he acted.[22]

While these foundation cases are now more than 120 years old, the Supreme Court has upheld the plenary power doctrine throughout the years, often through the sovereignty theory. In *Harisiades v. Shaughnessy* (1952), Justice Frankfurter wrote that the Supreme Court was not "to reshape a world order based on politically sovereign States" and noted that "ever since national States have come into being, the right of people to enjoy the hospitality of a State of which they are not citizens has been a matter of political determination by each State."[23] Similarly, in *Fiallo v. Bell* (1977), the Court reiterated that its cases "have long recognized the power to expel or exclude aliens as a fundamental sovereign attribute exercised by the Government's political departments largely immune from judicial control."[24]

Critics of the plenary power doctrine

Because of the judicial branch's lack of power in immigration matters, "the plenary power doctrine carves out a unique space in American public law: a realm where the Constitution does not always apply."[25] That is why many scholars condemn the plenary power doctrine,[26] which is founded on a case based on racist laws (the Chinese Exclusion Act and its expansion, the Scott Act) and results in the isolation of immigration law from constitutional law, thus denying prospective immigrants due process rights.

Due process ensures that the government respects all legal rights owed to a person, so without them, noncitizens seeking to immigrate to the United States do not enjoy the full spectrum of rights granted by the Constitution. As recently as 2003, the Supreme Court stated that "Congress may make rules as to aliens that would be unacceptable if applied to citizens."[27]

Among the theories justifying the limitation of rights to noncitizens, the sovereignty theory (discussed above) and the foreign-affairs theory are perhaps the most cited. Both are grounded in court decisions. The former, as discussed, relies on the concept that a state has the inherent power of decision for immigration matters. The latter is the idea that courts and judges cannot provide expert knowledge in foreign affairs, which are automatically and intrinsically connected to immigration. For instance, in *Harisiades v. Shaughnessy*, the Supreme Court stated that

> it would be rash and irresponsible to reinterpret our fundamental law to deny or qualify the Government's power of deportation. However desirable world-wide amelioration of the lot of aliens, we think it is peculiarly a subject for international diplomacy. It should not be initiated by judicial decision which can only deprive our own Government of a power of defense and reprisal without obtaining for American citizens abroad any reciprocal privileges or immunities. Reform in this field must be entrusted to the branches of the Government in control of our international relations and treaty-making powers.[28]

In 2001, Justice Scalia further explained the risks of allowing the judicial branch a voice in immigration matters in regards to foreign affairs. Dissenting from a Supreme Court decision that stated that the United States cannot detain immigrants under order of deportation for more than six months, even if no other country will accept them, Justice Scalia wrote:

> One of the more alarming aspects of the Court's new venture into foreign affairs management is the suggestion that the district court can expand or contract the reasonable period of detention based on its own assessment of the course of negotiations with foreign powers. The Court says it will allow the Executive to perform its duties on its own for six months; after that, foreign relations go into judicially supervised receivership.[29]

As noted, Justice Scalia wrote this in a *dissenting* opinion; indeed, although the plenary power doctrine is still in effect, it has evolved over the years as judicial courts throughout the United States have expanded the number and types of immigration claims they would hear.[30]

Evolution of the plenary doctrine

In 1984, about a century after the Chinese Exclusion Act, Stephen Legomsky predicted the doctrine's future, arguing that the Supreme Court would quickly "lay [it] to rest."[31] It didn't. A decade later, Legomsky revised his projection, stating instead that the plenary power doctrine would "wear away by attrition," that "little by little, exceptions and qualifications will reduce the doctrine to a shadow of its former self without an express overruling of contrary precedent."[32] In fact, this scenario was already "in progress," he observed. Indeed, "a chipping away of the plenary power doctrine"[33] had been happening for years. For instance, while the Supreme Court held in 1893 that a "deportation is not a punishment for crime,"[34] another case about half a century later brought the Court to the opposite conclusion, that "deportation is a drastic measure and at times the equivalent of banishment or exile. It is the forfeiture for misconduct of a residence in this country. Such a forfeiture is a penalty."[35]

A few such notable cases abandoned up to a century of precedents, which defined the power of Congress over immigration law broadly.[36] To cite *Knauff v. Shaughnessy*, a 1950 case of a German-born woman married to an American citizen after having worked for the U.S. War Department in her home country, immigration is "a privilege granted by the sovereign United States Government,"[37] and "the procedure authorized by Congress . . . is due process as far as an alien denied entry is concerned."[38] This premise almost crumbled in 2015, challenged by Fauzia Din, an American citizen, whose husband was denied a visa. Her husband, Kanishka Berashk, is an Afghan citizen and a former civil servant in his country, which was then under the Taliban regime. Din sued on her husband's behalf, advancing that the denial of his visa, a decision rendered with no specific reason, violated her constitutional right to due process of law as a citizen. The Supreme Court was divided on this case, but in a five–four decision, it concluded that the officials do not need to give reasons for denying visa applications. Justices Kennedy and Alito, in a concurring opinion with that of the Court, specified, citing precedent, "the Attorney General validly exercised the plenary power that Congress delegated to the Executive."[39]

Accordingly, while the plenary power doctrine seems more fragile than ever before,[40] it is still in effect. To this day, immigration is the one area in which Congress has the most power.[41] This "constitutional oddity"[42] means that aliens are often not even given a reason for the denial of their visa. As such, people who aspire to athletic careers in the United States, much like other foreigners, generally have very little recourse if their visas are denied—whatever the reason. Indeed, the laws do not provide any special treatment for gifted athletes; they are treated as ordinary immigrants seeking entry into the United States.

Sport Labor Migration

Most of the literature on labor migration has focused on men, with a tendency to focus on women migrating because of their role in the household when their husband decides to relocate.[43] Little research focuses on the migration of skilled women[44] and even less about that of female athletes. Reflecting the heteronormative and masculine culture often observed in sport,[45] "women's sport migrants have not yet found their place in academic literature on the subject of sport labor migration."[46] Indeed, the sport labor migration literature is composed mainly of research studying the most popular men's sports, especially soccer. Further, most of it focuses on either the migration phenomenon in sport through a global lens or the effects of that phenomenon on the athletes and the countries that receive them.[47] This case study, instead, brings to light the difficulties of the immigration process for athletes who do not take part in money-making sports but show high athletic skills nonetheless.

Precarity despite high skills

Michelle Carter, self-proclaimed "shot diva,"[48] became the first American woman to win a shot put Olympic gold medal in Rio in 2016. To support herself, she works as a makeup artist. Like Carter, many Olympic athletes, both men and women, must have a job on the side to survive, despite representing their nation on the most prestigious athletic stage.[49] This exemplifies that even highly skilled athletes (and someone who played on her country's national team in not one but three different—albeit related—sports undoubtedly belongs to the elite) can face financial precarity, forcing them to work in addition to practicing a sport at the highest level. This, of course, increases the risks of fatigue, and thus injury, which could in turn accentuate her precarity: an injured athlete who cannot compete is less likely to find sponsors and could lose out on possible contracts (however short and low paying they are). Because of the low number of professional women's leagues and the small salaries in the professional leagues that do exist, female athletes are more likely to be apprehensive about their finances.

The gender factor

"Identity is always gendered,"[50] and sport labor migration is a "case in point."[51] Looking at tennis and golf players, who travel the world every season, Joseph Maguire explains that "the enabling and constraining features that characterize their experiences may well be markedly different."[52] He continues, generalizing his conclusions to sport labor in general:

> Migrants in general have to do sport-work in various locations and, as a group, experience degrees of exploitation, dislocation and cultural adjustment. Although women are travelling more frequently and in greater numbers, the trend of men moving more freely and in greater

> numbers, over time and across space remains. This trend is based on a social structure that ensures that it is usually women who perform domestic and reproductive labour, whether in the company of their travelling partners or waiting "at home."[53]

Similarly, Thomas Carter sustains that the existence of the sex difference in how athletes experience migration in soccer is generalizable to all migrations:

> Gender is an important social distinction that unquestionably produces differentiated mobility within global football. That women soccer professionals will produce different forms of mobility than their male counterparts is both undeniable and in no way unique to women's soccer, soccer in general, or sport. Gender affects all forms of transnational migration. . . . What is abundantly clear is that for female soccer migrants to produce their own mobility, they are engaging with patriarchal institutions in which men and masculine worldviews about the nature of the world dominate the kinds of social relations engendered.[54]

This explains why women's decision to migrate depends on the gender system in both their country of origin and their country of destination.[55]

Among the sex differences in sport labor migration, one comes from the athletes themselves. Partly because women's sports have much less money involved than men's sports, women often advance motivations to migrate different from the men's. Moreso than economic reward,[56] the women often express the idea that their sport is, as Eliot Freidson put it, a "labor of love"—that is to say, something that we choose to do because we want to, sometimes with little financial reward.[57] In other words, women are more likely to move to another country to pursue their athletic career, not for the money but for either the possibility of having a sport career or the desire to play in a higher-quality league.[58] The latter is the reason Sandrine Rangeon wanted to live in the United States. She is what Jonathan Magee and John Sugden describe as an ambitionist:[59] skating is her passion, and improving her technique on skates is one of her priorities. Because the United States offers the most competitive playing field in her sports, she was set on settling there, but the immigration laws—including the plenary power doctrine, which leaves her no course of action once a visa has been denied—and the lack of opportunities in professional sports for women have forced her to reconsider.

RANGEON: SKATING ALIEN, PERSONA NON GRATA

Rangeon has always practiced various sports. Born and raised in the north of France, her parents were active, walking or riding bikes with her and her sister instead of driving whenever possible. Playing team handball, soccer, and basketball at recess, and practicing judo, swimming, and track and field as extracurricular activities, Rangeon fell in love with her first sport at nine years old, when she started skating.[60]

Hockey: The First Love

Rangeon grew up in Amiens, one of the few cities in the country where the local ice hockey club, Les Gothiques, has a bigger following than the local soccer team.[61] In fourth grade, Rangeon started playing roller-hockey with friends, led by her classmate Jérôme, who played for the youth Gothiques team. Soon after, she beat the odds and became the only girl to join Les Gothiques in her age group.

> And the boys, the players [were] offended that a girl [could] be on the ice with them. I got into a few fights because of it; guys wanted to get into fights against me, to show me that it's a guy's sport, and that I shouldn't be on the ice with them. Even people in the club, the coaches and managers, didn't want me to be on the ice, because it's like I'm "stealing" ice time from the boys.[62]

At 13 years old, Rangeon hung a poster of the Ice-Hockey Women's French National Team (IHWFNT) and learned the players' names and ages as well as any other basic information she could find about the women she hoped would become her teammates. Three years later, in 2002, she received her first letter calling her for an IHWFNT camp. At 16 years old, Rangeon became a staple of the IHWFNT, participating in five World Championships and two Olympic qualifying tournaments, until she retired from the sport in 2011 at only 25 years old. Overpowered by countries where hockey is king (such as Canada or Finland), France never qualified for the Olympics, a dream of Rangeon's, but the team did earn a bronze medal in the 2007 World Championships Division I (the second level after the Elite division).

Rangeon's biggest achievements at the international level happened on wheels rather than on the ice. A member of the In-Line Hockey Women's French National Team (ILHWFNT) from 2004 to 2011, she and her teammates earned three consecutive bronze medals in the sport's World Championships (2005 to 2007), losing to Canada and the United States but beating other powerhouses, such as the Czech Republic.

Studying to Skate Through America

The lack of institutional options for female hockey players in France did not stop Rangeon from having a successful career. In fact, it might even have helped her keep her spot despite her travels: in 2007, she studied abroad at the University of Connecticut, missing close to a year's worth of IHWFNT and ILHWFNT camps, but she still participated in the World Championships in both sports. Her year in the United States confirmed her wish to move there more permanently. "It's where the level is the highest in the sports I do," she explains. After returning to France to finish her bachelor's degree in kinesiology/physical education, she enrolled in a master's degree program in kinesiology and sports psychology at California State University, Fresno (Fresno State). There, in 2010, she discovered roller derby, the sport that would make her quit her first love just a year later: "I started playing roller derby when I lived in California, which wasn't a great place for women's hockey. So I thought I'd get into another skating sport to stay in shape for hockey. Then I fell in love with it and ended up quitting hockey for derby."

Having played at the highest competitive level in two other skating-based sports, Rangeon quickly became a roller-derby star: jammer for the French national team at the first Roller Derby World Cup in December 2011, where she was named most valuable player (MVP) for Team France. A few months later, she earned MVP Jammer at the 2012 Women's Flat Track Derby Association (WFTDA) Championships, the world's largest tournament in flat track roller derby, held in Atlanta, Georgia. That year, she was also voted second-best jammer of the year by Derby News Network readers, after Bonnie Thunders, whose success on the track earned her the nickname of "the Barry Bonds of Roller Derby."[63]

At the time, Rangeon lived in Denver, Colorado, on another student visa. She had successfully finished her research-track master's degree at Fresno State, even earning her college's "2011 Outstanding Thesis Award," but her next endeavor (a PhD program in Ottawa, Canada) made her understand that academic research was not her path. She signed up for an MBA with a specialization in entrepreneurship in Colorado (with the goal of focusing on sport management) and skated for the Denver Roller Dolls. At the time, Rangeon's wildest dreams had finally come true. When featured as the WFTDA player of the month in December 2012, she said:

> In my mind, living in the U.S. was the coolest thing I could ever do. Now, I'm not only lucky enough to be living here, but I'm also in a position where some American people look up to me because of derby. This is well beyond what I ever pictured in my childhood dreams.[64]

Her dream did not last long, though. While she was on a trip back to France, one of her professors dropped Rangeon from a class without notifying her. She found out about it too late: no longer a full-time student, she had lost her visa. Rangeon was "stuck"[65] in Ontario for a few months before yet another sport would open new doors for her.

Two Dreams Revived Thanks to One Sport

While she was in Canada, trying to figure out her next step to return to the United States, Rangeon signed up for a short-track training camp to stay in shape and "get better at roller derby." The camp went better than expected: "The coach, Sue Ellis [ex-Team USA coach] thought I had a lot of potential and should move somewhere to train full time." Rangeon followed her advice and revived her dream of becoming an Olympian by moving to Milwaukee, Wisconsin, to train with two-time Olympic medalist Katherine Reutter. In a blog post right after her move back to the United States, Rangeon said, "Being back in the U.S. and starting to practice again really feels like Christmas came early."[66] Although she did not qualify for an athlete visa, she was hopeful her immigration issues were coming to an end, as she was working to qualify for the 2018 Olympics in South Korea, which her coach admitted was definitely possible: "I think Sandrine . . . is one of the most talented athletes, and most fit athletes, that I've ever worked with, and it's really just about teaching her the skating," Reutter says. "I think it's pretty amazing what she's trying to do, and I think it's realistic, the goal she has set for herself."[67]

The Pettit National Ice Center where Rangeon trained cost about $600 a month for international athletes, a sum she was paying thanks to smart real estate investments and with help from her father. Both her American and Olympic dreams were back on track. In October of 2013, Rangeon enthusiastically posted on Facebook: "Speed skating in the morning, derby in the evening, rinse, repeat. Living the life!"[68]

But neither smart investments nor her father could help with what was to come: after 15 months in Milwaukee, Rangeon's B-1 visa (temporary business visitor visa) expired, and she once again had to leave the country. She had been looking for other avenues but failed to find any, despite help from immigration lawyers. Rangeon was never among the top in the world in short track, "just training toward that," which meant she did not meet the "extraordinary ability" in that particular sport. Roller derby, in her words, "isn't recognized enough," which meant the league could not sponsor her for an athlete visa. And even if she was willing to play hockey again, neither ice hockey nor in-line roller hockey had viable women's leagues.[69] Despite Rangeon's high athletic skills in four different sports, her American dream was crushed once again. Many of her fans made offers on social media to marry her[70] to help her through her immigration issues, but Rangeon was resolved to do things legally and on her own.

"The Best Way to Make Your Dreams Come True Is to Wake Up"[71]

As soon as she got back to France, Rangeon started her application for an E-2 investor visa, which few people can even afford to apply for because it requires one to invest tens of thousands of dollars into either purchasing an existing business or creating a new business in the United States. Rangeon, who owns two houses in the United States, started her own real estate company, for which she received an employer tax identification number from the IRS in late 2013.[72]

Working with an attorney, Rangeon started her visa application in the hopes of moving back to the United States in time for the 2015 roller derby season, in February 2015. She was allowed into the country on a couple of short-term visits to check on her houses, but she finished the year still living in France. To celebrate the arrival of 2016, she posted on Facebook a message full of hope:

> My main goals for 2015 were to get an E2 visa and play roller derby. I failed at both.
>
> I failed at both, but I ended up having a wonderfully surprising year. I wanted to spend the year growing my business, but instead ended up having to live on passive income and short-term gigs. Even if it was a bit stressful at times, I'm glad I had this experience. I got to travel to 12 different countries, and spent more time with family than I did in the previous 3 years combined. I discovered new sports, made new friends, and focused on doing things, rather than owning things.
>
> Maybe it wasn't a perfect year by usual standards, but maybe it's exactly what I needed. Bring it on, 2016.[73]

Indeed, Rangeon picked up two new skating sports in 2015 while the USCIS was reviewing her file, including a "hobby"[74] in which she has already made waves. Four years after first trying to participate in Red Bull Crashed Ice,[75] Rangeon finally joined the tour in early 2016. She was able to after entering one of six 2015 Riders Cup events, "an open competition that acts as a feeder event for skaters to qualify for the larger Crashed Ice series."[76] Her third-place finish in her first-ever ice cross downhill competition made her both "happy" and "frustrated,"[77] which shows her "ambitionist" approach,[78] her determination to always improve her skating technique and skills.

Rangeon's reputation as one of the best skaters in the world has also given her opportunities to travel to share her knowledge. "I get asked to coach leagues around the world. I love coaching and I'm always extremely flattered to receive invitations to teach at boot camps,"[79] she says. Yet, all of her hopes were once again crushed by the USCIS in February of 2016: visa denied.

At first, Rangeon was adamant on trying again, even if it meant spending "another $10k"[80] on a second E-2 visa application, but she writes,

> The more I tried to understand why my first application was denied, the less sense it made. Some rules for E2 visas completely contradict

> themselves, and you're left wondering how to tiptoe a line that isn't clearly traced. Take this example: I was refused entry into the U.S. at one point last year, for having hired an employee, which apparently I wasn't allowed to do. So I let the employee go, and then one of the reasons they gave for refusing my E2 this year was that I didn't have any employees . . . Um, what?[81]

After one J visa (as an exchange student), two F-1 visas (as a student in California and Colorado), and countless short-term and long-term B visas (tourist/business), Rangeon gave up. Her skepticism got the better of her, and she decided to switch her focus to Australia.

CONCLUSION: A NEW LIFE DOWN UNDER

When Rangeon decided to give up on a U.S. visa for the foreseeable future, she was left with two options: stay in France, which she describes as "settling down for simple, easy, and maybe a little lazy," or go somewhere new. She decided to do her best to "leave emotions out of it," so using the skills she learned in graduate school, she made a table to rate places "on a bunch of criteria, which included things such as real estate opportunities/work, immigration, quality of life, family, roller derby, Red Bull crashed ice training (skate parks + skiing + ice rink availability), etc." On top of that table came Australia, home of the "second best roller derby team in the world,"[82] so Rangeon once again packed her bags and flew down under on a three-month visitor visa, putting no pressure on the trip as she knew she could "easily return to France."[83]

Despite breaking her ankle in a roller derby practice soon after moving to Melbourne, Rangeon likes her new life. Granted a one-year working holiday visa,[84] Rangeon plans on staying in Australia much longer. She says the government offers "a lot of visa options leading to permanent residency, so [she] will most likely apply for a distinguished talent visa (athlete visa equivalent) as a roller derby player and inline hockey player. This would make [her] a permanent resident and [she] could potentially play on the Australian national teams for both of these sports."

She has not forgotten ice cross downhill either. Within a month of participation in the sport, Rangeon was ranked No. 9 in the world—the highest place for a European female athlete—and it was important to her to find a place that would allow her to practice ice cross effectively to improve her ranking.[85] When asked about how she envisions her near future, she says, "I see myself staying in Australia and hopefully being part of the first non-American team to win the Hydra (roller derby championships). I'd also like to keep racing Red Bull Crashed Ice and become a consistent top 5 finisher."[86]

From ice hockey and in-line roller hockey to roller derby and ice cross downhill, Rangeon has proven to be one of the most complete athletes of her generation, yet she has had to be flexible in where she lives because her American dream died one too many times.

Women's inclusion and exclusion in athletics is an international problem. Roller derby is one of the very few sports to break the "acceptable boundaries of who gets to participate in sports and what it means to be feminine and masculine."[87] It is "fun," Rangeon says, partly because players "don't have all the pressures that come with sports controlled by federations and clubs that don't really care about their women's teams."[88] The WFTDA's ethos to be "for the skaters, by the skaters"[89] helps tremendously in getting minorities to participate[90] and become active in the sport and in the league. Despite the WFTDA's growing popularity[91] and a recent agreement with ESPN3[92] and the sport's demands for fitness and athleticism, the league does not meet the USCIS's requirements that would allow visa sponsoring for athletes.

The narrow definitions for professional and amateur leagues in the COMPETE Act of 2006 and the limited categories of O visas, paired with the lack of opportunities in women's sports, have caused the United States to lose one of the best skaters in the world and a coach who is sought out at the international level. That immigrants are held to a higher standard than U.S. citizens for fewer rights is not a new notion,[93] but the standards required for an athlete visa put athletes of some minor sports at a major disadvantage. Because women's sports are often in the same lot as minor sports (lack of media coverage, difficulty of making a living, less recognition for athletes, etc.), immigration standards and the plenary doctrine, which blocks athletes from any judicial remedy, make migrating to the United States difficult, especially for women, creating yet another sex imbalance in the world of sport.

It also slows down the evolution of women's sports and hinders efforts at leveling the playing field. Indeed, athletes are more likely to thrive when competing against highly skilled opponents. In tennis, for instance, Serena Williams has often admitted that she "wouldn't be the player [she is] without Venus,"[94] her older sister. Similar observations—one athlete pushing the other and vice versa to increase the level of play—have been made about other great rivalries in various sports: Larry Bird and Magic Johnson in basketball; Annika Sorenstam and Karrie Webb in golf; Cristiano Ronaldo and Lionel Messi in soccer; Shelly-Ann Fraser-Pryce and Carmelita Jeter in track; and so on. Ultimately, obstacles to athletes' migration are a disservice to women's sports. Citing the example of Japan, which "foster[ed] the achievements of the national team" in women's soccer thanks to the emigration of its players to mainly European professional leagues, Sine Agergaard and Nina Tiesler conclude that "the transnational migration of players (and coaches) is the uttermost importance for the development of the game."[95]

Japan's performance in the 2010s (one World Cup win, one World Cup final, and one Olympic silver medal) is proof.

It is hard to believe that Rangeon is the only gifted athlete incapable of moving to the United States to improve her game and consequently that of others. Rangeon also happens to be a Western European with more freedom to move on her own and more financial stability than athletes from many other countries. Yet, the lack of viable leagues in women's professional sports still keeps her out of the United States. While new women's leagues have been created over the past few years in sports such as soccer and ice hockey,[96] that is not nearly enough for women to close the gap with their male counterparts. Future sociological research should consider these issues related to the immigration process—in addition to the existing research about the effects of migration. As the topic of immigration reform has been discussed in Washington for years, the timing to look into the issue seems particularly appropriate.

NOTES

1. David A. Martin, "Why Immigration's Plenary Power Doctrine Endures," *Oklahoma Law Review* 68 (2015): 29–56.
2. The U.S. code regulates the issuance of visas.
3. "Opening Day Rosters Feature 230 Players Born Outside the U.S.," *MLB.com*, last modified April 6, 2015, http://m.mlb.com/news/article/116591920/opening-day-rosters-feature-230-players-born-outside-the-us/.
4. "NBA Sets Record with 101 International Players from 37 Countries and Territories," *NBA.com*, last modified October 28, 2014, http://www.nba.com/global/nba_sets_record_with_101_international_players_37_countries_territories_2014_10_27.html.
5. "O-1 Visa: Individuals with Extraordinary Ability or Achievement," *Official Website of the Department of Homeland Security*, accessed July 13, 2016, https://www.uscis.gov/working-united-states/temporary-workers/o-1-visa-individuals-extraordinary-ability-or-achievement.
6. The COMPETE Act of 2006 expanded the category of people eligible for P-1 visas to include coaches and athletes from certain amateur leagues as well as athletes employed for theatrical ice skating productions.
7. "P-1A Internationally Recognized Athlete," *Official Website of the Department of Homeland Security*, accessed July 13, 2016, https://www.uscis.gov/working-united-states/temporary-workers/p-1a-internationally-recognized-athlete.
8. "Creating Opportunities for Minor League Professionals, Entertainers, and Teams through Legal Entry Act of 2006 (COMPETE Act of 2006), Pub. L. No. 109-463, 120 Stat. 3477 (2006) (admission as P-1 nonimmigrant)," memo, accessed on May 4, 2016, https://www.uscis.gov/sites/default/files/USCIS/Laws/Memoranda/Static_Files_Memoranda/competeact122806.pdf.
9. Ibid.

10. B. David Zarley, "Born to Skate," *Sports on Earth*, last modified February 19, 2014, http://www.sportsonearth.com/article/67915222/roller-derby-star-sandrine-rageon-tries-for-olympic-speed-skating.

11. Sandrine Rangeon (international athlete), personal communication with the author, July 2016.

12. *Chae Chan Ping v. United States*, 130 U.S. 581 (1889).

13. The United States' federal government is composed of three branches: the legislative (Congress), the executive (the president of the United States), and the judicial (federal courts, including the highest, the Supreme Court). The political branches are the legislative and the executive.

14. *Mathews v. Diaz*, 426 U.S. 67 (1976), 81.

15. Martin, "Plenary Power Doctrine Endures."

16. "Evolution of the U.S. Immigration Court System: Pre-1983," The United States Department of Justice, last modified April 30, 2015, https://www.justice.gov/eoir/evolution-pre-1983.

17. "About the Office," The United States Department of Justice, last modified September 8, 2015, https://www.justice.gov/eoir/about-office.

18. The Supreme Court's decision reads: "If there be nay just ground of complaint on the part of China, it must be made to the political department of our government, which is alone competent to act upon the subject." *Chae Chan Ping v. United States*, 609.

19. *Chae Chan Ping v. United States*, 603.

20. See for example *Nishimura Ekiu v. United States*, 142 U.S. 660 (1892) and *Fong Yue Ting v. United States*, 149 U.S. 698 (1893).

21. The system was abandoned because it raised "significant concerns about due process." "U.S. Immigration Court System: Pre-1983."

22. *Nishimura Ekiu v. United States*, 660.

23. *Harisiades v. Shaughnessy*, 342 U.S. 580 (1952), 596.

24. *Fiallo v. Bell*, 430 U.S. 787 (1977), 792.

25. Margaret H. Taylor, "Detained Aliens Challenging Conditions of Confinement and the Porous Border of the Plenary Power Doctrine," *Hastings Constitutional Law Quarterly* 22 (1995): 1127.

26. Martin, "Plenary Power Doctrine Endures."

27. *Demore v. Hyung Joon Kim*, 538 U.S. 510 (2003), 522.

28. *Harisiades v. Shaughnessy*, 591.

29. *Zadvydas v. Davis*, 533 U.S. 678 (2001), 712.

30. Jon Feere, "Plenary Power: Should Judges Control U.S. Immigration Policy?," Backgrounders and Reports, Center for Immigration Studies, February 2009, http://www.cis.org/plenarypower.

31. Stephen H. Legomsky, "Immigration Law and the Principle of Plenary Congressional Power," *The Supreme Court Review* 1984 (1985): 305.

32. Stephen H. Legomsky, "Ten More Years of Plenary Power: Immigration, Congress, and the Courts," *Hastings Constitutional Law Quarterly* 22 (1995): 934.

33. Feere, "Plenary Power," 7.

34. *Fong Yue Ting v. United States*, 730.

35. *Fong Haw Tan v. Phelan*, 333 U.S. 6 (1948), 10.

36. Ozan O. Varol, "Substantive Due Process, Plenary-Power Doctrine, and Minimum Contacts: Arguments for Overcoming the Obstacle of Asserting Personal Jurisdiction over Terrorists Under the Anti-Terrorism Act," *Iowa Law Review* 92 (2006): 320.

37. *Knauff v. Shaughnessy*, 338 U.S. 537 (1952), 542.

38. Ibid., 544.

39. *Kerry v. Din*, 576 U.S. (2015), Docket No. 13-1402.

40. Michael Kagan, "Plenary Power Is Dead! Long Live Plenary Power!," *Michigan Law Review First Impressions* 114 (2015): 21–29.

41. Legomsky, "Immigration Law."

42. Ibid., 255.

43. Parvati Raghuram, "Migrant Women in Male-Dominated Sectors of the Labour Market: A Research Agenda," *Population, Space and Place* 14 (2008): 43–57.

44. Sine Ageergard and Nina Clara Tiesler, "Introduction," in *Women, Soccer and Transnational Migration*, eds. Sine Ageergard and Nina Clara Tiesler (London: Routledge, 2014), 5.

45. Decades of research found that the world of sport is overly masculine and heteronormative. See, for example, the works of Michael A. Messner and that of Eric Anderson, including Michael A. Messner, *Out of Play: Critical Essays on Gender & Sport* (Albany, NY: SUNY Press, 2007), and Eric Anderson, *Out in Sport: The Experiences of Openly Gay and Lesbian Athletes in Competitive Sport* (Albany, NY: SUNY Press, 2016).

46. Sine Ageergard, "Elite Athletes as Migrants in Danish Women's Handball," *International Review for the Sociology of Sport* 43 (2008): 5–6.

47. Anthony Borgese, "Labor and Immigration Issues in Sports," *The Sport Journal* 12 (2009): 1–10.

48. The URL to her official website is http://www.shotdiva.com.

49. Kerry Close, "These Are the Day Jobs Olympians Work While They Chase Their Dreams, Why It's So Hard to Earn a Living as an Olympic Athlete," *Time*, last modified August 10, 2016, http://time.com/money/4428302/2016-rio-olympics-earning-side-jobs/.

50. Janet Wolff, "The Global and the Specific: Reconciling Conflicting Theories of Culture," in *Culture, Globalization and the World-System*, ed. Anthony D. King (London: Macmillan, 1991), 169.

51. Joseph Maguire, "Sport, Identity Politics, and Globalization: Diminishing Contrasts and Increasing Varieties," in *Sport: Critical Concepts in Sociology, Vol. II: The Development of Sport*, ed. Eric Dunning (London: Routledge, 2003), 399.

52. Joseph Maguire, "'Real Politic' or 'Ethically Based': Sport, Globalization, Migration and Nation-State Policies," *Sport in Society* 14 (2011): 1044.

53. Ibid.

54. Thomas F. Carter, "On Mobility and Visibility in Women's Soccer: Theorizing an Alternative Approach to Sport Migration," in *Women, Soccer and Transnational Migration*, eds. Sine Ageergard and Nina Clara Tiesler (London: Routledge, 2014), 168.

55. Vera Lucia Botelho and Bente Ovedie Skogvang, "Leaving the Core: The Emigration of Scandinavian Women Soccer Players," in *Women, Soccer and Transnational Migration*, eds. Sine Ageergard and Nina Clara Tiesler (London: Routledge, 2014), 119.

56. Maguire, "'Real Politic' or 'Ethically Based.'"

57. Eliot Freidson, "Labors of Love in Theory and Practice: A Prospectus," in *The Nature of Work*, eds. Kai Erikson and Steven Peter Vallas (New Haven, CT: Yale University Press, 1990).

58. Botelho and Skogvang, "Leaving the Core."

59. Jonathan Magee and John Sugden, "'The World at Their Feet': Professional Football and International Labor Migration," *Journal of Sport and Social Issues* 26 (2002): 421–37.

60. Sandrine Rangeon (international athlete), personal communication with the author, April 2016.

61. "L'Histoire des Gothiques: Episode VIII" [The Gothiques' History: Episode VIII], *lesgothiques.com*, last modified December 31, 2014, http://www.lesgothiques.com/lhistoire-gothiques-episode-viii/.

62. Zarley, "Born to Skate."

63. Carly Quick, "Best Roller Derby Players of All Time," *Devaskation*, accessed July 13, 2016, http://www.devaskation.com/Best-Roller-Derby-Players-of-All-Time.

64. "December 2012 Featured Skater: Sandrine 'Francey Pants' Rangeon," *WFTDA.com*, last modified December 7, 2012, https://wftda.com/featured-skater/francey-pants.

65. Sandrine Rangeon, "Glad There's Some Derby Online" (Facebook update), September 22, 2013, https://www.facebook.com/sandrine.rangeon/posts/10101485646399591.

66. Sandrine Rangeon, "Milwaukee/Chicago," Sandrine Rangeon (blog), last modified May 21, 2016, http://www.srangeon.com/milwaukee-chicago/.

67. Zarley, *Born to Skate*.

68. Sandrine Rangeon, "Living the Life!" (Facebook update), October 22, 2013, https://www.facebook.com/sandrine.rangeon/posts/10101536256262021.

69. Professional women's ice hockey now exists in the United States through the four-team National Women's Hockey League (NWHL), which launched in 2015.

70. Rangeon said in a private conversation that some of her fans have offered to marry her via Facebook private messages. Others do so in Facebook comments on various visa-related posts.

71. Rangeon said in a discussion with the author that among her favorite quotes, one from French author Paul Valéry stands out: *La meilleure façon de realiser ses rêves est de se réveiller* [the best way to make your dreams come true is to wake up]. After being asked to leave the United States, Rangeon decided to follow Valéry's advice to make her American dream come true: she decided to apply for an entrepreneur visa.

72. Sandrine Rangeon, "Officially a Business Owner" (Instagram post), November 6, 2013, https://www.instagram.com/p/gZGLasJ3kk/.

73. Sandrine Rangeon, "My Main Goals for 2015" (Facebook update), December 31, 2015, https://www.facebook.com/sandrine.rangeon/posts/10103049128084761.

74. Sandrine Rangeon, "So . . . I Have a New Hobby" (Facebook update), December 16, 2015, https://www.facebook.com/photo.php?fbid=10103020646257571&set=a.835189601271.2488147.9032668&type=3.

75. Red Bull Crashed Ice is the most prestigious series of events in ice cross downhill. Qualifying for the tour when Rangeon started trying was random, based on a lottery system, which selected as many as 200 men but only 20 women. Rangeon unsuccessfully tried to qualify through the lottery system in 2012, 2013, and 2014.

76. Andy Frye, "It's Like Roller Derby on Ice: Meet One of the Stars of the Red Bull Crashed Ice Series," *excelle sports*, last modified February 18, 2016, http://www.excellesports.com/news/sandrine-rangeon-ice-cross/.

77. Sandrine Rangeon, "I Took Third Place in the Race" (Facebook update), December 21, 2015, https://www.facebook.com/sandrine.rangeon/posts/10103027310592191.

78. Magee and Sugden, "The World at Their Feet."

79. Sandrine Rangeon, personal communication with the author, July 2016.

80. Sandrine Rangeon, "Something New," Sandrine Rangeon (blog), May 21, 2016, http://www.srangeon.com/something-new/.

81. Ibid.

82. Sandrine Rangeon, personal communication with the author, July 2016.

83. Rangeon, "Something New."

84. Rangeon was granted this visa thanks to an advantageous program between Australia and France that allows young citizens of these nations, aged 18 to 31, to discover the other country. See "Working Holiday Visa (subclass 417)," Australian Government Department of Immigration and Border Protection, accessed July 14, 2016, https://www.border.gov.au/Trav/Visa-1/417-.

85. Sandrine Rangeon, personal communication with the author, July 2016.

86. Ibid.

87. Alex Hanna, "Roller Derby Doesn't Enforce Gender Separation and Women Still Rule the Sport," *TheGuardian.com*, last modified August 19, 2015, http://www.theguardian.com/commentisfree/2015/aug/19/roller-derby-gender-separation-women-rule-the-sport.

88. Sandrine Rangeon, personal communication with the author, July 2016.

89. Ibid.

90. Roller derby is primarily played by women, including trans women, who are often excluded from women's sports. Women (trans or cis) are often perceived as a minority in the hypermasculine world of sport. Simon Copland, "Roller Derby Could Herald a Revolution for Gender Equality in Sport," *TheGuardian.com*, last modified June 17, 2014, https://www.theguardian.com/lifeandstyle/2014/jun/18/could-the-men-of-roller-derby-become-sports-first-male-feminists; Hanna, "Roller Derby Doesn't Enforce Gender Separation and Women Still Rule the Sport"; Rachel McKinnon, "Stereotype Threat and Attributional Ambiguity for Trans Women," *Hypatia* 29, no. 4 (2014): 857.

91. Adele Pavlidis and James Connor, "Men in a 'Women Only' Sport? Contesting Gender Relations and Sex Integration in Roller Derby," *Sport in Society*, advance online publication, accessed June 1, 2016, http://www.tandfonline.com/doi/abs/10.1080/17430437.2015.1067781?journalCode=fcss20.

92. Brandon Harder, "Roller Derby's Popularity in Saskatoon Shows No Signs of Toe Stopping," *TheStarPhoenix.com*, last modified May 15, 2016, http://thestarphoenix.com/news/local-news/roller-derbys-popularity-in-saskatoon-shows-no-signs-of-toe-stopping.

93. Immigrants to the United States can be banned from the country for issues that would have resulted in a monetary fine for U.S. citizens because they are expected to behave irreproachably, even though they are often granted less freedom than U.S. citizens; for instance, immigrants are often allowed to have one employer only, which limits opportunities to immigrate in underpaid occupations, such as women athletics. Further, traveling—even within the country—can be more difficult because it is regulated by the USCIS. Jackson Lewis, "The Top Five Immigration Mistakes Made by Foreign Athletes," *Immigration Blog*, last modified February 26, 2015, http://www.globalimmigrationblog.com/2015/02/the-top-five-immigration-mistakes-made-by-foreign-athletes/.

94. Bill Dwyre, "Serena Williams Beats Venus, but Little Else Is Revealed at Wimbledon," *Los Angeles Times*, last modified July 6, 2015, http://www.latimes.com/sports/la-sp-serena-venus-dwyre-20150707-column.html.

95. Ageergard and Tiesler, "Introduction," 13.

96. The National Women's Soccer League (NWSL) was established in 2012, shortly after the Women's Professional Soccer league (WPS) announced it was folding. Currently in its fourth season, it is the longest-running professional women's soccer league in the country, having surpassed the defunct Women's United Soccer Association and WPS (three seasons each). In ice hockey, the NWHL was established in March 2015, and its first game was in October 2015.

4

More Than One: What Happened When Multiple Black Female Athletes Excelled in Predominantly White Sports at the Rio Olympics

Rachel Laws Myers

INTRODUCTION

After the London 2012 Olympics came to a close, I wrote a piece entitled "African American Female Athletic Image: What We Should Take Away from the London 2012 Olympic Games."[1] That essay focused on two events that unfolded during the 2012 Games: the American Black community's issues with gymnast Gabby Douglas's hair, and the criticism of the media by hurdlers Dawn Harper and Kellie Wells in their sole focus on Lolo Jones leading up to the women's track and field competition at the Games. The events surrounding Gabby Douglas revealed a great deal about racism—structural, internalized, and interpersonal—and how it plays out in sport (particularly in a sport perceived as a "White" sport in the United States).

Douglas took a two-year hiatus from competitive elite gymnastics after the 2012 Olympics in order to write a book, tour, and develop her biopic *The Gabby Douglas Story* (2014). During that two-year absence from the national and international gymnastics stage, something remarkable happened: Simone Biles. While it's certainly *most* remarkable that Biles is the most decorated American female gymnast in history (she's been the World Gymnastics champion since 2013, earning 10 golds there, along with four more medals overall that comprise the most of any American), it is also momentous that she also happens to be Black.

With Gabby Douglas's successful return to elite gymnastics and the international domination of Simone Biles, aspiring gymnasts around the world and the populace of the United States that watches Olympic gymnastics in astounding televised numbers every four years looked to two young Black women to emulate and support as the Olympic trials unfolded in the second week of July 2016. Sure, this emulation and support of Black female athletes happens often in sports like basketball, track and field, and soccer, but two Black female athletes leading the team has *never* happened at the Olympic level in gymnastics. Historically, gymnastics has been dominated by nations without gymnasts of the African diaspora,[2] and the United States has never had more than one Black gymnast on an Olympic team. What happened when there was more than one? How did the media present Gabby Douglas and Simone Biles to the nation leading up to the 2016 Olympics in Brazil? How did the Black community support and criticize these gymnasts? What (if any) type of measurable progress has been made toward the diversification of USA Gymnastics since the 2012 Olympics? This essay will first present a brief background on Gabby Douglas, Simone Biles, and the history of the Black gymnast. Through the use of subheadings centered on issues of racism in predominantly White sports, the proliferation of the "tragedy to triumph" narrative, and discussion about where predominantly White sports should go from here, this work explores and analyzes how these Black gymnasts were portrayed by the media and public leading up to, during, and after the Rio Olympic Games. This essay concludes with a discussion of diversity within the sport of gymnastics in the United States and offers suggestions and predictions about the future of women's gymnastics and other predominantly White sports.

METHODOLOGY

In order to collect data for this essay, this researcher gathered a number of online periodicals, scholarly journals, and books that focused on race, culture, gender, and the media. In addition, it was invaluable to watch a number of live and prerecorded televised events: the 2016 U.S. Olympic gymnastics trials, the Oxygen series *Douglas Family Gold*, and the 2016 Olympics gymnastics and swimming competitions. After annotating the literature and taking copious notes on visual events, this researcher used qualitative data analysis methods (i.e., examining and organizing the data into specific categories) to form impressions and report them in the structured format of this essay.

A BRIEF HISTORY OF THE BLACK GYMNAST

If this researcher was asked who the first Black gymnast was when this researcher was a 12-year-old competitive gymnast in the year 1996, she would have said "Dominique Dawes" with absolute confidence. Yet, that's not the correct answer. While Dominique Dawes and Betty Okino became the first

Black American gymnasts to win an Olympic medal (a team bronze) in 1992, "Ron Galimore and Luci Collins Cummings are officially recognized as the first Black U.S. Olympic gymnasts."[3] However, Galimore and Cummings never got to compete after making the 1980 Olympic team due to the U.S. boycott of the Moscow Games. Galimore was recently inducted into the 2016 class of the USA Gymnastics Hall of Fame after winning multiple national titles before making the would-be competitive 1980 Olympic team and earning the first perfect 10 in National Collegiate Athletic Association (NCAA) Championships history on the vault for Iowa State in 1981. Gymnastics was just beginning to be televised during this time, thanks largely to the superstardom of Romanian gymnast Nadia Comăneci, in the 1976 Olympic Games. Galimore states that "as in any sport, all you need is a role model . . . that [1980] Olympics would have done quite a bit to attract new sets of eyes to our sport."[4]

Unlike Ron Galimore, Luci Collins Cummings did not receive much attention from the Black community at the 1980 Olympic trials. Being the child of Creole parents and having an address in the Inglewood section of California were not enough for outside viewers to see her Black identity through her very "White-looking" (i.e., light-colored eyes and skin, hair that isn't coarse) exterior features. Cummings admitted that "there were times [she] felt [she] wasn't a good enough representation . . . and all who followed [her] have created a wave of cultural support in the African-American community and a wave of African-American youth to dare to dream of trying gymnastics."[5] A number of other Black gymnasts have come and gone from the Olympic spotlight since Cummings and Galimore, such as Dianne Durham, Wendy Hilliard, Jair Lynch, Donovan Bailey, Tasha Schwikert, Betty Okino, and Dominique Dawes.

So what's changed in the landscape of exposure for Black gymnasts Douglas and Biles? There appears to be a number of things that set Douglas and Biles at an entirely new level of influence from those who came before them: social media, socioeconomics, and timing. Never had a Black gymnast won the Olympic All-Around title until Douglas clinched it in 2012 and then Simone Biles easily won it for herself in Rio. Douglas and Biles have set the stage for a new generation of elite Black gymnasts to emerge, as their titles will remain noteworthy in the public eye until the 2020 Tokyo Olympics. That's a total of eight years that will have elapsed with a Black woman representing the epitome of what has been known as a predominantly White sport. Black athletic success is not a genetic phenomenon but the result of the determination of Black individuals to overcome perceived arbitrary and deliberately contrived social barriers.[6] Douglas and Biles destroy the perception that gymnastics is a sport where only White people can find ultimate success and access. Douglas had her own reality television series on the Oxygen Network airing from late

May through early July 2016, and Biles *owns* the gym that she—and plenty of young White children—train at. The social barriers are now down, and a strong spotlight is showing the racialized blunders of White-controlled media outlets in their coverage of Biles and Douglas.

SIMONE BILES

At the age of six, Simone Biles was accidentally introduced to the sport of gymnastics. The extreme heat of a Texas day caused her school's field trip to divert indoors to a local gymnastics club rather than the ranch she and her classmates were supposed to visit. Biles was mesmerized and "began taking classes at Bannon's Gymnastix, in Houston."[7] Her coach, Aimee Boorman, saw her immense athleticism and began to train her. Similar to the majority of elite gymnasts in the United States, Biles spent her high school years being homeschooled so that she could have more hours of training in the gym. Biles lives with her parents, Nellie and Ron, in a suburb north of Houston."[8] In 2012, Biles was a year shy of the required Olympic age requirement. In the four-year span between the 2012 London Olympics and the Games in Rio, Biles became the first woman to win four U.S. All-Around titles in a row since Joan Moore Gnat did so between 1971 and 1974, *and* Biles amassed three World All-Around Champion titles between 2013 and 2015. In fact, Biles's "10 World gold medals is the most ever in women's gymnastics history."[9] This means that in four short years, Simone Biles had become the most dominant and successful gymnast in the history of the world.

GABBY DOUGLAS

Since making history in the 2012 London Olympic Games as the first Black gymnast to win the All-Around title, Gabby Douglas's life has changed drastically. When there were less than 100 days until the Rio Games, *Teen Vogue* reported that "the Virginia Beach, Virginia, native has a *New York Times* bestselling book; her own line of leotards, Gabbymojis; and a new docuseries [aired] on Oxygen called *Douglas Family Gold*."[10] Additionally, Douglas has been featured on cereal boxes and magazine covers and in a number of commercials for different products, and she has rubbed elbows with megacelebrities like Oprah Winfrey, Michelle Obama, and Alicia Keys. While Douglas left the London Olympics a 16-year-old girl, she arrived in Rio a 20-year-old woman with the financial stability to have moved her mother, brother, and two older sisters from Virginia Beach to an impressive home in the San Fernando Valley of California.

Douglas also made a coaching change since the London Olympics, leaving her former coach, Liang Chow, and Iowa to train at Buckeye Gymnastics in

Columbus, Ohio. With only her grandmother, "Miss Carolyn," by her side living in Ohio, Douglas was able to accomplish a rare return to a second Olympics appearance. Simply making a second Olympic team is a tall order for women;[11] Aly Raisman and Douglas were the only two of the London Games' "Fierce Five" that didn't retire before the Rio Games. With her return to the Olympic stage, Douglas was able to add another team gold to her medal collection. Unfortunately for Douglas, however, some of the same unwarranted criticism (along with some new) she had faced in London came back to haunt her in Rio. Why did this happen again? A simple answer: race.

THE PROLIFERATION OF THE "TRAGEDY TO TRIUMPH" NARRATIVE

Biles (at age five) and her sister Adria (at age three) were adopted by their maternal grandfather, Ron, and his wife, Nellie. Leading up to (and during) the Olympics in Rio, some media tried to portray Biles's family structure as a "tragedy to triumph" narrative, even though her adoptive parents are financially stable, enrolling her in costly gymnastics classes and even building her a gym:

> World Champions Centre, which is owned by Ron and Nellie Biles, who built it from the ground up as their retirement venture, consulting with architects on its family-friendly design. It's a 56,000-square-foot, light-filled and color-splashed oasis for gymnasts of all ages and abilities, as well as their parents and siblings. The Biles made sure to include the amenities they would have liked during the years they took turns watching Biles practice and compete in countless gyms around the country and world. There's an observation room above the gym floor for adults, with Wi-Fi and comfortable seating. There's a café; dance and taekwondo studios for siblings who aren't interested in gymnastics but need to stay busy; classrooms for use by families who home-school their children.[12]

It is interesting how often the media has chosen to highlight the fact that Simone's parents are not her birth mother and father, but media remain fairly silent about her family's economic stability. Of the dozen or so articles collected by this researcher on Biles, only two mentioned that Biles's parents built the gym in which she trains.[13] With a strong socioeconomic place in the world and chores and hobbies, such as "feeding her four German shepherds, taking her turn doing the dishes and cleaning her room each week . . . Netflix addiction, listening to Justin Bieber, shopping with friends at Woodlands Mall and daydreaming about one day meeting her crush, Zac Efron,"[14] keeping Biles's image as relatable as any other White gymnast, the media chose to hone in on the one thing they could to cast her into a tragic Black narrative: Biles's birth mother.

Biles was born in Columbus, Ohio, in March of 1997, and her birth mother struggled with drugs and alcohol. While *The New Yorker* tastefully writes that "at the age of two, [Biles] and three siblings were taken from their mother . . . and placed in foster care,"[15] in a detailed piece on Biles and the transformation of the point system in gymnastics, *People* magazine used the headline "How Gymnast Simone Biles Overcame Being Given Up by Her Mother to Become an Olympic Gold Hopeful"[16] to capture readers' attention. *People* magazine's choice to use the word "overcame" and the phrase "given up" in the title of their piece on Biles is laced with insidious racial stereotypes. When one overcomes something, one must have a struggle or difficulty to successfully work through. Yet, the author of this *People* piece does not mention Biles's difficulty with anything and simply quotes Biles saying of Ron and Nellie that "my parents make sure we have everything we need so that we compete to the best of our abilities."[17] Chances are high that any other Rio Olympic gymnast in the world with parents would have said the same of their own parents. Tom Leonard, a writer for the UK publication *Daily Mail*, chose an even more tragic headline for his August 12, 2016, piece on Biles: "Awesome Triumph: How the 4ft 8in Smiling Girl Who's Set the Olympics Alight Overcame an Appalling Childhood."[18] Yet Biles doesn't view her childhood as "appalling," nor does she believe that she had to "overcome" being raised by her adoptive parents rather than her biological mother. In fact, Biles told the *Daily Mail*, "When I was younger, I thought every kid was adopted . . . I didn't understand why people made it such a big deal. To me it's just normal."[19] In placing emphasis on her family structure—which is by all means stable and healthy—the media are clearly attempting to place Biles in the tragedy-to-triumph narrative that a number of successful Black athletes fall into due to socioeconomic hardship in their childhoods; the problem is that Biles doesn't fit into this box at all.

Even one of the most well-known NBC Sports commentators, Al Trautwig, chose to focus on Biles's family structure as a means to "other" her from the rest of the Olympic gymnasts. Fortunately, viewers called him out via social media for not accepting the fact that Ron and Nellie are indeed Biles's parents. Trautwig, whose career spans 40 years and coverage of multiple Olympic Games, first misspoke on air, stating that Biles "was raised by her grandfather and his wife and she calls them mom and dad," then tweeted, "They may be mom and dad but they are NOT her parents," after a profile piece aired on NBC on August 7.[20] Trautwig quickly deleted the tweet and offered an apology, but his comments ignited a discussion about biological versus adoptive parents online. The researcher argues, however, that Trautwig made his comments due to his racial bias toward Black Americans. After all, "Trautwig also consistently confused Biles with her teammate Gabby Douglas in his on-air commentary,"[21] and they were the only two Black Americans in the Olympic competition—not to mention they look nothing alike. Throughout her own meteoric rise, Gabby has overcome unthinkable odds—from starting out homeless and leaving her close-knit family behind at age 14 in pursuit of her Olympic dream to confronting racism along the way.[22] Just because Gabby Douglas's story *does* nicely adhere to the tragedy-to-triumph label, that doesn't mean Biles's story must also fit this narrative in order to be viewed as acceptably successful to Americans.

RACISM IN PREDOMINANTLY WHITE SPORTS

In his book *Promoting Racial Literacy in Schools: Differences That Make a Difference*, Howard Stevenson includes a section entitled "When Racial Hierarchy Is Challenged, Black and Brown People Become Expendable." While the focus of Stevenson's work is race relations in the school setting, a number of insights can be taken from his observations of predominantly White spaces (PWS) in education and applied to the predominantly White space that is competitive gymnastics. It is crucial to understand that "racial hierarchy defines diversity in predominantly White settings in a particular way."[23] Until four years ago, Whiteness—meaning "how individuals and groups construct meaning in a world in which racial hierarchy is a standard against which coping models are developed and evaluated"[24]—historically reigned supreme in the physical and psychological spaces of the gymnastics world. This means that physical representations of success and psychological mind-sets of aspiring Olympic gymnasts held the notion that the "best" and "better" gymnasts are White. Whiteness is "the standard by which we judge most of our successes and failures, our heroes, villains, and antivillains, our best and brightest, our leaders and followers."[25]

With the racial hierarchy in gymnastics holding White gymnasts as the epitome, it should be unsurprising that even with the success of Gabby Douglas in the London 2012 Olympics, some of the gymnastics world dismissed her accomplishments as an exception and not the beginning of a new racial hierarchy. In just a little more than a year after Douglas clinched gold, Biles won her first All-Around World Championship in Antwerp in October 2013. In doing so, Biles became the first Black gymnast to win the All-Around World title. For Italian gymnast Carlotta Ferlito (who placed 6th in the 2013 World All-Around competition and 21st in the 2012 London Olympics All-Around finals), Biles's win after the success of Douglas was too much change to her predominantly White sporting space. In an interview with an Italian reporter, Ferlito was asked, "What about the success of Biles, was it all planned?" She said, "I told [teammate Vanessa Ferrari] that next time we should also paint our skin Black so then we can win, too,"[26] and then she and the reporter began to laugh. Apparently two gold-medal-winning Black gymnasts equates to a conspiracy? Now there's something to laugh about.

Ferlito's comment highlights the discomfort and isolation that can often greet gymnasts of color in an international sport noted for its historical lack of color.[27] Douglas ran into this type of racist sentiment throughout her early years of gymnastics, which she discusses in her 2013 autobiography, *Grace, Gold and Glory: My Leap of Faith*.[28] Douglas was also slammed with negative racial commentary during the 2012 Olympics from within the Black community about her hair, as well as the White media that capitalized on her tragedy-to-triumph narrative and even ran an ad of a monkey doing gymnastics directly after reporting on Douglas's historic win of the All-Around gold medal. After social media erupted in disdain, NBC, the network responsible for the airing of the monkey commercial, apologized for the ill-timed advertisement of a new show called *Animal Practice* and said the network "intended no offense."[29] Similarly, after Ferlito's comments demeaning Biles's race and athletic talents went viral in the social media realm, she was quick to use Twitter to send out an apology, stating, "I want to apologize with the Americans girls. I didn't want to sound rude or racist. I love Simone and I'm a huge fan of USA gymnastics . . . I've made a mistake, I'm not perfect, I was too nervous and I didn't think about what I was saying. I'm just a human. I'm so so sorry."[30]

The thing is, it's difficult to accept that these types of incidents are really "mistakes" or "intend no offense." There is something insidious about the fact that viewers are supposed to believe that no one in the NBC control room stopped to think about how inappropriate airing a monkey doing gymnastics would be after the first Black gymnast won Olympic gold; it's common knowledge that Blacks were often referred to as "apes" and "monkeys" rather than as human in their racialized historical experience in the United States and abroad. And what about the Italian reporter who interviewed Ferlito? Ferlito answered the question without hesitation and with laughter, but the question itself was a loaded one that begged Ferlito to comment on the cause of the shift in racial hierarchy within elite gymnastics.

The media is not innocent in the propagation of a racial hierarchy that holds Whiteness as the ideal in predominantly White sports. Aside from trying to force Biles into the tragedy-to-triumph label via Al Trautwig, the NBC network tried to downplay the historic gold-medal victory of Black swimmer Simone Manuel in the 100-meter freestyle final. The 20-year-old from Sugar Land, Texas, had just become the first African American woman to win an individual gold medal in swimming, and her time of 52.70 seconds was an American and Olympic record.[31] Rather than show her historic and emotional medal ceremony right after her victory—as they did every time Michael Phelps won a medal—NBC chose to air it one hour after Manuel's historic race ended. An hour may not seem all that harmful in delaying a medal ceremony, but there is a powerful history around Black Americans and access to swimming pools that makes Manuel's accomplishment arguably equally or more significant than that of Douglas's gold in the sport of gymnastics.

A combination of anxiety and fear stemming from old Jim Crow laws has resulted in many Black Americans not knowing how to swim and being less likely to sign their children up for swimming lessons. Jeff Wiltse, a professor of history at the University of Montana and author of *Contested Waters: A Social History of Swimming Pools in America*, explains some of the history in an article in the *New York Times*:

> The few pools open to Blacks were small, poorly equipped, and often located in places like the basements of buildings . . . You had multiple generations of White families who had a cultural tradition of swimming and passed that interest to the next generation. And you had multiple generations of African American families who had no comparable tradition. Instead, their experience of swimming typically involved exclusion and, more dramatically, drowning. For generations of African American families, swimming has been associated with fear.[32]

The American public swimming pool period of growth came in the 1920s and 1930s, while the growth of private swim clubs in American suburbs took off in the 1950s and 1960s. This researcher's own father does not know how to swim because a couple of his family members drowned in bodies of water so his mother was afraid to let him near it. And this researcher's mother (a native of Fredericksburg, Virginia) was not allowed to swim at the nearest pool due to the color of her skin. It was not until her mother was required to pass swimming at her undergraduate alma mater, Hampton University, that her mother learned how to effectively swim without the threat of drowning. Fortunately for this researcher and her older sister, their parents decided to place their daughters in a Montessori program that had swim lessons because they didn't want their daughters to miss out on something that would be beneficial to them in life. Swimming *is* a life skill, especially when statistics show that "Black children drown at a rate nearly three times higher than their White peers."[33]

Thus, the NBC network's downplay of Manuel's victory, its attempts to reassign Biles's life into that of a tragedy-to-triumph narrative, and silencing of the history and current statistics surrounding the experience of Black Americans in the sports of gymnastics and swimming, is a means of upholding the White supremacist racial hierarchy within these predominantly

White landscapes. In upholding this hierarchy and maintaining historical ignorance for its viewers, NBC creates a sense of reassurance among some of its White viewers that American sports and its sporting culture are "postracial" (i.e., race doesn't matter). After the gold-medal performances of Manuel and Douglas, NBA star Lebron James received backlash from his White followers on Instagram for posting a congratulatory post to Biles and Manuel because he mentioned them *being Black*. Lebron's Instagram featured a picture of the Simones giving their gold medals a traditional bite of the teeth and the caption "Simone + Simone = Gold [two medal emojis]!!! Congrats young Queens!! Truly inspiring for so many especially young Black girls. My daughter was watching with me. #GoUSA #GoldStandard."[34] As of October 8, 2016, the post has been commented on 3,663 times, with the more critical comments stating things such as:

> There are also White people competing in the Olympics as well. It's so nice that our society still feels the need to point out how exceptional someone is due to the color of their skin.—Robert Filla
>
> The Black community always complain about segregation, that different races gets divided into certain groups etc etc. Now look at your status and see what you just did? You're not exactly helping the cause by separating Blacks from Whites. You very often hear 'look beyond race etc etc.' and I totally agree. But it doesn't make sense to complain about being exposed because of your skin color, and then based on exactly that (RACE←) isolate yourselves from everyone else. Cheer for America, not for races . . . —Albin Bondesson
>
> They are inspiring to ALL young girls! What's with the labeling!!! Why can't we just be AMERICANS? I think ALL young girls have something to learn from these two . . . —Lacie Eveland Murdock[35]

The reactions of these three White commenters point out two methods of misdirection that some who benefit from White privilege—the benefit of not having suffered or presently suffering race-related hardships—tend to rely on as a means to avoid talking about race and racism. Robert Filla went with the "let's not forget about the majority's accomplishments too" point, ignoring the historical absence of Blacks in the sports of gymnastics and swimming. Bondesson and Murdock employ the "look how far America has come, so let's not move backwards" point of contestation toward James's post, emphasizing that he should cheer for America and easily ask athletes of color to erase all other forms of their identities while at the Olympics. Perhaps if these viewers were exposed to the history and current statistics of participation of athletes of color in these two sports, it would have saved Lebron James from a lot of backlash and garnered Biles and Manuel much more respect.

Of course, "oppressions don't exist in isolation from each other; they're always intermeshed, reinforcing and contradicting each other."[36] This phenomenon is referred to as "intersectionality." There are different types of racism that when combined with other forms of oppression can be very hard for Black female athletes in predominantly White sports to navigate. The aesthetics surrounding hair were an issue for some members of the Black community in terms of how Gabby Douglas was viewed in 2012, and criticism emerged once again in Rio about her hair from the same source. After comments on Douglas's hair arose in 2012, this researcher's focus shifted toward the comments' impact on the gymnast with regards to internalized racism:

> Internalized racism should be understood as the "acceptance by members of stigmatized races of negative messages about their own abilities and intrinsic worth." The results of internalized racism are devastating. These members of society tend to view themselves and others who look like them as having limited humanity; limited self-determination, dreams, and self-expression.[37]

Douglas has admitted to feeling pain and loneliness around that first surge of comments about her hair in 2012. In watching her reality show on the Oxygen network, this researcher noticed that Douglas had a weave installed in her hair at all times unless she was in competition. This is a conscious effort on Douglas's part to show Black Americans that she does, in fact, care about the way her hair looks. One can also speculate that Marta Karolyi (the USA Gymnastics national team coordinator) likely required the five-woman team to wear their hair naturally for all international competitions; aesthetic uniformity is important in gymnastics. However, when the comments on Douglas's hair came again during the Rio Olympics, this researcher's attention turned more toward why Black women disparagers care so much about Douglas's hair looking good. The answer is that these Black disparagers view how Douglas wears her hair as a racial stereotype threat. Racial stereotype threat is the fear of confirming a racial stereotype about one's group;[38] in this case, it's confirming that Black people have "nappy" and/or "bad" hair. Black women want people to believe the myth that their hair is straight and "good."[39] Biles's hair seems to have gained the approval of these same Black disparagers, likely due to her hair appearing to benefit from chemical straightening.

One of the proudest moments of Douglas's gymnastics career was ruined shortly afterward because social media followers chose to shame her instead: "as Douglas took her third Olympic podium, she didn't do something her teammates did. She didn't place her hand over her heart as the national anthem played. Critics took to Twitter, calling her move 'disrespectful' and 'unpatriotic.'"[40]

Rather than place her hand over her heart, photographs depict Douglas standing at attention with her hands to her sides and smiling as the U.S. national anthem played. While Douglas did have a number of supportive tweets, she still had to deal with reading tweets from others who felt her poor hand placement was "shameful" and suggested that she "move somewhere else."[41] Douglas immediately explained herself on Twitter and even issued an apology that she didn't owe to anyone. Douglas attempted to move forward and focus on her individual bar finals.

As Biles and Aly Raisman wrapped up their All-Around finals in Rio as the gold and silver medalist respectively, their remaining teammates (Biles, Laurie Hernandez, and Madison Kocian) cheered from the stands. However, social media critics didn't think Douglas's enthusiasm was emphatic or genuine enough. Already disparaging Douglas for her alleged lack of patriotism, "the American darling of the 2012 London Olympics has been dubbed 'Crabby Gabby' in Rio by faceless trolls using social media to launch attacks that her own mother says have left her 'devastated.'"[42] Had something similar not happened in the 2012 Olympics with White teammate McKayla Maroney, one could perhaps take the harsh criticism of Douglas's facial expressions as warranted. Maroney's disappointed facial expression as she was awarded the silver medal in the vault was not criticized as "crabby" or a sign of bitterness. In fact, "a light-hearted meme quickly went viral and led to appearances on *The Late Show with David Letterman*, *Dancing with the Stars* and a recreation of the look with President Obama."[43]

The only distinguishing thing between Douglas and other athletes who have found themselves in controversial positions in the Olympics is their race. Maroney is White and doesn't have the "angry Black woman" stereotype looming over her; "not once was Maroney called jealous, angry or ugly."[44] When Michael Phelps laughed during the national anthem due to his friends from Maryland yelling out "O!" like they do at Orioles games, his patriotism wasn't questioned. When three other White male athletes failed to put their hands over their hearts, no outrage occurred:

> Of course it doesn't really matter to conservatives that Crouser, Kovacs, or Kendricks failed to put their hands over their hearts. They are White men. Their patriotism is in their blood . . . Gabby, on the other hand, younger than them all, got no such benefit of the doubt despite her excellent and dedicated service to our country. She's won more gold medals than those three combined, but that seemed to mean next to nothing when she failed to put her hand over her heart. She is, after all, a Black woman, and conservatives clearly started her off in a patriotic deficit she could never quite get out of.[45]

New York Daily News columnist and activist Shaun King is on to something in his reference to a "patriotic deficit." Stevenson explains that "as an ideology, the inferiority of Blackness is the perfect foil to the paternalistic hero Whiteness narrative of American racial politics."[46] This means that no matter what Douglas or Biles or Manuel do well in their respective sports, it will be viewed as *better* when a White athlete accomplishes the same thing.

On the reverse end of things, this means that when a White athlete does something poorly, it won't be seen as negatively in the public eye as it would if that person was Black. Take, for example, #Lochtegate from the Rio Olympics. Shortly after the swimming competition ended in Rio, a White person, Ryan Lochte, and three other U.S. swimmers alleged that they had been robbed at gunpoint. Lochte went on multiple news networks and proceeded to lie about what had actually occurred. Various pieces of evidence emerged—as well as admissions by other swimmers involved—that their original story of robbery in Rio was fabricated. In truth, Lochte and his fellow swimmers had drunkenly caused damage to a gas station bathroom then became belligerent with the security guard of the establishment when he tried to hold them accountable for the damage. Privileged by their Whiteness, Lochte and the rest of the swimmers were depicted not as liars or disgraceful American athletes but rather as "kids" who took "actions that [they] later regret."[47] Just imagine what the headlines would have read if Lochte and his teammates had been a group of Black male American athletes. When the benefit of the doubt is given freely to White men when they mess up—even in cases like this one where they actually may have broken the law—and yet withheld from others, it perpetuates entrenched systems of racism and sexism.[48]

CONCLUSION

The USA gymnastics team selected for the Rio Olympics is likely the most racially and ethnically diverse squad chosen to represent the country, and it's likely this trend will continue in the years to come. African Americans make up just 1.3 percent of USA Swimming's 337,084 members, according to the governing body's 2015 membership data.[49] What needs to change for predominantly White sports—specifically gymnastics and swimming—is twofold: organizational efforts to increase participation among people of color, and a shift in the way these athletes are presented by the media. These two changes can cause major shifts in the athletic landscape for generations to come, but they can also shift the place and value of Whiteness in the racial hierarchy.

There is only one professional sports league in the United States in which at least 50 percent of the players are not of a single race or ethnicity:[50] major league soccer. A study reported by *The Washington Post* in June of 2014 showed a direct correlation between player diversity and team results in competition, leading to the conclusion that diversity and success are very much related. The U.S. women's gymnastics team could certainly be viewed as an example of this conclusion ringing true; the gold medalist team of five finished eight points higher than second-place Russia. When interviewed after her historic victory in the pool, Manuel said she "would like there to be a day where there are more of us and it's not 'Simone, the Black swimmer' because the title 'Black swimmer' makes it seem like I'm not supposed to be able to win a gold medal or I'm not supposed to be able to break records and that's not true because I work just as hard as anybody else."[51] The success and presence of these Black female athletes in predominantly White sports is an improvement in race relations and a combatant to racial stereotypes.

More than ever, sports fans need to continue to hold the media accountable when they present deceptive narratives about Black female athletes. There's this fantasy world that the media tries to create for people, and the media teaches us to value deception and lying.[52] Fortunately, it appears that more people are noticing discrepancies in coverage and treatment of Black athletes—and Black female athletes in particular. As evidenced with the backlash toward Al Trautwig on Biles, "the tweets add up and have already forced some media members and outlets to issue mea culpas within days—even hours—of their remarks . . . the pushback from viewers is a solid start toward correcting behavior."[53] The more that Americans ask of the media in terms of delivering truth, equity of coverage, and attention to historical achievements, the better the Olympics and this country will become.

NOTES

1. See Rachel L. Myers, "African American Female Athletic Image: What We Should Take Away from the London 2012 Olympic Games," in *Race Still Matters: The Reality of African American Lives and the Myth of Postracial Society*, ed. Yuya Kiuchi (Albany: State University of New York Press, 2016).

2. The term "African diaspora" should be understood as describing the communities of people that have developed over time based on movement, whether forced or free, from the African continent to settle in new lands. See Colin Palmer, "Defining and Studying the Modern African Diaspora," *Perspectives on History*, September 1998, https://www.historians.org/publications-and-directories/perspectives-on-history/september-1998/defining-and-studying-the-modern-african-diaspora#.

3. Philip Hersh, "Simone Biles and Gabby Douglas Are Latest and Greatest Heroes in a Storied History of African-American Gymnasts," *TeamUSA.org News*, last modified February 29, 2016, http://m.teamusa.org/News/2016/February/29/Simone-Biles-And-Gabby-Douglas-Are-Latest-In-A-Storied-History-Of-African-American-Gymnasts.

4. Ibid.
5. Ibid.
6. Gary A. Sailes, "The Myth of Black Sports Supremacy," *Journal of Black Studies* 21, no. 4 (1991).
7. Reeves Wiedeman, "A Full Revolution: In the Run-up to the Olympics, Simone Biles Is Transforming Gymnastics," *The New Yorker* (May 30, 2016): 17. Published electronically May 30, 2016, http://www.newyorker.com/magazine/2016/05/30/simone-biles-is-the-best-gymnast-in-the-world.
8. Ibid.
9. USA Gymastics, "USA Gymnastics: Athletes," https://usagym.org/pages/athletes/athleteListDetail.html?id=164887.
10. Elaine Welteroth, "Comeback Kid: An (Almost) All-Grown-Up Gabby Douglas on Life since London, Growing Pains, and Going for the Gold—Again," *Teen Vogue* (August 2016).
11. Liz Clarke, "Four Years after Olympic Gold, Gabby Douglas's Reality Remains Riveting," *The Washington Post*, last modified May 22, 2016, https://www.washingtonpost.com/sports/olympics/four-years-after-olympic-gold-gabby-douglass-reality-remains-riveting/2016/05/22/073a79e6-1eb7-11e6-b6e0-c53b7ef63b45_story.html.
12. Ibid.
13. See Ibid. and Wiedeman, "A Full Revolution."
14. Clarke, "Four Years after Olympic Gold, Gabby Douglas's Reality Remains Riveting."
15. Wiedeman, "A Full Revolution."
16. Rose Minutaglio, "How Gymnast Simone Biles Overcame Being Given Up by Her Mother to Become an Olympic Gold Hopeful," *People*, last modified June 27, 2016, http://www.people.com/people/package/article/0,,20996464_21015150,00.html.
17. Ibid.
18. Tom Leonard, "Awesome Triumph: How the 4ft 8in Smiling Girl Who's Set the Olympics Alight Overcame an Appalling Childhood," *Daily Mail*, last modified August 13, 2016, http://www.dailymail.co.uk/news/article-3738356/Awesome-triumph-4ft-8in-smiling-girl-s-set-Olympics-alight-overcame-appalling-childhood.html.
19. Ibid.
20. Lawrence Yee, "NBC Sports Broadcaster Apologizes for Comments about Simone Biles' Parents," *Variety*, last modified August 9, 2016, http://variety.com/2016/tv/news/al-trautwig-apologizes-simone-biles-parents-nbc-sports-2016-olympics-1201833953/.
21. Ibid.
22. Welteroth, "Comeback Kid."
23. Howard C. Stevenson, *Promoting Racial Literacy in Schools: Differences That Make a Difference* (New York and London: Teachers College Press, 2014), 57.
24. Ibid.
25. Ibid.
26. Keli Goff, "Slur Highlights Race Problem in Gymnastics," *The Root*, last modified October 10, 2013, http://www.theroot.com/articles/culture/2013/10/black_world_champion_gymnast_simone_biles_is_slurred_by_italian_competitor/.

27. Ibid.

28. See pages 59, 66, 133, and 150 of this autobiography.

29. "NBC Forced to Apologise after Ill-Timed Ad Features a Monkey Doing Gymnastics—Right after Showing Gabby Douglas' Gold Medal Victory," *Daily Mail*, last modified August 4, 2012, http://www.dailymail.co.uk/news/article-2183284/Gabby-Douglas-NBC-forced-apologise-ad-features-monkey-doing-gymnastics-right-AFTER-victory.html.

30. "'Maybe Next Time We'll Paint Our Skin Black So We Can Win': Italian Gymnast Sparks Fury with Racist Jibe at 16-Year-Old New World Champion," *Daily Mail*, last modified October 14, 2013, http://www.dailymail.co.uk/news/article-2458533/Carlotta-Ferlito-sparks-fury-racist-jibe-new-world-champion-Simone-Biles.html.

31. Associated Press, "Simone Manuel's 100m Freestyle Olympic Gold Medal Is Not Just for Her," *NBCOlympics.com*, last modified August 17, 2016, http://www.nbcolympics.com/news/simone-manuels-100m-freestyle-olympic-gold-medal-not-just-her.

32. Gretchen Reynolds, "Hoping Olympic Gold Might End a Racial Divide," *New York Times*, August 16, 2016.

33. Associated Press, "Simone Manuel's 100m Freestyle Olympic Gold Medal Is Not Just for Her."

34. See Lebron James's Instagram post from August 12, 2016, via his Instagram account @kingjames.

35. Yesha Callahan, "Lebron James Upsets White Fans after Praising Black Olympic Athletes," *The Root*, last modified August 17, 2016, http://www.theroot.com/blog/the-grapevine/lebron-james-upsets-white-fans-after-praising-black-olympic-athletes/.

36. Jody Sokolower and Annika Butler-Wall, "Intersectionality: Gender, Race, and the Media," in *Rethinking Sexism, Gender, and Sexuality*, eds. Kim Cosier Annika Butler-Wall, Rachel L. S. Harper, Jeff Sapp, Jody Sokolower, and Melissa Bollow Tempel (Milwaukee, WI: Rethinking Schools, Ltd., 2016), 168.

37. Myers, "African American Female Athletic Image: What We Should Take Away from the London 2012 Olympic Games," 322.

38. Stevenson, *Promoting Racial Literacy in Schools*, 96.

39. Michael Kayode to Sports Nut, last modified August 8, 2016, http://sportsnut.sportsblog.com/posts/23216179/breaking-news--gabby-douglas-again-attacked-online-by-black-women-for-nappy-hair-and-bad-edges--is-simone-biles-next--.html.

40. Lawrence Yee, "Gabby Douglas Criticized for Not Placing Hand over Heart During Olympic Medal Ceremony," *Variety*, last modified August 10, 2016, http://variety.com/2016/tv/news/gabby-douglas-national-anthem-gold-medal-ceremony-1201834709/.

41. See Ibid.

42. Forbes Contributor, "Why Michael Phelps Can Make Faces but 'Crabby' Gabby Douglas Can't," *Forbes*, last modified August 17, 2016, http://www.forbes.com/sites/cartoonoftheday/2016/08/17/for-certain-top-athletes-some-things-never-change/#70c125ca6f9f.

43. Ibid.

44. Ibid.

45. Shaun King, "King: No Gabby Douglas Anthem Outrage for White Olympic Medalists," *New York Daily News*, last modified August 22, 2016, http://www.nydailynews.com/news/national/king-no-gabby-douglas-anthem-outrage-white-olympic-medalists-article-1.2760918.

46. Stevenson, *Promoting Racial Literacy in Schools*, 58.

47. Emma Gray, "White Male Privilege Is Why We Laugh at Lochte and Vilify Douglas," *The Huffington Post*, last modified August 19, 2016, http://www.huffingtonpost.com/entry/ryan-lochte-gabby-douglas-and-white-male-privilege-in-action_us_57b5e76de4b034dc73262f93.

48. Ibid.

49. Associated Press, "Simone Manuel's 100m Freestyle Olympic Gold Medal Is Not Just for Her."

50. Chris Hoenig, "The Measure of Diversity the Only One U.S. Pro Sport Meets," *DiversityInc*, last modified July 16, 2014, http://www.diversityinc.com/news/measure-diversity-one-u-s-pro-sport-meets/.

51. Associated Press, "Simone Manuel's 100m Freestyle Olympic Gold Medal Is Not Just for Her."

52. Butler-Wall, "Intersectionality: Gender, Race, and the Media," 171.

53. Sarah Spain, "Talking with Shawn Johnson and Jess Weiner about Sexism in Olympics Coverage," *ESPNW.com*, last modified August 16, 2016, http://www.espn.com/espnw/voices/article/17317860/said-sarah-spain-shawn-johnson-jess-weiner-sexism-olympics-coverage.

5

How to Become a Dominant Black Female Athlete and Get Paid: The Case of Serena Williams and Gains and Costs of Athleticism and Intersectionality

Scott Norman Brooks

> *The experiences of Black women do not fit within the traditional boundaries of race and sex discrimination as these boundaries are currently understood. The intersection of racism and sexism factors into Black women's lives in ways that cannot be captured wholly by looking at the race or gender dimensions of those experiences separately.*
>
> —Kimberlé Crenshaw[1]

INTRODUCTION

How can a Black woman from Compton, California, become a dominant athlete and be seen as highly marketable by multinational corporations? Inspired by Michele Lamont's "How to Become a Dominant French Philosopher: The Case of Jacques Derrida," this study explores the marketable legitimation of Serena Williams and develops a hypothesis about the legitimation process of dominant Black female athletes.[2] Heidi Parker and Janet Fink propose that a causal relationship exists involving athletes' behavior and public perception and marketability: "An athlete endorser who participates in an undesirable behavior will be rated less favorably on measures of trustworthiness than an athlete with identical credentials who has not engaged in undesirable acts."[3] However, I will illustrate how the marketability of Serena Williams is the result of her meeting racial expectations and failing to meet gender and class norms. Her position as Black, female, and from a working-class background intersect, leading to marketable gains and losses. Williams as a dominant athlete doesn't fit into the traditional ideas of athleticism and femininity that are stereotypically associated with race and gender. Nor does she share the class background of most professional tennis players. The majority of professional tennis players are White and often come from affluent backgrounds. She doesn't look like her peers, and her difference from them, in style, body type, and even actions, is magnified by the media. Black males are seen as the most natural and physically gifted athletes. Here again, Williams is out of place because she's not male. Yet, the presumption of natural and superior athleticism with Blackness works in her favor. Serena's dominant and aggressive image affords her greater leeway in being assertive, showing emotions like anger and frustration, and not conforming to narrow hegemonic forms of femininity. By possessing these characteristics, she benefits from creating social, cultural, and institutional "dilemmas and contradictions of status" and is marketable because she is unique, *the dominant female athlete*.

The goal here is to go beyond a common-sense understanding of Serena Williams's positionality and the effect on her potential earnings. By way of questioning, gathering data, and analysis, patterns may be found and conclusions drawn that can be further studied and applied to other people and situations. From here, the ideas of sexism, racism, and intersectionality are more than theorized; how they operate is revealed, at least in part, and plans for change can be developed, undertaken, and measured.

New Social Psychology of Race Prejudice

American sociologists have long been concerned with understanding race and race relations: how one becomes aware of one's own race and the race of others; how group racial formation occurs; and how race structures social experience. Symbolic interactionists think of race as a product of hierarchical social relations carrying meanings or stereotypes that are used to justify differential treatment, expectations, and outcomes. W. I. Thomas first identified race prejudice as a natural feeling, even an instinct, but something that could be unlearned.[4] Contact and exposure, Thomas and later Robert Park theorized, were important initial steps to lessening and ultimately eliminating prejudicial feelings over time and replacing them with sympathy and understanding.[5] Everett Hughes described how changing race and gender relations played out in mixed-group interactions.[6] Race, class, and gender are social status positions (what Hughes called "master statuses"), and occupations and activities are heavily associated with particular racial, class, and gender groups. For example, when we think of an occupation or activity such as football, our mind recalls men and boys, persons belonging to a specific race, class, and gender—this person in our imagination represents the norm. This is a cognitive matching process, and a person from a different race, class, gender, religion, and/or sexuality than expected would be considered strange or a "contradiction in status," and this creates an incongruity or "dilemma in status." How is this contradiction to be treated? It is not simply that the contradiction isn't whom we expected; it is also that there are institutionalized practices that have developed based on the interconnectedness of expected group membership and status and behavior. Hughes (writing in the 1940s) uses the Black doctor as an example. A Black man isn't generally respected by Whites, and yet, doctors are held in high esteem. The Black doctor's race allows for Whites to disregard him, to treat him as someone with low status, but his occupation typically grants him deference, reverence, and prestige. Herbert Blumer identified race formation as a social process, much like how a person comes to understand themselves as a distinct self; others must exist in order to know one's self because the self and society are twin born; one is not possible without the other.[7] The power of Blumer's thinking was not only awareness of self/one's own group in comparison to another group but the hierarchical organization and self-privileging that is often completed. People don't just join groups; they declare that their group is special, distinct, and inherently better than other groups. Most importantly, they feel that their group is entitled to certain things based on their elevated position. These classic pieces of scholarship outline an understanding of how race, gender, class, and sexuality are social constructions with real consequences. These social constructions carry meaning and expectations that often inform our behavior, perceptions, and interpretations of others and vice versa.

Since the civil rights movement, countless studies have been conducted that apprehend and comprehend the continuing marginality, racial attitudes and race prejudice, assimilation, and race as a system of hierarchy, privilege, and disadvantage across a variety of settings.[8] Current social psychological research regarding race relations and leadership tests perceptions and attitudes. Robert Livingston's work investigates how race and gender affect the experiences of Black executives. This research illuminates subconscious and covert feelings and attitudes that non-Blacks have about Blacks, which influences career mobility and evaluations of competence. Livingston and Nicholas Pearce assert that when evaluating a leader's competence and trustworthiness among other traits, evaluators are swayed positively and negatively by the race and sex of the leader.[9] Black males carry the stigma of being hypermasculine and violent without any performances or presentations; thus, a Black male who is dominant and assertive is "over the top," "out of control," to be feared, and a threat to others. Interestingly, when looking at male CEOs, Livingston and Pearce find a different, yet connected, pattern: Black baby-faced CEOs were rated as "warmer" than mature-faced Black CEOs, were leading more prestigious corporations, and were earning higher salaries. Baby-faced Black male CEOs were significantly more baby-faced than White male CEOs.

"Taken together, these findings suggest that baby-faceness is a disarming mechanism that facilitates the success of Black leaders by attenuating stereotypical perceptions that Blacks are threatening." The "teddy bear effect," as they call it, illustrates how the stigma of race and sex (being Black and male) operates in evaluations and in feelings connected to trust and perceptions of competence.

The perceptions and evaluations of White male CEOs do not follow the same pattern. Instead, White males are evaluated more positively if they are considered dominant and assertive and are not penalized for expressing anger and intensity. However, White females who perform dominance and show anger are evaluated negatively, like Black males; they are seen as "uptight" and *too* in control (i.e., power hungry and/or micromanaging). White females draw negative attention and appraisals when they use authoritative behavior because of the contradiction and dilemmas in status—White females' prescribed gender role is incongruous with being "strong" corporate leaders. Livingston, Ashleigh Rosette, and Ella Washington have extended this line of work to Black females and discovered that Black females differ from Black males and White females.[10] Black females who are described as assertive or "in charge" don't experience the same level of backlash. Black females, like White males, are allowed to express strong negative emotions with less sanctions and often receive praise or earn respect for exhibiting dominance. This thread of research connects social perceptions, racial attitudes, and feelings (only Whites and Asians were surveyed for each study) to interpretations of Blacks' actions and ascribed physical characteristics, which helps assess Black athletes' marketability where public opinion (the dominant group's opinion) is the reference point for speculation of an athlete's potential appeal and ability to sell goods.

Marketability, Intersectionality, and Serena Williams

To measure Williams's marketability, I use insights from sociological and psychological research on race relations and racial and gender attitudes. Attitudes and perceptions are connected to marketability because endorsers like Williams help to sell products to consumers. Therefore, companies look for endorsers who come across as attractive, approachable, and trustworthy, or who have an expertise or personal connection with their product, also known as the match-up hypothesis. A good match between the product and the endorser is critical for endorser effectiveness and endorsement success.[11] Although one could use a classic business definition of marketability,[12] a conceptual understanding of marketability based on social media research is most useful in the current era of globalization. Repucom, a marketing services company, has created a measure—Celebrity DBI—to quantify and qualify consumer perceptions of celebrities' clout and marketability.[13] Based on research,

Repucom measures eight different factors to determine the marketability of an athlete: awareness, appeal, aspiration, breakthrough, endorsement, influence, trendsetter, and trust. According to Repucom, awareness, or potential consumers' knowledge of an athlete, is the most important factor. There is an obvious correlation between marketability and awareness; identifiable endorsers have the biggest potential impact on consumers. But awareness does not simply equate to marketability, and awareness doesn't automatically lead to trust. Endorsement partnerships can sour quickly when a negative event occurs or negative information is learned about an endorser. Nicole Votolato and H. Rao Unnava found that negative information of an immoral nature about an endorser (athlete or celebrity) creates greater negative spillover on the sponsoring company than just negative information about an endorser.[14] Corporations are looking for endorsers who fit and create positive spillover. Therefore, an inquiry into Williams's marketability requires studying her as a dominant Black female athlete over time.

Sports is a powerful stratifying institution that reproduces and reinforces the ideas and social dynamics of the society in which it exists.[15] Professional female athletes don't earn as much money as male athletes, generally speaking or in the same sport. Female professional sports are not covered by the media to the same extent that male sports are covered;[16] female athletes are not considered as athletic and are not given the same respect and reverence for their hard work;[17] female athletes have fewer opportunities for playing professionally compared to male athletes;[18] female athletes work a "second shift," earning a majority of their income off the court, in non-sports-related activities;[19] female athletes who are deemed "pretty" are approached to be models of heterosexuality where they often wear "fake" uniforms or are out of their uniforms, are underdressed, and put into submissive "little girl" positions;[20] and female athletes are expected to fit neatly into a particular narrow "feminine" gender performance and femininity or risk being less or unmarketable and being perceived negatively by audiences.[21] Eileen McDonagh and Laura Pappano have identified this game that female athletes play in media and marketing as the "feminine bargain"—the implied promise that if they perform a recognized femininity and abide by the rules expected for girls and women, they will be allowed to engage in athletic performances while being exempted from unflattering stereotypes of female athletes.[22] All of this is justified by profit-making fueled by false notions that the demand for women's sports is not as high and the revenue is harder to earn—and a general view that women's sports are not as exciting, not as good. It must also be said that participation rates and opportunities vary greatly (and are less) for girls and women of color even after Title IX.[23] Black (as well as Latina, Native, and Asian) women are generally left out of scholarly discussions on race and sports *and* gender and sports because of their peculiar place—they're not men, and they're not White women.[24] This effectively omits the perspectives and lived experiences of some women, and the history of exclusion has a cumulative political, social, and economic impact.[25]

Today, it is difficult to understand sports separate from media; they are mutually beneficial and symbiotic.[26] Media is not objective but socially constructed,[27] and thus, portrayals and meanings must be inferred in analyses of media. The media coverage of female athletes is lacking,[28] and research across various mediums tells the same story—media maintains an underrepresentation and misrepresentation of female athletes.[29] Unbalanced coverage and under- and misrepresentations reinforce artificial sex and gender differences. Even with the advent of new women-specific media in the area of sport, we continue to see social constructions of traditional femininity,[30] although many feel that a progressive evolution is under way.[31] Blackness has been and continues to be produced in mass media and popular culture, acting as an immediate "cultural signifier" of difference.[32] Racism is institutionalized and occurs in media portrayals as both "common sense" and objective and fact based.[33]

THE STUDY

The first objective of this study is to develop hypotheses about the social legitimation process of Black female athletes through an examination of Serena Williams. The second objective is to understand how marketability varies across race, sex, and sport. In the case of Serena Williams, we see how her earnings are impacted by being a tennis player, a woman, and Black. My initial discussion will outline Williams's career via media coverage. This will illustrate her career arc and achievements in three decades of tennis and show how her success has made her a global figure. The next discussion asserts that distinction, an identifiable story, and visibility in the form of public "controversies" are prerequisites for her marketability and for staying on the list of highest earners for nearly two decades. The final discussion will consider how Serena Williams, widely regarded as the better and more successful athlete, has earned less than Maria Sharapova for 11 straight years and has often commanded only half of Sharapova's earnings from endorsements. All things being equal, how might this be explained?

My analysis is based on comparing tennis rankings, earnings per year, and controversies for the highest female athlete earners from 2005 to 2015. Data has been gathered via WTA.com, Forbes.com (for the annual lists of top-earning female athletes), and media coverage and public information, stories and reports from reputable mainstream, popular culture, and sports-specific news sources (*Washington Post*, *New York Times*, *Los Angeles Times*, and *ESPN*, *Sports Illustrated*, and *Tennis* magazines). To identify controversies,

I searched "Serena Williams controversy"; "Serena" and "Controversy"; and "Serena" and "controversies."

Williams's Career

Serena Williams's status as a tennis player stands apart from the success of women in other sports because of the global popularity of tennis, the amount of prize money, and because it is an individual sport. Tennis is an international sport, and the Women's Tennis Association (WTA) (the professional organization for female tennis players) began in 1970 with nine women signing $1 contracts to participate in the Virginia Slims series.[34] In its first year (1971), the nine women played in 19 tournaments with a total purse of $309,100. The tour has grown tremendously and now represents more than 2,500 players from 92 nations, competing for $137 million in prize money.[35] In 2016, the WTA tour included 57 events, 4 Grand Slams, and the Olympics, in 33 countries.[36] Each tournament varies in prize money, which comes from sponsors, television rights deals, ticket sales, and other on-site concessions. The four Grand Slams—Australian Open, French Open, Wimbledon (in England), and U.S. Open—represent the biggest tennis tournaments in terms of level of competition, media coverage and exposure, and prize money. Thus, playing and having success in the Grand Slams leads to global visibility. Over a 19-year career, Williams has amassed a win–lose record of 761–127: winning 70 WTA titles, 22 of which are Grand Slam titles, and winning a Grand Slam title in each of the last three decades.[37] She has ended the year as the No.1 player five times and has only been out of the Top 20 in the year-end rankings twice (1997 and 2006). Williams has also set benchmarks for prize money: she was the first to top $6 million in one season (2009), and she has earned the two highest season winnings—$12,385,572 and $10,582,642 in 2013 and 2015, respectively.[38] She has earned more than double the prize money of any other woman in history, raking in career winnings of over $80 million.[39]

Serena Williams's Legitimacy as a Dominant Female Athlete

There have been a number of female tennis players who have broken into the Top 10 earners list, but few can maintain this position. Breaking into the list is generally the result of sudden exposure/media attention due to big wins (having made a Top 10 ranking or near Top 10 ranking) or an athlete's potential for success (when greatness is anticipated because of a stellar junior career) *and* they have the "looks" to go along with the potential. Most don't stay in the Top 10 for long if their potential doesn't meet expectations or their success falters. The legitimation of female athletes is highly dependent on distinction, namely having an identifiable story, success, and visibility.

Williams has been unique and distinct because of (1) her race, class, and family; (2) her dominance in a highly visible sport for women; (3) her success fits a common and acceptable racial stereotype; and (4) all of this has enabled her to be marketable in a nontraditional way when compared to other women.

Serena Williams's story has been told and retold as a tennis version of *Hoop Dreams*.[40] The Williams family doesn't fit the common tennis story—they're not White, not wealthy, and the parents have served as long-time coaches and encouragers. Serena and sister Venus started playing at a very young age in Compton, California.[41] It was the dream and plan of their father, Richard Williams, who, while watching tennis on television, heard commentators speak about the prize money won by a female player. He hatched a plan to have two more daughters (they already had three) and make them tennis champions. Oracene Price, Williams's mother, was a nurse, and Richard ran his own security company. Both had great time flexibility in their jobs and invested heavily in the tennis dream for Serena and Venus.[42] Richard learned all he could from books, videos, and speaking with coaches and players and tried all kinds of methods to make the training fun, family oriented, and competitive. He took them to the courts day after day and exposed them to as much tennis as he could. Serena and Venus dominated the Southern California junior circuit, and Richard was bold in his predictions—Serena and Venus would become champions and the best players in tennis.[43] The family moved to Florida, putting the Williams girls in the Macci Tennis Academy to prepare them for going pro. Oracene and Richard racked up a lot of debt, and Richard gained a reputation for being more than eccentric; he was and continues to be described as "crazy," "insane," "arrogant," a "liar," and even a puppet master by those who believe that he fixed matches between the sisters.[44] The struggle of being poor and living in Compton strengthened the family bond, as Serena and Venus are and have been the best of friends. Oracene and Richard cautiously managed their daughters' pro careers, only allowing them to play sparingly in their first four seasons for fear of burnout. There was a youth movement afoot, an explosion of teenage tennis phenomes in the WTA at the same time: Monica Seles, Jennifer Capriati, Martina Hingis, Anna Kournikova, and soon afterwards Maria Sharapova and a host of teenage Russians. Still, as mentioned above, both Serena and Venus Williams have been different in self-promotion and by way of media portrayals and tennis's organizational public relations, representing an interest convergence that has been mutually beneficial for the Williams family, tennis, and its corporate sponsors.[45]

Serena Williams's claim to "Greatest of All Time" stands on winning—winning over top-ranked players and winning late in her career. Early success over Top 10 players foreshadowed her overall dominance of the sport. Williams made her pro debut in 1995 (but did not play all of 1996).[46] In her first full season, 1997, she became the lowest-ranked player (she was ranked No. 304) to defeat two Top 10 players in the same event. The following year, Williams had five wins over players ranked in the Top 10 (she is the fastest player to do so, in only 16 matches) and ended the year ranked in the Top 20. Serena stunned everyone in 1999 when she defeated the current and two future No. 1 players: Amélie Mauresmo at Paris, the legendary Steffi Graf at Indian Wells, and Martina Hingis at the U.S. Open. The year 2002 was her breakout year, as she won three Grand Slams (French Open, Wimbledon, and U.S. Open) and then won the Australian Open in the first Grand Slam of 2003. Winning each of the Grand Slam events once in a player's career is called a Career Grand Slam and serves as the hallmark of a great player. Williams held all four Grand Slam titles at once (within a 12-month period), becoming the only woman or man to have ever done so (she has done this twice), and this feat is named after her—the "Serena Slam." Williams's success since turning 30 punctuates her excellence. For six weeks in the summer of 2015, her WTA tour points (points are accumulated based on wins and the tournament importance) were more than double the tour points of No. 2 ranked Sharapova. She continues to set records: she's the oldest woman to earn a No. 1 ranking; she's had the biggest time gap between No. 1 rankings (seven years); she's the oldest to win a Grand Slam; and she is tied with Steffi Graff for the most Grand Slam titles in the modern era. In addition to dominating women's tennis individually, she has teamed with her sister Venus to win the second most doubles Grand Slam titles in history and three Olympic gold medals (2000, 2008, 2012).[47] The Williams sisters are the only two siblings to be ranked No. 1 and No. 2 in tennis history.

Tennis, like golf, is an old country club sport, and they are both associated with the wealthy. Therefore, tennis players are asked to endorse luxury, exclusive, high-cost products (watches, jewelry, high fashion, multinational banking, finance and technical corporations), in addition to the typical sports-related products and complements (sports drinks, soft drinks, fast food, shoes and apparel).[48] There are at least four female tennis players who appear on the list of Top 10 highest paid female athletes each year over the 10-year span 2005–2015, and their nationalities vary. Outside of tennis, few women stay on the list for more than three years except those who stay at the top of their sports or who are pioneers (e.g., stock car racer Danica Patrick). What this suggests is that tennis is a high-visibility sport. Moreover, women in tennis have an advantage in that tennis attracts a wealthy audience.

The focus of commentary regarding Williams is on her contradiction and incongruities. Jon Wertheim, a senior writer for *Sports Illustrated*, described Serena and Venus Williams in their first years on the WTA tour: "They were grunting, they were covering ground that no player would even try to get to, and the power—even at age 16—was nothing anybody had seen before."[49]

Wertheim helps to set the story in a conventional manner that we can all understand—Serena Williams is extraordinary, by definition—"nothing anybody has seen before." Considering the history of race relations and perceptions of race and group attributes, talk of Serena Williams's physicality and play take on deeper meaning. Interpretations of her behavior as demonstrative, aggressive, with attitude, angry, and intimidating reflect not only common themes when commentating on dominant Black athletes but a part of conventional sport and social thinking. Dianne Hagaman identified "sportsland" as a make-believe world in which certain aspects of our society are emphasized and serve as the basis for the entire description of a world. In this simplified world, only a few important things go on; there are only a few issues, only a few commonly held values.[50] Hagaman points out that the processes of conventionalization can be studied in sportsland because of the simplification of sports stories. Race is one of those stories. In sportsland, Blackness carries stereotypical biological and cultural advantages; those of African descent are believed to be physically advantaged due to genetics, which makes them quicker, faster, and better jumpers than all other races, and they have a hunger and persistence that comes from having endured racial discrimination and poverty. Gender-specific notions operate too. Patricia Vertinsky and Gwendolyn Captain write: "Attitudes toward the African-American woman's Amazonian work capacity, and lack of physical and emotional sensitivity, flowed easily into notions about the natural strength and 'manly' athletic abilities of black women in running, jumping and throwing activities."[51] As such, Williams's physical dominance makes sense; it is intelligible in a social context where race has meaning: she wins because she's Black and therefore naturally better than all others who are not Black.

Controversies

I proceed by highlighting the "controversies" Serena Williams has experienced. They are socially constructed and, according to media, are moments when Williams is othered/marked as deviating from norms. The labeling works as a form of social regulation that prescribes the normative behavior. I have identified these controversies by comparing the media representations and discussions regarding success and controversy for Williams against a representative sample of top-earning female athletes. The attributes and success of these top-earning women serve as the baseline for how a marketable female athlete is constructed by media and suggest the social expectations that go along with being a marketable woman athlete. Further study would be required to conduct a more thorough analysis of the changes in public perception, awareness of athletes, and marketability due to winning/losing a competition, relationship status/changes, and "controversies."

The controversies for the Williams sisters and Serena, in particular, have been made into lists, such as "Top-10 Williams sisters controversies" put together by ESPN research in 2004. This stands alone, as no other top earners have "lists" of their controversies, although other top earners have controversies that are easily found, and some are even known for being controversial (e.g., Martina Hingis). Starting with ESPN's "Top-10 Williams sisters controversies," I developed a new list that encompassed the most frequently cited events throughout Serena's career and decided to mine the list down to 15 incidents. After these 15, there was little more beyond scuttlebutt (such as a second but very small outfit controversy—known only to some Wimbledon fans). As a comparative, I did the same search for other No. 1 ranked women's tennis players (Martina Hingis, Kim Clijsters, Justine Henin-Hardenne, Monica Seles, Caroline Wozniacki, and Maria Sharapova) as well as others who have been on the highest-paid list (Anna Kournikova, Victoria Azarenka, Eugenie Bouchard). Studying controversy to understand social relationships has been a strategy previously used by scholars. Jaime Schultz analyzed Serena Williams's "catsuit" controversy in an intersectional and comparative manner to reveal the production of a hegemonic racialized order in women's tennis.[52] She studied this controversy as a specific "sporting moment" to highlight how power operates through media. I build on this method by enlarging the sample size to give a sense of the whole (top-earning female athletes), adding breadth (considering multiple sporting moments), and offering a comparative look at Williams's counterparts.

Athletes are celebrities, and the most visible ones are often followed, the subject of popular news—good, bad, and otherwise. The controversies for top-earning women athletes have been conventionalized. Their sportspersonship is questioned (they quit in tough situations, blame others when they fail, stretch and violate rules, are coached illegally) and they gossip and fight over men and compete for attention. Sportspersonship is behaving in a "sporting" way, in a manner that is in line with good muscular Christianity, exhibiting dominant values and morals. But female athletes are held to a gendered standard as well. Their sportspersonship can be questioned because they're not behaving as a "lady" as well as not acting as a good sport. A majority of the controversies for women tennis players that happen on the court reinforce that they are women, the traditionally perceived inferior sex, and more childlike than their male counterparts. Tantrums, glares, having a bad attitude, grunting, pouting, cursing, tight outfits, and short skirts all fit into this type of deviance labeled as controversy by the media. In fact, in many of the on-the-court controversies, the fans signal a controversy or that a norm has been broken by whistling and booing. Off the court, women athletes are measured against a hegemonic femininity that is classed, raced, and sexed, although this is changing. Are they sexy, and how are they presenting their sex appeal? How does their appeal fit with expectations of their race, class, gender, and sexuality?[53] The list below is in chronological order and marks Williams's career in the public eye.

1998 Wimbledon: Serena Williams withdraws rather than face Venus Williams in the next round.

2001 Indian Wells semifinals: Venus Williams contends she can't play, allowing Serena Williams a walkover to the finals. This is when questions arise about whether or not the family is "fixing the matches."

2002 U.S. Open: Williams wears a "catsuit," causing a stir at Flushing Meadows.

2003 French Open semifinals: Williams accuses Justine Henin-Hardenne of "lying and fabricating" about a controversial service call. Williams was also booed continually during the match by the fans and held back tears in the postmatch press conference.

2003 Wimbledon: Serena and Venus Williams are accused by media and fans of collusion and predetermining the outcome of the match.

2004 Olympics: Williams backs off the flight to Greece at the last minute—just a few hours prior to takeoff—and her Olympic spot could not be filled.

2004 U.S. Open quarterfinals: An umpire awards a point to Jennifer Capriati that should have been given to Williams in the third and deciding set. TV replays also appear to show at least two other incorrect calls that went against Williams in the final game. Afterward, an official apology from the U.S. Open is made to Williams.

2009 U.S. Open: Williams is called for a foot fault in the third set of the finals against Kim Clijsters. Outraged, she threatens the line judge and is punished by the WTA for her behavior.

2012 Olympics: After winning an Olympic gold medal, Williams celebrates by doing the "Crip Walk," a dance affiliated with a notorious Los Angeles–based gang.

December 2012, Sao Paulo: Caroline Wozniacki imitates Williams in an exhibition match and is called racist. This followed Novak Djokovic doing a similar but pared-down imitation of Serena a month earlier.

2013 Australian Open: Williams loses to Sloane Stephens in the Australian Open quarterfinal. Later, Stephens speaks out about Williams cutting off communication after losing.

2013 Wimbledon: Maria Sharapova responds after Williams, quoted in a magazine, made some biting comments referring to Sharapova's boyfriend and fellow tennis player, Grigor Dimitrov, who was also Williams's ex-boyfriend.

2013 Charleston: Jelena Janković and Williams have a testy on-court exchange after Williams makes Janković wait to serve. "How long do I have to wait?" Janković asks the chair. "'Til I'm ready," Williams replies. "I'm not slow." At the year-end championships, the Serb questions whether Williams's fluctuations during matches are gamesmanship.

2015 *Sports Illustrated*: *Sports Illustrated* names Williams Sportsperson of the Year and puts her on the cover. Social media is set ablaze as some people feel that the horse American Pharoah should have been named, and others body-shame Williams, posting remarks about her sex, body type, muscle tone, and attractiveness.

2016 *People* magazine: Williams is named one of the "Most Beautiful Women of 2016," and she posts a photo to her Instagram account that followers believe she has heavily Photoshopped.[54]

This list largely covers the conventional sportsland controversies of women athletes—spats with competitors, attitude or "unladylike" responses to others, including umpires or line judges, but also adds another element that highlights how Williams creates dilemmas and contradictions in women's tennis and athletic femininity. (The exceptions are those incidents involving her and her family that may reflect notions of Black families and deviance.) The controversies over body image and race spotlight Williams's distinction from all of the other top earners (except for her sister). She doesn't look like the other women in "lady" sports. Moreover, spats and complaints of calls, even tirades, rants, and cursing are common behaviors, but they don't become controversies for others, as they do for Williams, and part of a public record of perceived misbehavior and deviance that is maintained and retold. (I found that Sharapova and others had similar events but no list of "Top 10" had been created nor are the events well documented like Williams's.) These specific controversies, those that can be tied to race via body difference and threatening attitude, illustrate how Williams is portrayed as authentically Black.

In their imitations of Williams, Novak Djokovic, the No. 1 ranked men's player, and Caroline Wozniacki, the former No. 1 ranked women's player, stuffed their shirts with towels and Wozniacki stuffed her skirt and then stuck her bottom out to get a laugh from the crowd during an exhibition in Brazil. At an exhibition match in Slovakia, Djokovic shifted into his impersonation without warning, midgame, by going to his players' station, pulling out a towel, putting it up his shirt, and then adjusting the form of the towel. Without Djokovic mentioning whom he was imitating, the television announcer described what Djokovic had done and that he was mimicking "Serena Williams." As with both impressions, Williams's body is symbolically represented and can be alluded to and known by the audience without words.

Arguably the biggest controversy of Williams's career is the 2009 U.S. Open cursing of the line judge. During a U.S. Open semifinal match against Kim Clijsters, Williams was called for a foot fault. This call is rarely made at an important point in a significant match; it happened to come one point from match point.[55] The foot fault resulted in a double-fault for Williams and moved Clijsters one point from victory. Williams took a moment, received a new ball to serve again, and then paused before stepping toward the line judge, screaming, cursing, and shaking a ball at her. Williams was penalized for this outburst, and Clijsters was awarded another point, which was match point, and the match was over; the semifinal ended without playing the deciding two points. The controversy is not simply that Williams cursed in public. U.S. Open tournament director Jim Curley said that Williams protested the call in "a threatening manner." This description of "threatening" speaks to how Williams is read as a Black deviant, easily carrying the stigma of being physically imposing and possibly criminal. Williams was fined by both the United States Tennis Association (USTA) and U.S. Open, totaling $82,500, a record level of punishment, plus put on probation for two years where she had to avoid having another "major offense." The public controversies of Serena Williams illuminate that she not only gets the female athlete treatment but also a racialized treatment for being at the intersection of race, class, and gender.[56]

THE COST AND BENEFIT OF BEING A STRONG BLACK WOMAN ATHLETE

Serena Williams is the greatest women's tennis player of all time. And yet, she has been second behind Maria Sharapova for 11 straight years in endorsement income and total earnings. The streak has only recently been broken (2016) after Williams entered rarified air with her record making *and* Sharapova tested positive for a performance enhancement drug and lost some endorsement deals. This, more than any other detail, illustrates what it means to be a dominant Black female athlete.

Serena Williams fits an antihero/counterhero dominance. She has benefited from the myth of "natural Black athleticism" to explain her ability.[57] She is praised for dominance, strength, power, muscle, toughness, and athleticism. And this drives awareness. Williams's image fits with how male athletes are often marketed, making her a good spokesperson for sporting goods and performance products, such as Gatorade, Nike, tennis racquets, and so on.[58] The focus on her physical strength and abilities has displaced the typical marketing script where female athletes are sought after largely based on their "attractiveness" and meeting White standards of beauty. This has increased respect for her athleticism and game, while at the same time implicitly tagged her as nonattractive and atypical for female tennis players. While controversies might spell disaster or laughter for other women's tennis players, for Williams they have been punishable but also excused. After the 2009 U.S. Open, some questioned the price Williams would pay in endorsement opportunities for "losing her cool." But she has suffered little to no losses in her existing deals, and she has only gained more since the incident.[59] One advertising executive, postcontroversy, believed that Williams would not lose ad campaigns and went as far as to say that it could lead to new endorsement deals. "Serena's outburst could become the subject of a campaign for an antiperspirant, herbal tea, mattress or other product designed to help you stay cool, calm and relaxed."[60] This seems counterintuitive. How does behaving "poorly" hurt some but help Williams?

Going back to Livingston, Rosette, and Washington's research on leadership and agentic Black women, I believe that Williams suffers fewer marketability losses because she is a Black female seen as a "real" athlete with intensity, fight, and physicality.[61] Like dominant male athletes, Williams is partially excused because she was in competition and it got the best of her. Her dominance and Black femaleness affords her some latitude in expression, difference, and dominance with costs and benefits in the endorsement marketplace. Kurt Badenhausen reflected on Williams's late-career success, which has made Williams an attractive endorser for marketers and the top-earning female athlete. "Williams ranks second among active athletes, behind only LeBron James in the U.S., on Repucom's CelebrityDBI . . . Her 89% awareness level ranks in the top 3% of the nearly 4,000 celebrities Repucom follows, and she scores highly on the aspiration and influence attributes in particular."[62] Still, Williams has only twice been the highest-earning female athlete during her career, in 2004 and 2016, and her endorsement dollars lagged far behind Sharapova's; in 2014, Williams pulled in $11 million compared to Sharapova's $22 million.[63] To top Sharapova this year, Williams has remarkably nearly doubled her endorsement earnings (reaching $20 million for the first time).

Sharapova's long-standing reign of 11 years as the "highest-earning female athlete" is easily understood where "popular media reproduces the hegemonic racialized order in women's tennis."[64] Tennis is a "ladies' and gentlemen's" sport, which gives women an additional boost in terms of marketability. Female tennis players are boosted by the perception of normative femininity inside their high-class sport. Sharapova's earnings are greater than most male athletes' because she competes in an upper-class global sport where the financial rewards are higher than in most other sports. She has earned more than her tennis competitors off the court because she fits the normative femininity and feminine performance—she is tall, has a slight build, and is White, with blonde hair and blue eyes, known for "avoiding" controversy—meaning that it is not constructed or maintained by media. Sharapova has had great success in major tennis tournaments, completing the Career Grand Slam—winning each of the four Grand Slams once. Her total income was the highest for female athletes from 2004–2015 ($250 million) and she ranks in the Top 20 for *all* athletes (male and female) over the 10-year span of 2005–2015, with the lion's share coming from endorsements, an average of about $15.5 million over her whole 16-year career, and averaging more than $18 million per year off the court for the last eight years.[65]

It's difficult to make sense of the disparity in Williams's and Sharapova's endorsement dollars without considering a possible interrupting effect of Williams's dominance and race and class. "Maria Sharapova also earns significantly more, and it's likely because she's willowy, white, and blonde, while Williams is a black woman with prominent, athletic muscles—as is often pointed out, sometimes disparagingly."[66] Williams's physical gifts supposedly give her an obvious and inherent advantage that lessens her "amazing" story of success.[67] Thus, her current level of success can be tempered: her achievements are forgone conclusions, any loss is more telling; when she loses it suggests that she's really inferior, not so good, skilled, mentally tough, smart, or tactical. In addition to her being the "bully," another interpretation of the effect of controversies is that negative stories can feed racial stereotypes of Black deviance and justify maintenance of the status quo.[68] Black athletes are often stereotyped as deviant, connecting to an urban Black masculinity, and the construction of bad stories of Williams's behavior can effectively support a "self-fulfilling prophecy" that Blacks are inherently inferior—in other words, that Williams naturally cannot control herself.[69]

CONCLUSION

So how does a Black woman from Compton, California, become a dominant athlete and come to be seen as highly marketable by multinational corporations?

It used to be said by Blacks that a Black person has to be at least two or three times better than a White person to be afforded the same amount of respect, earn the same pay, and be considered an equal. This logic fits here. First, the dominant Black female athlete needs to be the best in her sport. We'd have little awareness of Williams if she wasn't at the top of the rankings. Second, the woman needs to be physically dominant. The focus on Williams's body is reminiscent of the Hottentot Venus, highlighting the difference and distinction of Williams. In the late 1700s, Sara Baartman, a South African Black woman, was paid to tour as a freak show attraction in Europe and exhibit her "abnormal" body. Special attention was paid to her bottom, and even after her death, her body was dissected and put on display.[70] Baartman, given the show name "Hottentot Venus," was helpful in illustrating racial difference and justifying unequal treatment. The dominance of Williams necessitates explanation, and this comes in the form of commentary by media and her peers that puts her body on display and highlights particular differences between Williams and others, as though those are the only differences that exist and that are important to understand Williams and her success. Third, the dominant Black female athlete needs to have controversies. There is less news of her sister Venus and even less about other Black tennis players (e.g., Sloane Stephens, Madison Keys) and Black female athletes in other sports. Williams is a target, which raises awareness, albeit with some potential negative effect. Serena Williams's marketability is high but capped because of her deviation from the norm, while this difference has created a niche that is stable and durable. Her sustained greatness and exceptional athleticism have allowed her to break new ground. Last, a dominant Black female athlete has to have patience. Williams has the race, dominance, and her Compton urban background to be presented and read as authentically Black. She is an image of strength, and this can sell to a broader public; it has a bigger appeal where ideas are changing in regards to the perception of women's athleticism and the significant growth in the women's sports market. But this is a timing issue, and Williams happens to be in this position at the perfect moment. Sporting apparel companies have learned that the old, narrow, and White models of femininity (as fragile, diminutive, and "cute") no longer have as broad an appeal as they once did. Instead, post-Title IX women are inspired by strong athletic women, and Williams epitomizes this and models self-empowerment.[71] The cultural shift toward "real body types" is very recent, and now Williams is being heralded for her "nontraditional" body type and has been proclaimed a new body image role model by *Vogue* magazine.[72] Even this signals that Williams is different—"new"/"nontraditional"—and not the norm. However, Williams crosses over as a "real" athlete while still paying a price for not fitting the ideal. Shane Aaron Miller writes about the case of South African track star Caster Semenya, wonderfully articulating the complexity of dominant Black female athletes:

> The existing rhetorical ancestry of female athletes in general, black athletes in particular, and female black athletes specifically, invoked a framework of difference and Otherness that placed Semenya in a position of particularity. Semenya's story and image readily supported the historical reading of the black female athlete as freak. Although the stories written about Semenya were sympathetic and insisted on her innocence, her ability to continue competing, and glorified her success and fortitude, the history of the black female athletic freak lurked as a specter outside of the stories.[73]

Serena Williams continues to face the specter and has had a public career filled with "controversy" when compared to other female athletes on the highest earners list, and her endorsements have been relatively consistent and low compared to Sharapova's. I propose that stigma is inherent to the Black athlete, female or male, and therefore, the creation of her negative events or "controversies" by the media and general public is a reminder of the negative repercussions that coincide with being a dominant Black female athlete. In order for Williams to reach maximum earning power, she must maintain her success in the field of women's tennis, be physically dominant, and face body-shaming and suspicion surrounding her femininity—a dilemma for women athletes and a contradiction to traditional femininity, which garners the highest-paying endorsement opportunities. And, this must happen in combination with less dominant White female tennis players being unable to compete with her, failing miserably behind her, and/or being found out as poor sportspersons/cheaters.

NOTES

1. Kimberlé Crenshaw, "Mapping the Margins: Intersectionality, Identity Politics, and Violence against Women of Color," *Stanford Law Review* 43, no. 6 (July 1991): 1244.

2. Michele Lamont, "How to Become a Dominant French Philosopher: The Case of Jacques Derrida," *American Journal of Sociology* 93, no. 3 (November 1987): 584–622.

3. Heidi M. Parker and Janet S. Fink, "Arrest Record or Openly Gay: The Impact of Athletes' Personal Lives on Endorser Effectiveness," *Sport Marketing Quarterly* 21 (2012): 72.

4. William I. Thomas, "The Psychology of Race-Prejudice," *American Journal of Sociology* 9, no. 5 (March 1904): 593–611.

5. Robert Ezra Park, *Race and Culture* (Glencoe, IL: Free Press, 1950).

6. Everett C. Hughes, "Dilemmas and Contradictions of Status," *American Journal of Sociology* 50, no. 5 (1945): 353–59.

7. Herbert Blumer, "Race Prejudice as a Sense of Group Position," *Sociological Perspectives* 1, no. 1 (Spring 1958): 3–7.

8. Race relations has been studied across many different real contexts. See Elijah Anderson, *Cosmopolitan Canopy: Race and Civility in Everyday Life* (New York: W. W. Norton, 2011); Lawrence D. Bobo, James R. Kluegel, and Ryan A. Smith. "Laissez-Faire Racism," in *Racial Attitudes in the 1990s*, eds. Steven Tuch and Jack K. Martin (Westport, CT: Praeger, 1997), 15–42; Eduardo Bonilla-Silva, "Rethinking Racism: Toward a Structural Interpretation," *American Sociological Review* 62, no. 3 (1997): 465–80; Eduardo Bonilla-Silva, *Racism Without Racists* (Lanham, MD: Rowman and Littlefield Publishers, 2010); Sharon M. Collins, *Black Corporate Executives: The Making and Breaking of a Black Middle Class* (Philadelphia, PA: Temple University Press, 1997); Joe R. Feagin, "The Continuing Significance of Race: Antiblack Discrimination in Public Places," *American Sociological Review* 56, no. 1 (February

1991): 101–17; Devah Pager, *Marked: Race, Crime, and Finding Work in the Era of Mass Incarceration* (Chicago, IL: University of Chicago Press, 2007); Deidre Royster, *Race and the Invisible Hand: How White Networks Exclude Black Men from Blue-Collar Jobs* (Berkeley: University of California Press, 2003).

9. Robert W. Livingston and Nicholas A. Pearce, "The Teddy-Bear Effect: Does Having a Baby Face Benefit Black Chief Executive Officers?," *Psychological Science* 20, no. 10 (2009): 1229–36.

10. Robert W. Livingston, Ashleigh Shelby Rosette, and Ella F. Washington, "Can an Agentic Black Woman Get Ahead? The Impact of Race and Interpersonal Dominance on Perceptions of Female Leaders," *Psychological Science* 23, no. 4 (2012): 354–58.

11. Thomas C. Boyd and Matthew D. Shank, "Athletes as Product Endorsers: The Effect of Gender and Product Relatedness," *Sport Marketing Quarterly* 13, no. 2 (2004): 82–93; Brian D. Till and Michael Busler, "The Match-Up Hypothesis: Physical Attractiveness, Expertise, and the Role of Fit on Brand Attitude, Purchase Intent, and Brand Beliefs," *Journal of Advertising* 29 (2000): 1–14.

12. Marketability is defined as (1) fit to be offered for sale, as in a market: marketable produce, (2) in demand by buyers or employers; salable: marketable goods; marketable skills.

13. Repucom.net.

14. Nicole L. Votolato and H. Rao Unnava, "Spillover of Negative Information on Brand Alliances," *Journal of Consumer Psychology* 16, no. 2 (2006): 196–202.

15. Harry Edwards, *Sociology of Sport* (Homewood, IL: Dorsey Press, 1973). For an example of work that suggests White players received a disproportionate share of positive character comments and Blacks received more negative comments, see James A. Rada and K. Tim Wulfemeyer, "Color Coded: Racial Descriptors in Television Coverage of Intercollegiate Sport," *Journal of Broadcasting & Electronic Media* 49, no. 1 (2005): 68–85; and another work that found the performances of Black and White athletes was often reduced to physical gifts, with Black success being attributed to their physical superiority and White failure understood as a result of their natural physical deficits is Andrew C. Billings, Kelby K. Halone, and Bryan E. Denham, "'Man, That Was a Pretty Shot': An Analysis of Gendered Broadcast Commentary Surrounding the 2000 Men's and Women's NCAA Final Four Basketball Championships," *Mass Communication & Society* 5, no. 3 (2002): 295–315.

16. Margaret Carlisle Duncan, Michael A. Messner, and Linda Williams, *Coverage of Women's Sports in Four Daily Newspapers* (Los Angeles, CA: Amateur Athletic Foundation of Los Angeles, 1991).

17. Michael S. Messner, *Taking the Field: Women, Men and Sports* (Minneapolis: University of Minnesota Press, 2002); Leslie Heywood and Sharon Dworkin, *Built to Win: The Female Athlete as Cultural Icon* (Minneapolis: University of Minnesota Press, 2003).

18. Messner, *Taking the Field*.

19. Duncan, Messner, and Williams, *Coverage of Women's Sports*.

20. Messner, *Taking the Field*; Heywood and Dworkin, *Built to Win*.

21. Interestingly, the 1990s marks what many sports cultural scholars have identified as the time in which men have become sexualized as boy-toys and measured

against an athletic, "hard body" reference point. See Heywood and Dworkin, *Built to Win*, and Toby Miller, *Sportsex* (Philadelphia, PA: Temple University Press, 2002).

22. Eileen L. McDonagh and Laura Pappano, *Playing with the Boys: Why Separate Is Not Equal in Sports* (New York: Oxford University Press, 2008).

23. Richard Lapchick, Eric Little, Colleen Lerner, and Ray Matthew, *The 2008 Racial and Gender Report Card: College Sport* (Orlando: University of Central Florida, 2009).

24. Stephanie A. Tryce and Scott N. Brooks, "'Ain't I a Woman': Black Women and Title IX," *Journal for the Study of Sports and Athletes in Education* 4, no. 3 (2010): 243–56.

25. Angela Davis, *Women, Race & Class* (New York: Vintage, 1981).

26. Sut Jhally, "Advertising as Religion: The Dialectic of Technology and Magic," in *Cultural Politics in Contemporary America*, eds. Lan Angus and Sut Jhally (New York: Routledge, 1989), 217–29; Walter LaFeber, *Michael Jordan and the New Global Capitalism* (New York: W. W. Norton, 2002).

27. John Fiske, *Understanding Popular Culture* (London: Routledge, 1989); Margaret Carlisle Duncan and Barry Brummett, "The Mediation of Spectator Sport," *Research Quarterly for Exercise and Sport* 58, no. 2 (1987): 168–77; Michael A. Messner and William S. Solomon, "Outside the Frame: Newspaper Coverage of the Sugar Ray Leonard Wife Abuse Story," *Sociology of Sport Journal* 10 (1993): 119–34.

28. James Bryant, "A Two-Year Selective Investigation of the Female in Sport as Reported in the Paper Media," *ArenaReview* 4 (1980): 32–44; Pamela J. Creedon, "Women, Media and Sport: Creating and Reflecting Gender Values," in *Women, Media and Sport: Challenging Gender Values*, ed. Pamela J. Creedon (Thousand Oaks, CA: Sage Publications, 1994), 3–27; Mary Jo Kane and Lisa J. Disch, "Media Coverage of the Female Athlete Before, During and After Title IX: Sports Illustrated Revisited," *Journal of Sport Management* 2 (1988): 87–99.

29. Duncan, Messner, and Williams, *Coverage of Women's Sports*; Elaine M. Blinde, Susan L. Greendorfer, and Rebecca J. Shanker, "Differential Media Coverage of Men's and Women's Intercollegiate Basketball: Reflection of Gender Ideology," *Journal of Sport and Social Issues* 15 (1991): 98–114; Nancy Theberge, "A Feminist Analysis of Response to Sports Violence: Media Coverage of the 1989 World Junior Hockey Championship," *Sociology of Sport Journal* 6 (1989): 247–56; Mary Jo Kane and S. L. Greendorfer. "The Media's Role in Accommodating and Resisting Stereotyped Images of Women in Sport: Challenging Gender Values," in *Media, Women and Sport: Challenging Gender Values*, ed. Pamela Creedon (Thousand Oaks, CA: Sage Publications, 1994), 28–44; Daniel L. Wann, Michael P. Schrader, Julie A. Allison, and Kimberly K. McGeorge, "The Inequitable Newspaper Coverage of Men's and Women's Athletics at Small, Medium and Large Universities," *Journal of Sport and Social Issues* 22, no. 1 (1998): 79–87.

30. Janet S. Fink and Linda Jean Kensicki, "An Imperceptible Difference: Visual and Textual Constructions of Femininity in Sports Illustrated and Sports Illustrated for Women," *Mass Communication and Society* 5, no. 3 (2002): 317–39.

31. Heywood and Dworkin, *Built to Win*.

32. Herman Gray, *Watching Race: Television and the Struggle for "Blackness"* (Minneapolis: University of Minnesota Press, 1995).

33. Johnnie Frances Harris, "Nobody Knows Her Name: The Depiction of the Black Female Athlete in National Sports Telecasts," Master's thesis (University of Texas, Austin, 1991); Jhally, *Advertising as Religion*.

34. WTA.com.

35. Ibid.

36. Ibid.

37. WTA.com, "Player Biography/Career in Review/Career Highlights," Women's Tennis Association, accessed July 1, 2016, wtatennis.com/.

38. Ibid.

39. Kurt Badenhausen, "Serena Williams Tops Sharapova as the World's Highest-Paid Female Athlete," *Forbes.com*, last modified June 6, 2016, http://www.forbes.com/sites/kurtbadenhausen/2016/06/06/serena-tops-sharapova-as-the-worlds-highest-paid-female-athlete/#2765737e4f79.

40. Nancy E. Spencer, "From 'Child's Play' to 'Party Crasher': Venus Williams, Racism and Professional Women's Tennis," in *Sport Stars: The Cultural Politics of Sporting Celebrity*, eds. David L. Andrews and S. J. Jackson (London: Routledge, 2001), 87–101.

41. S. L. Price, "Who's Your Daddy," *Sports Illustrated*, May 31, 1999; Serena Williams with Daniel Paisner, *On the Line* (New York: Grand Central Publishing, 2009).

42. Williams, *The Line*.

43. Williams, *The Line*; Price, "Daddy."

44. Price, "Daddy."

45. Delia D. Douglas, "To Be Young, Gifted, Black and Female: A Meditation on the Cultural Politics at Play in Representations of Venus and Serena Williams," *Sociology of Sport Online* 5 (November-December 2002), http://physed.otago.ac.nz/sosol/v5i2/v5i2_3.html; Delia D. Douglas, "Venus, Serena, and the Inconspicuous Consumption of Blackness: A Commentary on Surveillance, Race Talk, and New Racism(s)," *Journal of Black Studies* 43, no. 2 (2005): 127–45; Janell Hobson, "The 'Batty' Politic: Toward an Aesthetic of the Black Female Body," *Hypatia* 18 (2003): 87–105; Spencer, "Child's Play"; Nance E. Spencer, "Sister Act IV: Venus and Serena Williams at Indian Wells: 'Sincere Fictions' and White Racism," *Journal of Sport and Social Issues* 28 (2004): 115–35.

46. WTA.com.

47. Ibid.

48. Badenhausen, "Tops Sharapova."

49. Price, "Daddy."

50. Dianne Hagaman, "'The Joy of Victory, the Agony of Defeat': Stereotypes in Newspaper Sports Feature Photographs," *Visual Sociology* 8 (1993): 48–66.

51. Patricia Vertinsky and Gwendolyn Captain, "More Myth Than History: American Culture and Representations of the Black Female's Athletic Ability," *Journal of Sport History* 25, no. 3 (1998): 544–45.

52. Jaime Schultz, "Reading the Catsuit: Serena Williams and the Production of Blackness at the 2002 US Open," *Journal of Sport and Social Issues* 29 (2005): 338–57.

53. It is important to note that media is not the only place where the behavior of female athletes is scrutinized. Scholars also debate the feminist politics (see Heywood and Dworkin, *Built to Win*). Are they being exploited or taking advantage of the system?

Are they only thinking of themselves and personal game or the impact on women overall when they pose in bikinis or nude? This is also magnified on social media.

54. "Top-10 Williams Sisters Controversies," 2004 ESPN Research, September 10, 2013, retrieved on July 12, 2016, http://espn.go.com/sports/tennis/usopen04/news/story?id=1876882. http://espn.go.com/blog/espntennis/post/_/id/1035/2013-controversies-of-the-year;retrievedonJuly12,2016,http://www.cnn.com/2009/US/09/15/serena.williams.outburst/index.html?eref=rss_topstories&utm_source=feedburner&utm_medium=feed&utm_campaign=Feed%3A+rss%2Fcnn_topstories+%28RSS%3A+CNN+-+Top+Stories%29&utm_content=Google+Feedfetcher; retrieved on July 12, 2016, http://espn.go.com/sports/tennis/columns/story?id=3952939;http://abcnews.go.com/Sports/story?id=99759; retrieved on July 12, 2016, http://espn.go.com/sports/tennis/news/story?id=4699850 (6) http://www.nytimes.com/2009/09/29/business/media/29adco.html; retrieved on July 12, 2016, http://www.nbcnews.com/news/other/was-it-racist-caroline-wozniacki-imitates-serena-williams-stirs-controversy-v15845710; retrieved on June 20, 2016, http://www.si.com/tennis/2015/07/14/serena-williams-body-image-wta-tennis; retrieved on June 20, 2016, http://www.cosmopolitan.com/style-beauty/fashion/news/a57705/serena-williams-people-magazine-photoshop/.

55. ESPN.com, "Clijsters Wins after Controversial Ending," last modified September 13, 2009, http://www.espn.com/sports/tennis/usopen09/news/story?id=4468762.

56. This is also called "multiple jeopardy," see Deborah K. King, "Multiple Jeopardy, Multiple Consciousness: The Context of a Black Feminist Ideology," in *Words of Fire: An Anthology of African American Feminist Thought*, ed. B. Guy-Sheftall (New York: New Press, 1995), 294–315.

57. Scott N. Brooks and Michael A. McKail, "A Theory of the Preferred Worker: A Structural Explanation for Black Male Dominance in Basketball," *Critical Sociology* 34, no. 3 (2008): 369–87; Jay Coakley, *Sport in Society: Issues and Controversies* (St. Louis, MO: Mosby, 1990); Harry Edwards, "The Myth of the Racially Superior Athlete," *Intellectual Digest* 44 (1972): 32–38; D. Stanley Eitzen and George Sage, *Sociology of American Sport* (Dubuque, IA: Brown, 1989); Gary Sailes, *Sport Socialization Comparisons among Black and White Adult Male Athletes and Nonathletes*, Unpublished doctoral dissertation (University of Minnesota, 1984); Gary Sailes, "A Socioeconomic Explanation of Black Sports Participation," *Western Journal of Black Studies* 11, no. 4 (1987): 164–67; Gary A. Sailes, "The Myth of Black Sports Supremacy," *Journal of Black Studies* 21, no. 4 (1991): 480–87; Eldon E. Snyder and Elmer Spreitzen, *Social Aspects of Sport* (Englewood Cliffs, NJ: Prentice-Hall, 1983).

58. Kate Fagan, "Sex Sells? Trend May Be Changing," *ESPNW.com*, last modified 2014, http://espn.go.com/espnw/w-in-action/nine-for-ix/article/9604247/sex-sells-trend-changing-espnw.

59. Andrew Adam Newman, "Serena Williams's Ad Deals Survive Her Outburst on Court," Business, *NewYorkTimes.com*, last modified September 28, 2009, http://www.nytimes.com/2009/09/29/business/media/29adco.html; Rich Thomaselli, "No Marketing Fallout Expected for Serena Williams: Brands Stick with Tennis Star after Profane Outburst; Others See Opening for Champ Clijsters," *Adage.com*, last modified September 15, 2009, http://adage.com/article/news/marketing-fallout-expected-serena-williams/139030/.

60. Thomaselli, "Fallout."

61. Livingston, Rosette, and Washington, "Agentic Woman."

62. Badenhausen, "Tops Sharapova."

63. Forbes.com, "The World's Highest Paid Female Athletes 2016."

64. Schultz, "Catsuit," 339.

65. Kurt Badenhausen, "The Athletes Who Have Made the Most Money Over the Past 10 Years," *Forbes.com*, last modified September 24, 2015, http://www.forbes.com/sites/kurtbadenhausen/2015/09/24/the-athletes-who-made-the-most-money-the-past-10-years/#a7ff03e264d9; Kurt Badenhausen, "How Maria Sharapova Earned $285 Million During Her Tennis Career," *Forbes.com*, last modified March 8, 2016, http://www.forbes.com/sites/kurtbadenhausen/2016/03/08/how-maria-sharapova-earned-285-mill-during-her-tennis-career/#e10b6d766fdc.

66. Marc Bain, "Why Doesn't Serena Williams Have More Sponsorship Deals," *The-Atlantic.com*, last modified August 31, 2015, http://www.theatlantic.com/entertainment/archive/2015/08/serena-williams-sponsorship-nike-us-open/402985/.

67. Susan K. Cahn, *Coming on Strong: Gender and Sexuality in Twentieth-Century Women's Sport* (New York: Free Press, 1994); Jessica Edwards, "The Black Female Athlete and the Politics on (In)Visibility," *New Political Economy* 4, no. 2 (1999): 278–82.

68. Laurel R. Davis and Othello Harris, "Race and Ethnicity in US Sports Media," in *Media Sport*, ed. Lawrence Wenner (London: Routledge, 1998), 154–69.

69. Cheryl L. Cole and Harry Denny, "Visualizing Deviance in Post-Reagan America: Magic Johnson, AIDS, and the Promiscuous World of Professional Sport," *Critical Sociology* 20, no. 3 (1994): 123–47.

70. bell hooks, *Black Looks: Race and Representation* (Boston: South End Press, 1992); Clifton Crais and Pamela Scully, *Sara Baartman and the Hottentot Venus: A Ghost Story and a Biography* (Princeton, NJ: University of Princeton Press, 2009); Anita Little, "Serena Williams, the Hottentot Venus and Accidental Racism," *ms.Magazine.com*, last modified December 15, 2012, http://msmagazine.com/blog/2012/12/15/serena-williams-the-hottentot-venus-and-accidental-racism/.

71. Heywood and Dworkin, *Built to Win*; Fagan "Sex Sells"; Adrianne Pasquarelli, "Adidas Taps Squad of Female Athletes in New Global Campaign Created by 72andSunny, Series Continues Trend of Female-Centric Marketing from Sports Brands," *Adage.com*, last modified February 4, 2016, http://adage.com/article/cmo-strategy/adidas-taps-squad-female-athletes-global-campaign/302516/; Katie Richards, "Why Brands Are Finally Choosing More Female Athletes for Big Endorsement Deals: Women Are No Longer Sitting on the Sidelines," *Adweek.com*, last modified September 20, 2015, http://www.adweek.com/news/advertising-branding/why-brands-are-finally-choosing-more-female-athletes-big-endorsement-deals-167007.

72. Patricia Garcia, "Why Serena Williams and Jennifer Lawrence Are Our New Body Image Role Models," Culture, *Vogue*, last modified July 14, 2015, http://www.vogue.com/13283545/serena-williams-jennifer-lawrence-body-image/.

73. Shane Aaron Miller, "'Just Look at Her!': Sporting Bodies as Athletic Resistance and the Limits of Sport Norms in the Case of Caster Semenya," *Men and Masculinities* 18, no. 3 (August 2015): 312.

6

"It Was a Historic Game That No One Saw": Evaluating the Cultural Citizenship and Moral Legitimacy of Women's Professional Hockey through the Inaugural Women's Winter Classic Outdoor Ice Hockey Game

Cheryl MacDonald, Courtney Szto, and Jonathon Robert James Edwards

INTRODUCTION

Part of the hegemony of men's professional sports is signified by the fact that it is visibly more apparent in mainstream media than women's sports. According to the Tucker Center for Research on Girls and Women in Sport at the University of Minnesota, 40 percent "of all sports participants are female, yet women's sports receive only 4% of all sport media coverage."[1] Men's sports, of varying types, are televised regardless of their cultural or economic significance, as illustrated by televised darts, five-pin bowling, and even Little League baseball all being available for viewing on major sports networks (e.g., ESPN). Finding television coverage of women's sports, however, remains a "scavenger hunt." Aside from the Olympics, this has been a prominent concern for supporters of women's hockey in North America. For example, the 2016 National Collegiate Athletics Association (NCAA) Division I women's hockey final was broadcast on a tape delay one week after the game took place; yet it received higher ratings than any of the men's games from the 2016 tournament.[2] This raises the question: Does a lack of coverage indicate low interest in women's hockey? The ratings for the NCAA women's tape-delayed final and the reception of the first ever women's Winter Classic outdoor ice hockey game would suggest that the answer in *no*. Indeed, when the National Hockey League (NHL) announced that it would host its annual premier outdoor event in partnership with the Canadian Women's Hockey League (CWHL) and National Women's Hockey League (NWHL), fans took to social media to find out where they would watch the game.

The NHL Winter Classic tradition began in 2008 and sought to memorialize hockey's roots as a game played on frozen outdoor ponds. The inclusion of women in the 2016 Winter Classic intended to increase the visibility of women's professional ice hockey. However, as this chapter will demonstrate, both fans and members of the participating teams were critical of the way the event was organized.

On December 28, 2015, the NHL officially announced the inaugural women's Winter Classic outdoor ice hockey game (hereafter referred to as the Women's Classic) on its website. The game—between the CWHL's Les Canadiennes de Montréal and the NWHL's Boston Pride—was scheduled just three days later on December 31. Earlier in December, news of the Women's Classic had been leaked, but there were no official announcements made until weeks later.[3] Additionally, no tickets were sold for the Women's Classic. As was stated on the NHL's website, "fans that have a ticket to the 2016 NHL Winter Classic Alumni Game can use that ticket to gain early entry into the stadium to watch the Outdoor Women's Classic."[4] The game itself consisted of two 15-minute periods (as opposed to the usual three 20-minute periods); the NHL referred to this as an "abbreviated exhibition game."[5] The contest between Les Canadiennes and the Pride ended in a one-one tie, without an overtime or shoot-out. Perhaps most important, however, was the fact that the game was not officially televised and no tickets were sold.

The central focus of this study is to examine the question, What does the lack of a televised broadcast for a so-called historic development in women's ice hockey say about the value or legitimacy of the sport? According to the global governing body of women's ice hockey, the International Ice Hockey Federation,[6] "the modern era of organized women's hockey began in the late 1980s," and women's hockey has experienced significant growth over the past five years in North America. Since 2010–2011, the number of registered female hockey players in Canada has increased from 85,827 to 87,494 in 2014–2015.[7] In the United States, the number of registered female hockey players was just under 70,000 during the 2014–2015 season,[8] up from 65,609 in 2010–2011.[9] Yet, while the popularity of women's hockey is expanding by participation, research on the CWHL (and NWHL) has been limited in scope. As a result, the purpose of this study was to explore the perceptions and experiences that were fostered by the first ever Women's Classic and determine the value of women's professional ice hockey within the larger hockey landscape.

Guided by theories of cultural citizenship and moral legitimacy, we conducted a social media content analysis of posts about the Women's Classic on Twitter, the world's leading form of microblogging. We also interviewed members of Les Canadiennes in order to obtain firsthand accounts of how the game operated behind the scenes. Our account of the study begins with an introduction of the CWHL and Les Canadiennes, is followed by relevant theoretical and methodological deliberations, and concludes with a discussion of the status of women's professional hockey in light of the lack of broadcasting of the Women's Classic.

THE CANADIAN WOMEN'S HOCKEY LEAGUE AND LES CANADIENNES DE MONTRÉAL

After the original National Women's Hockey League (there is now a new iteration of the "NWHL") disbanded in 2007, the CWHL formed a professional, player-driven league initiated on both sides of the Canada–United States border in 2007.[10] The CWHL consists of five teams—the Boston Blades, Les Canadiennes, the Toronto Furies, the Brampton Thunder, and the Calgary Inferno—and was founded by contemporary iconic players Sami Jo Small, Jennifer Botterill, Allyson Fox, Kathleen Kauth, Kim McCullough, and Lisa-Marie Breton-Lebreux.[11] Each team plays 27 regular season games and then competes for the Clarkson Cup, which was provided by and named after former Canadian governor-general Adrienne Clarkson.[12]

For league cofounder Lisa-Marie Breton-Lebreux, former player and now coach of Les Canadiennes, the goal of the CWHL is to provide a place for elite female hockey players to continue their development beyond university and outside of national programs. In her words,

> there are more and more young girls who want to play hockey. We're at the stage where we need to feed them, they need to know they can go somewhere in a hockey career, and someday become paid professionals. We want the league to have the best players in the world—Russian, German, Italian. We want them to come play with us. That's the ultimate goal.[13]

Originally, CWHL players were not paid, revenue was shared equally by each team,[14] and the league covered costs such as travel, uniforms, and some equipment.[15] More recently, Montreal, Toronto, and Calgary have formed partnerships with their local NHL counterparts, receiving support in the form of thousands of dollars in funding, ice time, and exposure to assist in the development of the league.[16] The NHL's Ottawa Senators also partnered with the CWHL in 2016 to host the Clarkson Cup.[17] Nonetheless, Breton-Lebreux is an example of the many players who have long been dedicated to the advancement of women's ice hockey purely out of their passion for the game.

Les Canadiennes, which has roots in Montreal dating as far back as the 1930s, has won three CWHL Clarkson Cups, and its current roster includes Quebec native Olympians Caroline Ouellette, Charline Labonté, and Marie-Philip Poulin.[18] Indeed, journalists and authors Elizabeth Etue and Megan Williams note in their book on the history of women's ice hockey in Canada that

> while the female game has a long history in Québec, the powerful national position of the province's female players is nothing short of extraordinary given the comparatively low number of women who play hockey here. . . . Québec has consistently supplied a plentiful crop of talented women to the Canadian national team.[19]

Thus, Breton-Lebreux comes from a deep-rooted and unique hockey tradition and has played a key role in the development of the CWHL, which is now the longest-standing women's professional sporting league after the Women's National Basketball Association. Still, despite the long tradition of women's hockey in Canada and the sport's growing popularity in the United States, the game rests on precarious ground with regard to its economic, social, and cultural value.

CULTURAL CITIZENSHIP AND THE SIGNIFICANCE OF TELEVISED SPORTS

Cultural citizenship has been defined in numerous ways; however, for our purposes, it refers to the ability of citizens to coproduce or coauthor "the cultural context (webs of meaning) in which one participates."[20] Furthermore, cultural citizenship assumes that the basic levels of political and social citizenship have (more or less) been achieved and are now trying to turn equal opportunities into lived equalities. It does not seek to incorporate individual culture into political citizenship but rather to position citizenship as relevant in matters of culture.[21] Pieter Boele van Hensbroek contends that participation in culture itself does not signify citizenship because one must be able to have an impact on the cultural activity in question. In other words,

> the idea of the whole exercise is to provide reinterpretations of history, to challenge or enrich existing views, in short, to have an impact on the cultural consensus. This deeper aspect of participation is captured well in the idea of co-authorship, for if deviant historical interpretations remain in a cultural niche and the ruling images are not challenged, then there may be cultural freedom but no co-authorship.[22]

Relating this approach to the Women's Classic, we argue that allowing the women to participate in the NHL's Winter Classic is representative of cultural freedom, whereby women have been included, but their inclusion has had very little impact on the landscape of professional hockey. Furthermore, the absence of television coverage of the Women's Classic challenges the cultural citizenship of both the players and fans because there was a lack of a shared experience to create meaning and value. Due to the cross-border nature of this event, the term "citizen" should not necessarily be interpreted as one with nationalistic connotations; rather, we situate citizenship very simply as a valued, equal, and contributing member of society.

The significance of televised sport reaches well beyond economic value. Nancy Theberge has observed that the men's hockey system has historically overshadowed the women's game.[23] From a practical standpoint, having televised (and recorded) games affords the opportunity for instant replays, a feature that is normalized and valorized as part of the high production value that has become men's sport.[24] Perhaps more importantly, legends are born and sustained through the instant replay. The ability to select which parts of history are replayed and which stories are downplayed is an exercise of power.[25] Thus, televised sports games not only reproduce what is, supposedly, economically valuable through broadcast rights; they also reproduce particular histories and cultural value. As Cheryl Cooky, Michael Messner, and Robin Hextrum argue, "as longitudinal research on the televised news media coverage demonstrates, women's sports is consistently ignored and sports media silences women's sports."[26] After Title IX legislation in the United States was passed in 1972, the belief was that women's sports coverage on television and in newspapers would catch up to the growing number of women and girls participating in sport. Conversely, research has observed that coverage of women's sports has in fact declined in the 21st century.[27]

Jay Scherer and David Rowe have argued free-to-air sporting events represent an important service and responsibility for public broadcasters because citizen's rights should not only be limited to basic needs.[28] Access to television and radio was once thought of as equivalent to a citizen's right to access social services such as education and health care. Moreover, publicly available television programming, such as news, documentaries, game shows, children's shows, and sport, were considered "simply part of the 'national estate'";[29] this content was seen as valuable to a nation's culture. If we understand what is televised as relevant to society and those who are televised as valuable citizens, then both women's hockey and the fans that support them were barred from contributing to the cultural consensus of what hockey is and means. It is difficult to change, resist, and/or support that which is not visible. Consequently, instead of writing onto hockey history as coauthors, this chapter argues that, in 2016, women's professional hockey continues to be a footnote with the Women's Classic demonstrating how far the sport is from achieving lived equalities and being considered a legitimate cultural artefact.

MORAL LEGITIMACY AND THE VALUE OF WOMEN'S PROFESSIONAL ICE HOCKEY

The construct of moral legitimacy is used here as a means of understanding the results of the NHL's actions to add a women's game to the NHL Winter Classic. Legitimacy can be understood as a social evaluation of organizations by constituents, stakeholders, and society.[30] Mark Suchman states that legitimacy is "a generalized perception or assumption that the actions of an entity are desirable, proper, or appropriate within some socially constructed systems of norms, values, beliefs and definitions."[31] In addition, "legitimacy emerges when organizational activities align with constituents' expectations."[32] While legitimacy has been extensively researched, there has been limited research that has explored how organizations are evaluated with regards to establishing and maintaining legitimacy.[33] Audience-based evaluations can be understood through media legitimacy,[34] which is reflected through "communication through printed media, TV, or radio broadcasts."[35] In the case of this study's empirical setting, women's professional hockey is trying to establish its legitimacy and is thus seeking the approval of the constituents interested in women's hockey to advance the popularity of women's hockey in North America.

Organizational legitimacy originates from the notion that societal acceptance is based on an organization's actions and/or managerial decisions.[36] This societal acceptance is based on the idea that "once an action is perceived, social judgements form based on its congruence with a constituent's expectations for appropriate practice."[37] Furthermore, Alex Bitektine[38] stated that granting or withholding legitimacy represents a mechanism of social control by conferring legitimacy on organizations, structures, or practices; social actors encourage these organizations and promote structures and practices that they perceive as beneficial to themselves, their social group, or the entire society.

Legitimacy can ultimately dictate an organization's survival within a particular environment. Furthermore, legitimacy is "an anchor-point of a vastly expanded theoretical apparatus addressing the normative and cognitive forces that constrain, construct, and empower organizational actors."[39] Material resources, legal standing, and cultural status are all sources of legitimacy.[40]

Social actors evaluate an organization based on the features, structural attributes, and outcomes of an activity.[41] This evaluation is determined through the use of analytical processing where types of judgments can be established: cognitive or sociopolitical legitimacy.[42] Cognitive legitimacy is understood as the knowledge of certain organizational forms that are identifiable and recognizable.[43] While sociopolitical legitimacy comes from "the observed features of an organization, its structural attributes and outcomes of its activity are benchmarked against the prevailing social norms: the actor renders a judgment as to whether the organization [or event in the case of this study], its form, its processes, its outcomes, or its other features are socially acceptable and, hence, should be encouraged."[44] In this study, we examine sociopolitical legitimacy by comparing the women's outdoor hockey game to the men's outdoor hockey game to assess the legitimacy of the NWHL, CWHL, NHL, and women's hockey in North America.

Moral legitimacy, as identified by Suchman, is one of three types of legitimacy. The other two are pragmatic and cognitive.[45] Pragmatic legitimacy, as defined by Donna Wood,[46] occurs when "audiences are likely to become constituencies, scrutinizing organizational behavior to determine the consequences for them, of any given line of activity."[47] Pragmatic legitimacy can be subdivided into three areas: exchange, influence, and dispositional legitimacy. Cognitive legitimacy is described by Suchman as an "affirmative backing for an organization or mere acceptance of the organizations as necessary or inevitable based on some taken-for-granted cultural account."[48] There are two types of cognitive legitimacy: comprehensibility and taken-for-grantedness.

Moral legitimacy "rests not on the judgments about whether a given activity benefits the evaluator, but rather on judgments about whether the activity is 'the right thing to do.'"[49] Essentially, this type of legitimacy is based on the reflection of beliefs about whether an activity is socially acceptable and constructed by an "audience's socially constructed value system."[50] There are four types of moral legitimacy: consequential, personal, procedural, and structural legitimacy (see Table 6.1). That which is most appropriate for the

Table 6.1 Moral Legitimacy

Types of Moral Legitimacy	Definitions
Consequential Legitimacy	This type of legitimacy is based on the accomplishments of the organization. If the organization is compliant with the institutional expectations of the stakeholder(s), then a reward is given. If a reward is given, the organization is deemed legitimate.
Personal Legitimacy	Personal legitimacy is when actors perform acts that exercise personal influence, which leads to personal rather than organizational legitimacy.
Procedural Legitimacy	Organizations can "garner moral legitimacy by embracing socially accepted techniques and procedures."[1] When an organization exemplifies sound organizational procedures, there is an increased likelihood of legitimacy.
Structural Legitimacy	"Audiences see the organization as valuable and worthy of support because its structural characteristics locate it within a morally favored taxonomic category."[2] Structural characteristics are described as an organization's socially constructed capacity to perform a specific task.

[1] Mark C. Suchman, (1995). "Managing Legitimacy: Strategic and Institutional Approaches," *Academy of Management Review* 2 (1995): 571–610, accessed March 27, 2016, 580.

[2] Ibid., 581.

study was determined throughout the analysis and will be presented during the discussion.

METHODOLOGICAL APPROACHES TO CITIZENSHIP AND LEGITIMACY

This study poses the question, What does the lack of a televised broadcast for a so-called historic development in women's ice hockey say about the value or legitimacy of the sport for both fans and Les Canadiennes? The analysis employs mixed methods, including a social media content analysis and semistructured interviews. These procedures involved the combination of qualitative and quantitative techniques, a practice that methodologists contend will add depth to the findings and provide opportunities to cross check information in the event that conflicting findings would further complicate analysis.[51] The research question was examined in two phases. First, a quantitative content analysis of social media posts on Twitter was conducted in order to determine public reaction to the event. Twitter was deemed a viable site for data collection because of its popularity, its ease of access to public information, and because sports fans often take to Twitter to discuss relevant events, such as hockey games.[52]

A search was conducted for any tweets containing the words "Women's Winter Classic" and the hashtag "#womenswinterclassic." Hashtags are used to filter conversations and topics, essentially operating as a common thread. The challenge associated with this search is that it excluded tweets that were private and those that may have been about the game but did not explicitly use the keywords in question, making the sample nonexhaustive. We contend, however, that our sample is relevant because we suspect that the tweets containing the exact keywords were likely produced with more intent to be active in the broader public conversation about the event than those that did not specify to the same extent.

Once located, the tweets were coded into categories according to their content, the date they were produced, who tweeted them, and how many times they were retweeted or liked by others. The data were then entered into the Statistical Package for the Social Sciences (SPSS) in order to determine frequency distributions and to determine the usefulness of the data set for running tests for statistical significance. Typically, this would involve running cross tabulation tests, such as Pearson's Chi Square Test of Independence, in order to determine if there is a statistically significant relationship. For example, this test could be used to verify whether or not the accounts tweet out particular content or what kind of content was more likely to obtain retweets or likes. This was not possible, however, because the categories sometimes had counts of less than five tweets and thus could not produce reliable results.

A possible alternative could have been to run a Fisherman's Exact Test or Monte Carlo analysis; however, such calculations are typically reserved for larger and more meaningful data sets; therefore, we elected to portray our data set as descriptive and exploratory instead. The frequency distributions still produced an image of who engaged with the event on social media, when it was most popular, and which information garnered most attention.

The second phase of data collection and analysis involved conducting semistructured qualitative interviews with four members of Les Canadiennes—the general manager (Meg Hewings), assistant coach (Lisa-Marie Breton-Lebreux), and two players (Ann-Sophie Bettez and Julie Chu), all of whom volunteered to participate. The interviews were meant to glean the team members' perceptions of the event and to obtain firsthand accounts of the ways in which the first ever Women's Classic may have contributed to the current status—or, perhaps more accurately, the legitimacy—of women's professional hockey in Canada and North America. The interviews lasted between 25 and 45 minutes and were focused on three themes: the participants' accounts of participating in the event in their respective capacities as team members, their thoughts on the organization of the event, and their perspectives on what the Women's Classic means for the development of women's professional hockey as an active and legitimate citizen of hockey culture. Probes were occasionally used to shore up the discussion, such as "What was the most enjoyable part of the experience?" "Were you consulted in the planning of the event?" and "How has the NHL's involvement with the CWHL affected your team?"

ANALYSIS: A SERIES OF MISSED OPPORTUNITIES

The Twitter analysis was conducted in two phases, one of which provided more substantial results than the other. Much to our surprise, the search for "#womenswinterclassic" revealed 87 results, whereas "Women's Winter Classic" produced 836 tweets between December 2015 and April 2016. This was unexpected given the knowledge of the effectiveness of the hashtag for bringing social media users together and grouping information in one location in order to follow trends or events.[53] With that said, no official event hashtag was created by the NHL or other participants, despite one having been created for the men's game (#WinterClassic), therefore those who used #womenswinterclassic did so on their own, resulting in fewer occurrences. This, in turn, created a limited sample of tweets and a narrow scope.

As a result, we opted to focus on the search results for "Women's Winter Classic" and suggest that without an official hashtag, not only is the opportunity missed to create online engagement, but also from a research perspective, it is more difficult to locate relevant tweets because they are less easily aggregated. This challenge connects back to the nonexhaustive limitation of the study sample. Nonetheless, the 836 other tweets do provide a sufficient canvassing of public reaction to the inaugural Women's Classic and will be discussed at length here. No direct quotations will be shared because, although the tweets observed were made visible to the public by the users, it could be considered unethical to collect and disseminate their tweets without consent.

Social media can ethically "toe the line" between public and private despite privacy settings, and this is still being worked out in academia where ethics are concerned. Twitter scholar Michael Beurskens notes that "privacy is an important issue at the core of social networking" and that, as a result, from a research perspective, "even though legal claims are unlikely, university administration tends to be careful with regard to approving research on Twitter data."[54] By omitting direct quotations, we avoid this issue, and we believe our interview data complements our content analysis quite well.

The primary investigator examined 836 tweets from over 300 different Twitter users. The first tweet was posted on December 5, 2015, speculating about the CHWL and NHL discussing a Women's Classic. The most recent tweet collected in the study was posted April 17, 2016, about Denna Laing, a Boston Pride player who was paralyzed as a result of a fall on the ice during the game, which garnered substantial media attention. The following analysis combines the themes that were consistent across both social media and interview data.

The timeline of Twitter activity surrounding the event was divided according to posts produced in the days leading up to the game, on game day, and afterward.

Table 6.2 below demonstrates the frequency distribution of when tweets were posted. Approximately half of the tweets about the Women's Classic were produced before game day, which suggests that it did indeed garner some attention prior to the event, albeit in a relatively small time frame given that the game was officially announced on December 28. Just under a third of tweets were posted the day of the game, and just under a quarter of them were posted after the game. According to the Twitter website, "TV and Twitter have a special connection" because of the real-time forum created for engagement with exponentially more tweets generated during shows that intentionally seek participant interaction. Consequently, our content analysis seems to confirm that without intentional engagement with fans (and potential fans) and providing the broadcast to foster disparate, yet collective, engagement, events such as the inaugural Women's Classic miss out on important opportunities to grow the sport, brand, image, or fan base.

Table 6.2 When Tweets Were Posted

		Frequency	Percent	Valid Percent	Cumulative Percent
Timeline	Before Game Day	417	49.9	49.9	49.9
	Game Day	227	27.2	27.2	77.0
	After Game Day	192	23.0	23.0	100.0
	Total	836	100.0	100.0	

The content of the tweets created a robust image of the ways in which the Women's Classic was perceived by social media users. In descending order of frequency, the content of the 836 tweets were as follows: articles previewing the game; criticism of the lack of broadcasting; tweets about Denna Laing's injury; criticism of USA Hockey for not releasing its Olympians on the Boston Pride team for the game; commentary on the game being a "good first step" in the development and visibility of women's professional hockey; criticism of the NHL's organization of the game (including running time, two periods, short notice, no specific tickets); scores and updates; spotlight tweets and articles on specific teams and players; articles recapping the game; positive commentary on women's hockey; questions and information about the Periscope streaming of the game; negative commentary on women's hockey; and lastly, tweets asking where and how to obtain tickets to the game.

Ten tweets were categorized as "other" because they appeared sparingly. These included the following: two tweets stating that the game would have received far less coverage had it not been for the Laing injury; two tweets about where and how to obtain Women's Classic merchandise; one tweet about low attendance at the game; one tweet stating that the CWHL and NWHL should merge in order to be a stronger force in the development of the sport; one tweet in which the user accuses the NHL of being sexist; and finally, one tweet stating that there should be an official hashtag for the event. Table 6.3 below illustrates the frequency distributions by count, and Figure 6.1 constitutes a visual representation of the same. When combined with our interview data, three consistent themes emerged across both data sets: the lack of a television broadcast as a significant problem, viewing the game as an important "first step" for women's hockey, and the poor organization of the Women's Classic.

The Twitter search revealed that many fans of women's hockey wanted to view the Women's Classic and were eager to take part in this historic event. Across all tweets analyzed, fans wanted to know where they could view the game and, later on, demanded to know why it would not be

Table 6.3 Content of Tweets

		# of Tweets	Percent	Valid Percent	Cumulative Percent
Content	Article previewing game	222	26.6	26.6	26.6
	Lack of broadcast	115	13.8	13.8	40.3
	Laing	108	12.9	12.9	53.2
	Criticism of USA Hockey	81	9.7	9.7	62.9
	View game as "good first step"	78	9.3	9.3	72.2
	Criticism of organization of game	64	7.7	7.7	79.9
	Score/updates	62	7.4	7.4	87.3
	Team/player spotlights	30	3.6	3.6	90.9
	Article recapping game	30	3.6	3.6	94.5
	Positive commentary on women's hockey	12	1.4	1.4	95.9
	Other	10	1.2	1.2	97.1
	Periscope streaming	10	1.2	1.2	98.3
	Negative commentary on women's hockey	7	.8	.8	99.2
	Asking where to get tickets	7	.8	.8	100.0
	Total	836	100.0	100.0	

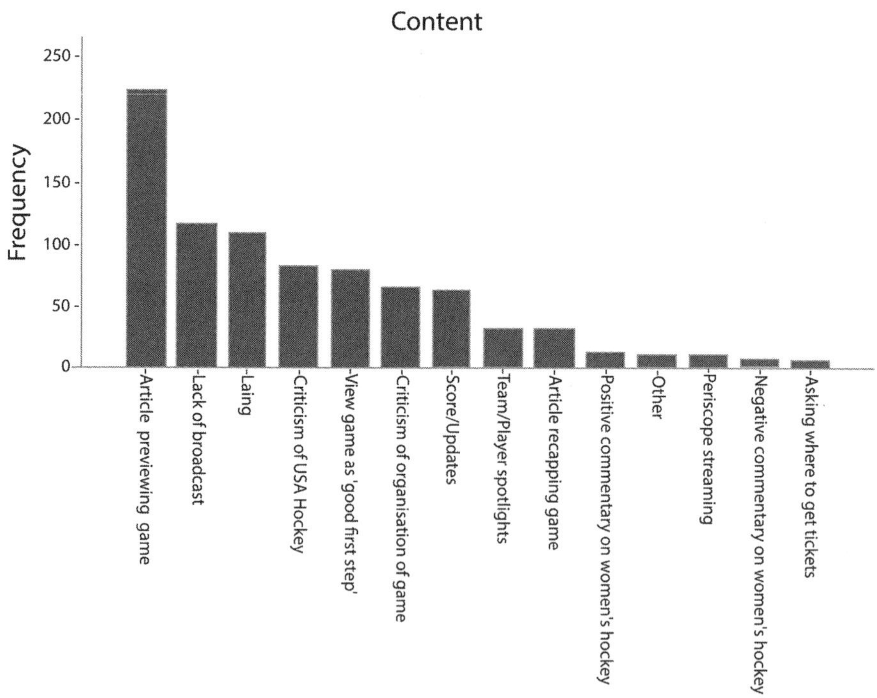

Figure 6.1 Visual Representation of Tweet Contents

broadcast. This sentiment was echoed by members of Les Canadiennes. Coach Breton-Lebreux suggested that even if not broadcast on television, perhaps the game could have been streamed online because "it was a historic game that no one saw!" Along similar lines, Bettez contends that women's hockey needs to be viewed in order for the game to grow: "It needs to be televised. It's unfortunate that we have so little time to shine and if you look at the guys, they have all the TV time they want. It is what it is, but it makes no sense to me that we're professionals and not on TV." General Manager Hewings also commented that because that game was not televised this historic event was unable to capitalize on reaching the younger audiences who are necessary in growing the game. Drawing on the work of Scherer and Rowe, if televised sport is supposed to serve as part of the "national estate" for citizens (whether American or Canadian in this instance), that the Women's Classic was not televised leads us to question not only *what* is included in the nation's estate but also *who*.[55] Moreover, our Twitter analysis suggests the existence of a public demand from both men and women for the event to be broadcast. This challenges the argument that there is no viable market for women's sports and corroborates Cooky, Messner, and Hextrum's longitudinal study on the (lack) of televised coverage for women's sports.[56]

In a Yahoo! Sports interview with Patrick Burke, director of NHL player safety, he explained, "There are five or six [people] in the NHL who formed an unofficial group to do things involving women's hockey."[57] The fact that the Women's Classic was a last-minute effort made by a small group of women's hockey supporters within the NHL headquarters was certainly evident to fans and viewers; thus, the lack of a television broadcast, while hardly acceptable, is understandable. Unsurprisingly, the most dominant theme discussed in the interviews was the last-minute organization of the event.

Participants noted that, under ideal circumstances, the planning for the Women's Classic would have started at least a year in advance. However, the rush to make the event happen from the NHL's side resulted in an "abbreviated game," which was less than ideal for the players. Some interview participants spoke of wanting to "play a real" game, discursively marking the Women's Classic as not real and/or as a less valuable game in a sense, at least in comparison to NHL hockey, which was also consistently articulated as the pinnacle of competitive hockey. Significantly, there were no change rooms allocated for the women at Gillette Stadium; instead the players got dressed at a nearby arena and were bussed to the stadium.

There were conflicting reports from participants as to how many players were allowed to participate (ranging from 15 to 18) in the Women's Classic, but according to the NHL's press release on the CWHL website, each team brought 18 players (including two goaltenders) and three coaches. Therefore, the Canadiennes cut three players and five coaching staff from the roster that appears on their official webpage. Julie Chu, U.S. Olympian and a Les Canadiennes veteran, recounted,

> We have a playing roster of twenty-five players and we could only dress eighteen. So our coaching staff and general managers did what they thought was right—going with seniority and then which players are playing better. Even though Marie-Philip Poulin is—well, technically she's not a rookie, but either way, she was going to play in that Winter Classic!

Chu continued to explain that there was a conscious effort made by the team to not let the Women's Classic divide the team between those who got to play and those who did not because nonplaying team members were not allowed in the VIP areas: "Like there was always 'Okay, for the roster players' and 'Okay, for the non-dressing players' and they had to do it that way to be specific but it creates a divide on the team." Similarly, Coach Breton-Lebreux discussed how the NHL provided clothing for the roster players and some members of the coaching staff:

> They were also only giving out things to wear—outfits—to those eighteen players, coach, and General Manager. But the coach and General Manager were nice enough to share the package with us, so we had mittens, toques [knitted hats], jackets with the nice logo. But, you know, we're a team of twenty-three. We, as a team, decided to bring everyone and the club paid extra for the hotel rooms and bus and for them to have tickets, but that created a bit of a separation. How do we make decisions—who is going to play on the team? We did veterans first, then scoring leaders, but it was really hard for the coaches.

While not denying the significance of the event and important contributions made by the NHL to make it happen, it is hard to imagine an instance where a professional men's team would have had to face similar circumstances.

The inclusion of the Women's Classic was definitely a progressive statement for gender equality, yet the conditions of this historic occasion whisper of the continued marginalization of women's sports more broadly. In this way, it is important for future organized efforts toward equality to try to level experiences in addition to providing the opportunity. Even though the differences may seem trivial to some, they reproduce a pattern whereby women's sporting events are treated like a sideshow.

The last theme to be discussed is the notion that the Women's Classic was an integral "first step" for the promotion of women's hockey in North America. Hewings described the NHL's Winter Classic as "the biggest stage in hockey" and stated "we were very privileged to participate and to know that we were going to make history in this way." Chu also commented that the tangible results are yet to manifest because the Women's Classic was viewed as a starting block of sorts. What is interesting about these comments is that, while this event occurred during the NWHL's first season as a league, the CWHL has been trying to make an impact for almost 10 years now. Hewings continued her thought, explaining "that what we were doing was making history and setting the groundwork for future events and future large stages for the female game outside of the Olympics." However, at what point does the notion of "laying the groundwork" become irrelevant? The number of "firsts" for women's sports increases every year, but we fail to see these firsts amount to much in the way of tangible equality. Interview participants also reflected on the 1998 Nagano Olympics as being key to the development of women's hockey, so should we really be considering the Women's Classic, 18 years later, as part of that same foundational "groundwork," or is hockey merely playing catch-up given that one of its most recent significant historic events was not televised?

INTERPRETING THE OUTCOMES OF THE INAUGURAL WOMEN'S OUTDOOR WINTER CLASSIC

When applying cultural citizenship and moral legitimacy to our study results, we concluded that both theories address the actions of all of the parties involved (i.e., NWHL, CWHL, and NHL). Indeed, using both, we arrived at the conclusion that women's professional ice hockey is undervalued by organizations like the NHL, despite being valued by fans, and that this issue runs deeper than a lack of broadcasting of the Women's Classic. We found that the NHL was attempting to maintain legitimacy through the inaugural Outdoor Winter Classic. Raymond Dart indicated that "organizations [or events] reflect and embody important social ideas as much as they deliberately perform certain tasks."[58] Drawing on the work of Suchman, our findings suggest that the involvement of two women's professional leagues in the Outdoor Winter Classic was a strategic managerial decision by the NHL that "emphasizes the ways in which organizations instrumentally manipulate and deploy evocative symbols in order to garner societal support."[59]

What is seemingly apparent is that the NHL used the gender of the leagues (i.e., NWHL and CWHL) to promote itself to fans as an inclusive league that is willing to partner with the NWHL and CWHL. To reiterate, Dart explained that "moral legitimacy refers to legitimacy that is normative and based on an evaluation of whether an activity of a focal organization [NHL] is the proper one (relative to external norms) rather than whether it specifically benefits those who are making the evaluation";[60] thus, moral legitimacy is established through the preferred models of a sport and recreation delivery system with the broader social and political ideologies.

The preferred model in this setting is the NHL male model where the Outdoor Winter Classic is heavily promoted and accessible and generates revenue for the NHL. In an attempt to replicate that model, the CWHL and NWHL agreed to participate in the inaugural Outdoor Winter Classic, which was not received well on a societal level because of lack of broadcasting, and Laing being paralyzed, which resulted in negative media coverage. We identify this as consequential legitimacy because of the organizations' hopes that they would gain a reward and acceptance with regards to their participation in the event. The maintenance of legitimacy through a moral legitimacy category in this setting, we argue, was not successful for all of the parties involved despite being the best fit.

Some of the Twitter data and members of Les Canadiennes indicate that legitimacy was established from a "better than nothing" perspective, meaning at least there was a Women's Classic to begin with. Les Canadiennes also discussed the differences between women's and men's hockey, articulating that there is a desire for fans to appreciate the women's game as a sport unto itself. To these points, we contend that, from a cultural citizenship perspective, women were given an opportunity for equality, to skate on the same stage as NHL players and NHL legends and make a name for themselves, yet the impact they had on that stage was mitigated by numerous structural constraints.

There was no television coverage, no unique tickets, a lack of promotion, a truncated game format, a lack of facilities, and a shortened roster. Judith Vega and Boele van Hensbroek explain that cultural citizenship is meant to draw a connection between culture and citizenship;[61] "it brings citizenship into a new area of concerns . . . [implying] that citizenship has [more] than merely political connotations."[62] Our study illustrates Vega and Boele van Hensbroek's theoretical framework as a tool for addressing issues of dominance rather than an absence of fundamental rights. We are not arguing that the women were being consciously discriminated against; however, the way events unfolded does point to a pattern whereby female athletes are forced to accept lesser conditions and expected to be pleased with these opportunities (e.g., the United States Women's National Soccer team's battle for equal pay and real turf conditions, or when the Japanese women's soccer team flew coach to the 2012 London Olympics while the men's team flew business class).[63] Would a professional men's team be asked to bring a *portion* of their team to a game? Would a professional men's team have to share merchandise because there was not enough for every team member? Would a historic men's event neither have its own ticket nor be televised?

To further contextualize our argument, we draw on Mary Louise Adams's analysis of the intersections of hockey and gender in the Canadian context.

She asserts that "in its roles as national symbol and everyday pastime, hockey produces a very ordinary and pernicious sense of male entitlement: to space, to status, to national belonging."[64] Although the fact that the NHL even included the Women's Classic could be viewed from a "better than nothing" perspective, it is equally symbolic of that "pernicious sense of male entitlement" that Adams references. The entitlement to space is evident in our interviews with regards to a lack of change rooms for the women. Sadly, women and girls who play hockey are all too familiar with the lack of a designated change room at ice rinks or shared facilities.[65] Arguably, the lack of tickets also greatly changed the atmosphere of said space. As far as status goes, it is quite apparent that women who are currently professionals and Olympic medalists are positioned as economically, socially, and culturally less valuable than even retired NHL players.

CONCLUSION

At the end of 2015, the *New York Times* sports section published an article titled "Women Stole the Show in 2015,"[66] celebrating the great strides made by women's sports across the board in the past year, and yet women's sports coverage continues to hover around the 1 percent mark for both regular television and ESPN coverage.[67] As a result, "the historic game that no one saw" could be the accurate tagline of not just women's professional hockey but also for all women's sports.

Indeed, the freedom of opportunity was extended to women's professional ice hockey players through the Women's Classic. Yet, the relevant lived equality is simply not yet existent because the game took part on the NHL's terms and not under circumstances that could effectively promote the sport. The members of Les Canadiennes with whom we spoke argued that lived equality would be made possible through relying on the NHL for the moment. However, this raises broader and more fundamental questions about men being the gatekeepers to both cultural citizenship and legitimacy. This is something that future studies of this nature should take up.

Future studies should also consider following Cooky, Messner, and Hextrum's model of a longitudinal study of television coverage of women's sports and piece together the ways in which any future Women's Classics evolve over time. We contend that women's professional hockey will be better accounted for by analyzing the ways in which future events of this nature are organized. Should the argument that the inaugural Women's Classic was "a good first step" hold any weight, we can only assume that the event will improve and become available for viewing, thus maintaining the legitimacy and cultural citizenship that the athletes have worked so hard to establish.

NOTES

1. "Media Coverage & Female Athletes: A Tucker Centre/tptMN Video Documentary," Tucker Center for Research on Girls and Women in Sport, last modified December 1, 2013, http://www.cehd.umn.edu/tuckercenter/multimedia/mediacoverage.html.

2. Brian Stensaas, "Tape-Delay Coverage of Women's Frozen Four Out-Earns Men's Live Coverage," *Star Tribune*, last modified April 6, 2016, http://www.startribune.com/tape-delay-coverage-of-women-s-frozen-four-out-earns-men-s-live-coverage/374820641/.

3. Ken Campbell, "Blunder Over Women's Game at Winter Classic Has NHL Scrambling," *Hockey News*, last modified December 11, 2015, http://www.thehockeynews.com/ blog/blunder-over-womens-game-at-winter-classic-has-nhl-scrambling/.

4. "NHL to Host First-Ever Outdoor Women's Classic Presented by Scotiabank," *NHL.com*, December 28, 2015, https://www.nhl.com/news/nhl-to-host-first-ever-outdoor-womens-classic-presented-by-scotiabank/c-794629.

5. Ibid.

6. "IIHF Ambassador and Mentor Program," *International Ice Hockey Federation*, 2015, last modified May 4, 2016, http://www.iihf.com/iihf- home/sport/women/ambassadors.html.

7. "2015 Annual Report," *Hockey Canada*, 2015, last modified May 4, 2016, http://cdn.agilitycms.com/hockey-canada/Corporate/About/Annual-Report/2015-nov/2014-15_annual_report_e.pdf.

8. "2014–2015 Season Final Registration Reports," *USA Hockey*, last modified May 4, 2016, http://assets.ngin.com/attachments/document/0077/6505/2014-15_Memebership_Reports.pdf.

9. "2010–2011 Season Final Registration Reports," *USA Hockey*, last modified May 4, 2016, http://assets.ngin.com/attachments/document/0043/6193/2010-11_Final_Report.pdf.

10. "Our Story," Canadiennes de Montréal, last modified February 18, 2016, http://pointstreaksites.com/view/lescanadiennes-en/home/our-story-1.

11. Martin Cleary, "Dreaming of a League of Their Own," *Ottawa Citizen*, last modified September 30, 2007, http://www.canada.com/ottawacitizen/columnists/story.html?id=b649a ca4-4560-49af-b3f0-525e14891b75.

12. Donna Spencer, "Clarkson Cup: Montreal, Calgary to Play for Women's Hockey Title," *CBC*, last modified March 10, 2016, http://www.cbc.ca/sports/hockey/nhl/news/clarkson-cup-cwhl-1.3484904.

13. Mike Burse, "Possible NHL and CWHL Partnership in the Works," *Bleacher Report*, last modified July 17, 2010, http://bleacherreport.com/articles/421458-possible-nhl-and-cwhl-partnership-in-the-works.

14. "About Us," *Canadian Women's Hockey League*, last modified February 18, 2016, http://www.cwhl.ca/view/cwhl/about-us.

15. Cleary, "Dreaming of a League of Their Own."

16. "The Montreal Canadiens Enter a Partnership with the Montreal Stars," *Canadiens de Montréal*, last modified March 12, 2016, http://canadiens.nhl.com/club/news.htm?id=758859; "Calgary Inferno New Look and Name Unveiled at Flames-Rangers

Game," Calgary Flames, last modified March 12, 2016, http://flames.nhl.com/club/news.htm?id=683782; "Leafs Announce Partnership Agreement with Toronto Furies," Toronto Maple Leafs, last modified March 12, 2016, http://mapleleafs.nhl.com/club/news.htm?id=645484.

17. "Meet Us in Ottawa for the 2016 Clarkson Cup," Canadian Women's Hockey League, last modified January 25, 2016, from http://www.cwhl.ca/view/cwhl/news-644/news_383918.

18. "Roster," Les Canadiennes, last modified May 25, 2016, http://cwhl_mon.stats.pointstreak.com/teamroster.html?teamid=277086.

19. Elizabeth Etue and Megan K. Williams, *On the Edge: Women Making Hockey History* (Toronto: Second Story Press, 1996), 125.

20. Pieter Boele van Hensbroek, "Cultural Citizenship as a Normative Notion for Activist Practices," in *Cultural Citizenship in Political Theory*, eds. Judith Vega and Pieter Boele van Hensbroek (London: Routledge, 2012), 73–86.

21. Ibid., 76.

22. Ibid., 82.

23. Nancy Theberge, "'It's Part of the Game': Physicality and the Production of Gender in Women's Hockey," *Gender & Society* 11 (1997): 69–87; Nancy Theberge, "'Same Sport, Different Gender': A Consideration of Binary Gender Logic and the Sport Continuum in the Case of Ice Hockey," *Journal of Sport & Social Issues* 22 (1998): 183–98.

24. Richard Gruneau, "Making Spectacle: A Case Study in Television Sports Production," in *Media, Sports and Society*, ed. Lawrence Wenner (London: Sage, 1989), 134.

25. Gruneau, "Making Spectacle," 135.

26. Cheryl Cooky, Michael A. Messner, and Robin H. Hextrum, "Women Play Sport, but Not on TV: A Longitudinal Study of Televised News Media," *Communication & Sport* 1 (2013): 204.

27. Terry Adams and C. A. Tuggle, "ESPN's SportsCenter and Coverage of Women's Athletics: 'It's a Boy's Club,'" *Mass Communication and Society* 7 (2007): 237–48; C. A. Tuggle, "Differences in Television Sports Reporting of Men's and Women's Athletics: ESPN SportsCenter and CNN Sports Tonight," *Journal of Broadcasting & Electronic Media* 41 (1997): 14–24.

28. Jay Scherer and David Rowe, "Sport, Public Service Media, and Cultural Citizenship," in *Sport, Public Broadcasting, and Cultural Citizenship: Signal Lost?*, eds. Jay Scherer and David Rowe (New York: Routledge, 2014), 1.

29. Ibid., 4.

30. Alex Bitektine, "Toward a Theory of Social Judgements of Organizations: The Case of Legitimacy, Reputation, and Status," *Academy of Management Review* 36 (2011): 151–79, accessed March 25, 2016, http://journals.aomonline.org/amj; Jonathon R. Edwards and Marvin Washington, "Establishing a 'Safety Net': Exploring the Emergence of College Hockey Inc. and the Legitimizing Strategies of NCAA Division I Universities and Colleges," *Journal of Sport Management* 29 (2015): 291–304; Daniel Lock, Kevin Filo, Thilo Kunkel, and James L. Skinner, "The Development of a Framework to Capture Perceptions of Sport Organizations Legitimacy," *Journal*

of Sport Management 29 (2015): 362–79; Mark C. Suchman, "Managing Legitimacy: Strategic and Institutional Approaches," *Academy of Management Review* 2 (1995): 571–610, accessed March 27, 2016, http://www.aom.pace.edu/amr.

31. Suchman, "Managing Legitimacy," 574.

32. Lock et al., "The Development of a Framework," 362.

33. Bitektine, "Toward a Theory of Social Judgments"; Lock et al., "The Development of a Framework."

34. Bitektine, "Toward a Theory of Social Judgments"; David L. Deephouse, "Does Isomorphism Legitimate?" *Academy of Management Journal* 39 (1996): 1024–39; Ralph C. Hybels, "On Legitimacy, Legitimation, and Organizations: A Critical Review and Integrative Theoretical Model," *Academy of Management Best Papers Proceedings* (1995): 241–45; Kai Lamertz and Joel A. C. Baum, "The Legitimacy of Organizational Downsizing in Canada: An Analysis of Explanatory Media Accounts," *Canadian Journal of Administrative Sciences* 15 (1998): 93–107; Timothy Pollock and Violina P. Rindova, "Media Legitimation Effects in the Market for Initial Public Offerings," *Academy of Management Journal* 46 (2003): 631–42.

35. Bitektine, "Toward a Theory of Social Judgments," 154.

36. Suchman, "Managing Legitimacy," 572.

37. Lock et al., "The Development of a Framework," 362.

38. Bitektine, "Toward a Theory of Social Judgments," 152.

39. Suchman, "Managing Legitimacy," 571.

40. Benjamin D. Golant and John A. A. Sillince, "The Constitution of Organizational Legitimacy: A Narrative Perspective," *Organization Studies* 28 (2007): 1149–67, doi:10.1177/0170840607075671; Jeffrey Leiter, "Structural Isomorphism in Australian Nonprofit Organizations," *International Journal of Voluntary and Nonprofit Organizations* 16 (2005): 1–31; Tom E. Thomas and Eric Lamm, "Legitimacy and Organizational Sustainability," *Journal of Business Ethics* 110 (2012): 191–203, doi:10.1007/s10551-012-1421-4.

41. Bitektine, "Toward a Theory of Social Judgments,"151.

42. Howard E. Aldrich and C. Marlene Fiol, "Fools Rush In? The Institutional Context of Industry Creation," *Academy of Management Review* 19 (1994): 645–70.

43. Bitektine, "Toward a Theory of Social Judgments"; John W. Meyer and Brian Rowan, "Institutionalized Organizations: Formal Structure as Myth and Ceremony," *American Journal of Sociology* 83 (1977): 340–63.

44. Bitektine, "Toward a Theory of Social Judgments," 157.

45. Suchman, "Managing Legitimacy," 577.

46. Donna J. Wood, "Corporate Social Performance Revisited," *Academy of Management Review* 16 (1991): 691–718.

47. Suchman, "Managing Legitimacy," 578.

48. Ibid., 582.

49. Ibid., 579.

50. Ibid.

51. John Creswell, *Research Design: Qualitative, Quantitative, and Mixed Methods Approaches*, 4th ed. (Thousand Oaks, CA: Sage Publications, 2014); Chris Gratton and Ian Jones, *Research Methods for Sports Studies*, 2nd ed. (New York: Routledge,

2010); William Lawrence Neuman, *Social Research Methods: Qualitative and Quantitative Approaches*, 6th ed. (Boston: Pearson Education Inc, 2006).

52. Katrin Weller, Axel Bruns, Jean Burgess, Merja Mahrt, and Cornelius Puschmann, *Twitter & Society* (Berlin, Germany: Peter Lang Publishing Inc., 2014).

53. Weller et al., *Twitter and Society*.

54. Michael Beurskens, "Legal Questions of Twitter Research," in *Twitter & Society*, eds. Katrin Weller, Axel Burns, Jean Burgess, Merja Mahrt, and Cornelius Puschmann (Berlin, Germany: Peter Lang Publishing, Inc., 2014).

55. Scherer and Rowe, "Sport, Public Service Media," 4.

56. Cooky, Messner, and Hextrum, "Women Play Sport," 204.

57. Jennifer Neale, "Patrick Burke on Bringing NHL, Women's Pro Leagues Together at Winter Classic," *Yahoo! Sports*, last modified December 30, 2015, http://sports.yahoo.com/ blogs/nhl-puck-daddy/patrick-burke-on-women-s-outdoor-game-logistics--bringing-nhl--nwhl-cwhl-together--q-a-070839753.html.

58. Raymond Dart, "The Legitimacy of Social Enterprise," *Nonprofit Management & Leadership* (2004): 14–416.

59. Suchman, "Managing Legitimacy," 572.

60. Dart, "The Legitimacy of Social Enterprise," 417.

61. Judith Vega and Pieter Boele van Hensbroek, eds., *Cultural Citizenship in Political Theory* (London: Routledge, 2012).

62. Ibid., 1.

63. Caitlin Murray, "USWNT Push for a New Deal and Make Clear: We Are Not Playing on Artificial Turf," *Guardian*, last modified January 28, 2016, https://www.theguardian.com/football/2016/jan/28/uswnt-collective-bargaining-agreement-artificial-turf; Mark McDonald, "Japanese Women Fly Coach to the Olympics; the Men Go Business Class," *New York Times*, last modified July 19, 2012, http://rendezvous.blogs.nytimes.com/2012/07/19/japanese-women-fly-coach-to-the-olympics-the-men-go-business-class/?_r=0.

64. Mary Louise Adams, "The Game of Whose Lives? Gender, Race, and Entitlement in Canada's 'National' Game," in *Artificial Ice: Hockey, Culture, and Commerce*, eds. David Whitson and Richard Gruneau (Toronto: Broadview Press, 2006), 71.

65. Jose Colorado, "Why No One Cares about Women's Hockey—and Why That Should Change," *The Province*, last modified January 6, 2016, http://www.theprovince.com/sports/cares+about+women+hockey+that+should+change/11637507/story.html.

66. Christopher Clarey, "Women Stole the Show in 2015," *New York Times*, last modified December 23, 2015, http://www.nytimes.com/2015/12/24/sports/women-stole-the-show-in-2015.html?_r=2.

67. Cooky, Messner, and Hextrum, "Women Play Sport," 221.

7

UConn Women's Basketball: Dynasty and Dominance versus Gender Inequality in Sports Media Coverage?

Kenneth Nathanial Robinson

> *Most of us don't care about the women's tournament. Sorry. I know this is not the politically correct stance and I know there are young women all over the nation who rightfully look up to the Huskies as role models, but the fact remains most red-blooded American fans don't give a hoot about women's basketball and the dominant Huskies are a big part of the problem.*
>
> —Dan Shaughnessy[1]

STATEMENT OF THE PROBLEM AND THEORETICAL PERSPECTIVES

Between the years 1995 and 2016, the University of Connecticut's (UConn) "women's" basketball teams won a history-making 11 national championships, including six undefeated seasons. In 2016, the team won their fourth straight National College Athletic Association (NCAA) national championship while maintaining a 100 percent graduation rate. President Barack Obama, who has hosted the team more than once, referred to them as the best team of any sport, irrespective of sex, and lauded them for being role models to his own daughters.[2] Despite their successes, the team has not been without their detractors. In 2016, during their march to a fourth consecutive NCAA tournament championship, Dan Shaughnessy, a male reporter from the *Boston Globe*, diminished their dominant play as bad for women's basketball. His comments, while widely viewed as controversial, had the effect of reigniting debate on the subject of gender inequalities in sports media coverage. Through the use of secondary data analysis, research in this chapter shows that although major for-profit media corporations, such as ESPN and CBS, cover NCAA men's and women's basketball, these media outlets generally provide greater, disproportionate coverage of the men's games. Additionally, media coverage of women's basketball is plagued by sex typing—a form of linguistic sexism where differentiation replete with masculine and feminine connotations is pronounced and more common during coverage. Consequently, women's basketball is disadvantaged by a *hierarchy of naming*, which reinforces status differences between men's and women's basketball, with references to the respective sports by sex (i.e., NCAA Women's Basketball vs. the Men's game—NCAA Basketball), in media reporting.[3] Furthermore, numerous research studies show the differences in media coverage are especially pronounced during March Madness, which encapsulates the annual NCAA men's and women's basketball tournaments.

A review of content studies also shows various media platforms from electronic to print, and even Internet-based sources, continuing this trend of covering and promoting men's basketball to a greater extent than the women's games, despite both NCAA tournaments being hosted at the same time. Even more revealing, not-for-profit media outlets, such as the NCAA, campus newspapers, and conference websites, have been found to exacerbate these disparities in media attention accorded to men's basketball over women's basketball.

LITERATURE REVIEW

Historically, sports competition was essentially a domain for boys and men. Title IX legislation changed the backdrop of sports competition, which resulted in a surge of girls and women participating in competitive sports. This landmark legislation, passed by Congress in 1972, prohibits discrimination against women in sports. It also seeks to engender greater equality between males and females in access and opportunities to play sports at colleges and universities that receive federal funding.[4] James Hallmark and Richard Armstrong[5] reported that the participation of women in sports was greatly advanced by Title IX. Prior to its passage, females accounted for a mere 7 percent of all high school athletes, and the idea of college scholarships for women was fundamentally nonexistent.[6] Some of the earlier yields from the law's enactment show that, by 1982, the number of females participating in high school sports increased to 35 percent.[7] Three years later, basketball became the most popular sport for young women athletes, as colleges awarded over 10,000 scholarships.[8] It was also in 1985 that UConn hired Coach Geno Auriemma, who would build his program's dynasty amid the growing popularity of women's basketball and the greater distribution of college scholarships for athletes. The proportionate awarding of athletic scholarships to attend college for female and male athletes is required by Title IX to help remedy sex inequalities in sports participation.[9] The increase in girls participating in high school sports led to a similar rush in women participating in collegiate sports, all of which had a positive impact on the expansion of NCAA Division I women's college basketball in general and the UConn women's team in particular.

As of 1996, it was estimated that upward of 100,000 women were competing in intercollegiate athletics.[10] This period coincides with a dramatic shift toward wider acceptance of women's sports and the growing popularity of their participation in basketball. The UConn women's team won their first NCAA Women's Basketball National Championship in 1995. In addition, the 1996 Olympics ushered in a greater measure of appreciation for women's sports and basketball in particular. To underscore this latter point, the women's basketball games were moved from Morehouse College to the larger Georgia Dome to accommodate the demand. These increases in participation and mainstream attention to sports featuring women were indicators of progress. A new beacon of light, the bourgeoning UConn women's basketball program, took shape in the face of glaring inequities. However, despite the greater involvement of women in intercollegiate sports, inequalities have persisted when considering coinciding enrollment rates. Hallmark and Armstrong[11] found that in 1996, women accounted for approximately half of all undergraduate students but only 33 percent of participants in college sports. The latter issue raises questions of compliance as it pertains to Title IX enforcement of proportionality, given the overall representation of females on college campuses versus their participation in sports. Marie Hardin et al.[12] reported that Title IX's growing influence is observable today, where women compete in over 9,000 intercollegiate sports teams. In the last 15 years, 3,000 women's sports teams were added at the collegiate level.[13] These progressive outcomes notwithstanding, there is still much work to be done to ensure that women realize equitable treatment when compared to men in sports competition. Adrienne Milner and Jomills Braddock[14] take a decidedly different tact, objecting strongly to sex-segregated sports participation as unconstitutional. The authors use the premise of *Brown v. the Board of Education*, the landmark Supreme Court case that struck down "separate but equal," dismantling legal segregation in America, to argue that Title IX's "no sports contact" prohibition is a problem that exacerbates inequalities that favor men over women participating in sports competition. While the inequalities between men and women are indeed expansive, such disparities are especially apparent in media coverage, where gendered allocations in sports reporting have only magnified the problem.

MEDIA COVERAGE AS A PROBLEM

In an analysis of sex equity in NCAA televised broadcasts of men's and women's Division I basketball national championships, from 1991 to 1995, Hallmark and Armstrong[15] found women's college basketball experienced increased popularity and acceptance in the United States in the 1990s. Despite such growing acceptance, women's sport was shortchanged during this time with uncomplimentary labeling, where their sex, an ascribed status, became a master status in sports media coverage. For example, the NCAA Division I women's basketball tournament was subordinated by the men's game, which was defined as the "NCAA tournament," along with the NCAA Final Four. Conversely, the women's game was typecast as the "NCAA Women's Tournament" and "Women's Final Four" respectively. Consequently, the men's game is treated as the standard, while the women's game is viewed as "secondary" or marginalized as "other."[16] Such media coverage is indicative of what has been referred to as "sex typing."[17] The social harm associated with sex typing involves profiling female participants in sports by their ascribed statuses, which leads to gender stereotyping. To further underscore this point, Michael Messner et al.[18] studied the NCAA Division I women's and men's basketball tournaments in 1989, and men's and women's professional tennis matches, and found widespread instances of "gender marking" and "hierarchy of naming." For example, the late Pat Summitt, the Hall of Fame head coach of the University of Tennessee's women's team, transcended gender boundaries with her coaching expertise. She holds the record for most wins for an NCAA basketball coach, be it men's or women's, at any divisional level.[19] Yet, during television broadcasts, she was often referred to as "a legend in women's basketball."[20] Through the early 1990s, CBS covered both the men's and women's game and used gender marking expressly in the case of the women. Over the course of three games, which included the Final Four and National Championship, there were 25.7 instances of gender marking of women per game, using verbal and graphic content. During the analysis of commentary and content of the three men's games, which, like the women's, included the Final Four and National Championship, there were no instances of gender marking recorded.[21] When the researchers expanded measures of gender marking to include team names (i.e., "Lady Vols"), the unequal coverage was more pronounced. In the three women's games, the average rate of gender marking (verbal and graphic) more than doubled to 59.7 times per game when including the team's name.[22] The gender disparities have also been observable in other media platforms, such as television, print media, and the Internet. The various forms of for-profit media sources, including the likes of ESPN and CBS, as well as print media sources like *Sports Illustrated*, have contributed to disparities in gendered allocations of media coverage favoring men's basketball over the women's game in the association (major NCAA Division I). While for-profit media sources operate with surplus value in mind, given the undergirding need to make money, not-for-profit media sources have been just as problematic.

The NCAA news sites, websites, campus newspapers, and even major conferences have been known to exacerbate gender inequalities in sports media coverage.[23] Donations for men's sports in the NCAA are disproportionately greater than for women's sports.[24] Most NCAA women's basketball teams operate in the red, at approximately $2 million annually. Such disparities have contributed mightily to the uneven distribution of revenue and sports media coverage by both for-profit and not-for-profit media outlets covering major NCAA Division I women's and men's basketball.

Several theories help explain the social effects associated with gender inequalities in sports media coverage of NCAA women's basketball when compared to the men's game. Such perspectives include equity, gender schemata, and labeling, which help describe how the master status of "women's basketball" is a problem in the social construction of media coverage and the persistence of gender inequalities in sports reporting.

EQUITY THEORY

Proponents of equity theory assert that inequities persist in media coverage because of the greater economic value placed on NCAA men's basketball over women's basketball when it comes to measures like revenue and television ratings. Milner and Braddock argue that the unequal distribution of resources and media attention accorded to men's sports has the effect of devaluing women's sports.[25] Several studies of NCAA women's basketball have sought to examine not merely the quality of media coverage accorded but the quantity.[26] Moreover, factors that contribute to the inequities include a disconsolate view of women's basketball as lacking economic value. Mary McDonald observed that the advent of the WNBA, fueled by the economically powerful, male-dominated NBA, created a consumption culture in an attempt to capitalize off the $15 billion sports retail industry by selling licensed apparel to foment a postfeminist climate.[27] Despite the height of success that followed the 1990s, when women's basketball became more popular, the sport today is seen as lacking in economic viability, thus providing a disincentive for major for-profit media outlets like CBS and others to cover the sport.[28] With television ratings for women's basketball games being relatively low, networks see less of a return on their broadcasts. Advertisers, much like the television networks, see ratings and revenues as intertwined. Additionally, most business marketing corporations advertising on sports television target men, particularly in the 18–44 range. There is also evidence that NCAA Division I-A women's basketball is devalued by the lower price of tickets to attend their games, which is far less than the men's basketball game.[29]

Michelle Hebl et al. employed equity theory in their study of 303 NCAA Division I programs to determine if the sex of a basketball team influences the price of a ticket to their game.[30] The researchers found significant differences in pricing for tickets, with the cost to attend a women's basketball game being far less than the cost to attend a men's game. The study found "discrepancies in financial indicators lead to differences in perception of value."[31] Consequently, NCAA men's basketball is seen as having more value because the cost of tickets is greater. This rationing may help to explain why women's basketball games, including those of UConn's very successful teams, have been plagued by poor attendance. In 2013, when UConn defeated Louisville in the NCAA women's title game, the New Orleans Arena, which hosted the game, was half empty.[32] In 2015, the UConn's women's basketball team had less than half their usual attendance, which the head coach termed "embarrassing" given their success.[33] The poor attendance at games is only exacerbated by the relatively poor television ratings of women's college basketball, generally speaking, and for UConn in particular. The Huskies women's team has the honorable distinction of having won more National Championships than any team in history. On the other hand, the team also owns the dubious distinction of having played in four of the five least-watched women's National Championship games since ESPN began broadcasting the contest in 1996. Although ESPN has the contract to broadcast the NCAA women's basketball tournament, research studies have found that the network has provided more coverage to the men's NCAA tournament.

This discrepancy has also been noted both on the ESPN website's main page[34] and on their television station's premier broadcast, *Sportscenter*.[35] Even more discouraging, in 2016, it was revealed that ESPN was using in-studio broadcasters for the first two rounds of the NCAA women's tournament rather than having them courtside as they are in the men's games. The network reasoned that they were able to save money by not sending broadcasters to the games, which lessened the costs of production overall.[36] In an interview I conducted with Shaughnessy, he opined that ESPN "overpaid" for the NCAA women's tournament.[37] Although ESPN reasoned that the savings gained would be put into other facets of their broadcast of the women's tournament in later rounds, the public revelation further devalued the sport. UConn's head coach, Auriemma, felt little consolation in ESPN's explanation, proffering that he could not imagine the men's basketball tournament would be subject to such devaluing in their broadcasts.[38] Auriemma has a point. Edward Kian et al.[39] estimated the association garners 90 percent of its revenues from the three-week NCAA men's basketball tournament. The annual NCAA men's basketball tournament suffers no shortage of media coverage from print, the Internet, or television sources, which allows it to grow in popularity and revenue generated. Equity theorists would certainly argue that ESPN cutting the production costs for the women's basketball tournament further devalued it. All of this might explain the lackluster television ratings of the women's tournament when compared to the men's.

Aside from ticket prices, the women's game is also diminished by the percentage of donations that come to their basketball programs. For example, it was reported that both NCAA football and men's basketball receive donations that greatly inflate revenues, since such donations are required in order to purchase season tickets.[40] Interestingly, this linkage of "donations" for the rights to purchase season tickets is akin to for-profit entities like the National Football League (NFL), which charges patrons for PSLs (personal seat licenses) to purchase season tickets. Like NFL teams, the financial rewards are significant. Estimates show that such donations to the top NCAA football and basketball programs can be twice as much as revenues procured from television.[41] To put this in perspective, the University of Alabama's football team raised $18.6 million through such donations, while the university's women's basketball team raised none. In the Southeastern Conference (SEC), Bowman found that for every $1 donated for women's basketball, $6.02 was donated to men's basketball.[42] For every $1 donated to women's basketball, $67.03 was donated to Alabama's football program.[43] Such disparities go to the heart of why NCAA women's basketball, and the UConn women's team in particular, suffers unequal media coverage.

Equity theory helps to explain how the women's and men's games are valued differently. The value of the men's game appreciates through higher ticket prices, greater revenues from donations, and higher television ratings, which results in better overall media coverage. Conversely, the women's game is devoid of all such benefits, and consequently its game depreciates in value, which exacerbates the gender inequities in sports media coverage. But why are these disparities such an endemic part of the sports landscape in the NCAA despite Title IX legislation, which increased the participation rates of women in sports? Milner and Braddock state that Title IX was originally met with resistance, and the NCAA's executive director as well as several football coaches lobbied to exempt men's revenue-generating sports from the legislation.[44] Consequently, the association and its member institutions developed a creative mechanism to ensure men's sports teams continued to be cash cows through the aforementioned donations to teams for season tickets, which favors men's basketball and football. Additionally, Milner and Braddock argue that Title IX created a two-tier system whereby girls are consigned to sex-segregated sports of lower status than those of boys.[45] Moreover, using dominant gender ideology, the researchers assert, the notion of "coed" sports participation is misleading, as the majority of sports competition is not integrated by sex.[46] The fact that Title IX has increased participation rates but has not had an appreciable effect on how women's sports have been carried out, covered, or valued, speaks to age-old attitudes about what roles women and men should play in society, and this ideology is maintained through gender socialization.

GENDER SCHEMATA THEORY

In probing gender inequities in media coverage of women's basketball generally, and the UConn women's team in particular, gender socialization emerges as a tenable explanation. Historically, men and women were expected to fulfill certain social roles, which begin in infancy. The onset of gender differentiation begins at birth when boys are wrapped in blue blankets and girls are wrapped in pink.[47] Messner et al. found that CBS's televised broadcast of professional tennis matches used pink graphics for the women's game and blue graphics for the men's.[48] To underscore how relative this socially constructed phenomena is, Milner and Braddock note that in the early 20th century, men wore pink to show strength and women wore blue to convey "daintiness."[49] Gender schemata theory also examines gender socialization in the way males and females develop their interest in careers. This socialization begins with the social roles males and females are given in the household. Boys are told to take out the garbage, mow the lawn, and help fix things that are broken. On the other hand, girls are expected to help cook, clean, and wash the dishes. Shaughnessy, whose views on UConn women's basketball team were derided as sexist, conceded during our interview that he was raised in such a household, where duties were demarcated by sex (male or female) and gender (masculine or feminine).[50] Although he denies being sexist, the sports reporting media is certainly a male-dominated industry. Such gender socialization, like the aforementioned, leads to gender stratification in terms of career pursuits. Males are socialized to gravitate toward careers that are more mechanical and technical, such as computer science, engineering, and even business, which often pay more. On the other hand, women are expected to go into roles like teaching, child care, and health care, where their nurturing skills are expected to benefit them. It is worth noting that such gender schisms in the world of work contribute to women earning less income than men, where they make between 70-80 cents on the dollar. These same social tendencies have manifested themselves in sports.

Amy Jones and Jennifer Greer found that "sport is a major sector in society that depicts stereotypes of American culture."[51] In discussing gender schemata theory, Jones and Greer stated that "individuals learn the differences between the classifications of male and female from society and then adjust their behaviors to meet these expectations."[52] The theory is also useful in explaining the inequities in gendered allocations in sports media coverage that reinforce gendered stereotypes.[53] Hence, females get more quality media coverage for participating in sports that exude more femininity. For example, tennis, which is considered more of an individual sport, is also considered more gender appropriate for a woman. Hence, media coverage of men's and women's professional tennis has been described as more symmetrical.[54]

Conversely, while some see basketball as a gender-neutral sport, Jones and Greer's research found basketball was perceived as a more masculine sport.[55] Their study of whether photographic content portraying women's sports participants as either feminine or masculine would influence the interest level of male and female readers in an accompanying article produced some interesting findings. Men who saw women playing basketball reported less interest in the accompanying article, since, in their view, the women appeared more masculine. Conversely, women subjects appreciated the image of women playing a sport like basketball even if the photographs projected a more masculine affect.

These findings may help to explain why, generally speaking, women's basketball, and the UConn women's team's dominance in particular, receives less quality media coverage and why television ratings have been poor. Shaughnessy was emphatic in noting that a sport like women's basketball does not appeal to men, and consequently, they will not watch it.[56] Most sports media outlets are either headed by or heavily influenced by males, who determine what stories or storylines get coverage. If there is a perception that male consumers of sport would rather not see women playing basketball, it could indeed help to explain the problem of gendered coverage allocations in media that favors men. Shaughnessy pointed out that he writes what readers want to read[57] and estimates that most of his readers are men.[58] The NCAA women's basketball tournament's poor ratings are but another indicator that a good portion of the male-dominated sports world follows the warped logic that most men would rather not see women play sports like basketball. Other studies have shown that publications like *Sports Illustrated* would rather accentuate the feminine qualities of women athletes to make them more palatable to men, who make up 80 percent of their readers.[59] McDonald emphasized that the advent of the Women's National Basketball Association (WNBA) was about making women more heterosexual and feminine.[60] Women were spotlighted as having careers, husbands, boyfriends, and children. Sports media outlets would rather punctuate the sexuality of women than focus on their athletic abilities to make them more appealing to the general public, even in a sport like basketball.

In 2007, this phenomenon in the media was brought to center stage. In the aftermath of the NCAA women's basketball championship game between the University of Rutgers and the University of Tennessee, CBS radio talk show host Don Imus stated that the Lady Vols were "cute" but demeaned the Rutgers's women's team in racially derogatory terms, referring to them as "nappy-headed hos." Although there was no merit to Imus's erroneous comparisons, his statements gave credence to research findings that show the perceived attractiveness of women participating in sports will influence the quality of media coverage accorded by men. Perhaps the greatest encumbrance that

NCAA women's basketball has encountered in gaining equality in media coverage is the hierarchy of naming and labeling associated with the women's game versus the men's game.

HIERARCHY OF NAMING AND LABELING THEORY

One of the biggest factors contributing to disparities in gender allocations in sports media coverage is the hierarchy of naming brought on by labeling. A hierarchy of naming has been described as a linguistic vehicle used to reinforce status differences, in this case between men and women competing in NCAA basketball tournaments.[61] One of the distinct advantages of the NCAA hosting both basketball tournaments in March is that researchers can compare the way the men's and women's games are covered in the media. Consequently, a hierarchy of naming has been observed in several forms, including what is often referred to as sex typing and gender typing. While the terms are often used interchangeably, sex typing more readily identifies male and female athletes by their ascribed statuses (i.e., men and women). On the other hand, gender typing speaks to the attribution of masculine and feminine characteristics in the sports reporting media in describing male and female participants (e.g., referring to a female athlete as "ladylike"). The phenomenon of sex typing and gender typing is observable when the NCAA Women's Basketball Tournament is distinguished from the NCAA Basketball Tournament—the latter, of course, refers to the men's tournament. When I asked Shaughnessy about the appropriateness of such sex typing of the respective tournaments, he asserted there was nothing wrong with it. He stated: "It's necessary to distinguish the respective sports. The Little League World Series is distinguished from Major League Baseball's World Series."[62] It can be argued that Shaughnessy's analogy of the Little League World Series to MLB's World Series is reminiscent of the media's tendency to infantilize women[63] in sport. The difference, however, is that the NCAA is the umbrella organization sponsoring both men's and women's basketball tournaments. Worse even, the association has also been cited for providing unequal media coverage of men's and women's basketball. As noted, the NCAA Basketball Tournament is the men's game, as is the NCAA Final Four. Conversely, the NCAA Women's Basketball Tournament and NCAA Women's Final Four speaks for itself. To further underscore the tendency to reinforce this hierarchy of naming through sex typing, Shaughnessy added, "When you say Final Four, people are expecting to see Duke [University's men's team] not UConn [women's team]."[64]

When the "NCAA Final Four" is both an implicit and explicit reference to the men's game versus NCAA Women's Final Four, referring ostensibly to the women's, it creates the impression that the latter has an asterisk by it.

The disparaging distinction gives the impression that the "women's game" is of secondary importance. Feminist scholars have asserted that the institution of sport has been established in the 20th century for men to be a "homosocial sphere of life," which only buttressed "male superiority."[65] Hence, studies in the late 20th and early 21st centuries have noted the persistence of gender inequities in sports media coverage generally speaking, and particularly with NCAA women's and men's basketball. Sports commentators have been documented referring to white men by their last or whole names, while women and other underrepresented groups are often referred to by their first name only. This hierarchy of naming conveys a greater sense of substance and distinction to sports athletes who are called by their last name, which connotes greater consideration for their male identity. Traditionally, when men and women have married, the woman has taken the man's last name. Conversely, for athletes referred to only by first name, it bears no distinction, nor does it differentiate their participation in sports from any other activity whereby their first name typically identifies them. Such disparate treatment in naming leads to the onset of pejorative labeling.

Labeling theory suggests that those in positions of power and influence, like major television networks and other media outlets, can label others, and in particular, marginalized members of society, such as women, as they see fit. Thus, labeling is a process, which in turn influences the interaction between those doing the labeling and those who have been labeled. The effects of this hierarchy of naming and subsequent labeling is explicable through the theory of gender stratification. Thus, sports media as an institution "constructs and legitimizes men's overall power and privilege over women."[66] Furthermore, most of the network executives, producers, writers, and journalists of various media platforms are men, which makes the pejorative labeling of women easier to achieve. Women's basketball is often marred by gender marking, where references to sex or perceived femininity occurs often during a broadcast, thus amplifying the problem of labeling. Moreover, when the name of the team is included in the commentary (i.e., "the Lady Vols"), the level of gender marking doubles. Even more disconcerting, such labeling can foster a definition of the situation, where women athletes and their advocates can develop a sense of learned helplessness. In my interview with Shaughnessy, he was asked if media coverage of women's NCAA basketball would improve. He offered that it would, and the process would be "organic,"[67] in his view; it would evolve over time, naturally. But, after more than 20 years of basketball supremacy, the UConn women's basketball team should have emerged as a model of gender equity in sports media coverage. Instead, their rise and subsequent rejection by the likes of Shaughnessy, and the television viewing public, has made them a symbol of gender inequality in sports media coverage.

UNIVERSITY OF CONNECTICUT DYNASTY AND DOMINANCE, 1995–2016

In the last 20-plus years, the University of Connecticut women's basketball team has become a sports dynasty that has completely altered the landscape of America's sports culture. Under the guidance and direction of Auriemma, the Huskies have achieved unparalleled success, shattering records and glass ceilings along the way. In the last two decades and counting, no sports organization, intercollegiate or professional, has won more championship titles than the UConn women's basketball team. Even more impressive is that this level of success has been sustained over one-fifth of a century, with a different group of female athletes who have consistently yielded the same results: NCAA National Championships.

Since 1995, when Coach Auriemma and the Huskies began their championship tradition, they have won a record-breaking 11 NCAA National Championships. The most recent, in 2016, broke the record for national titles held by John Wooden, the legendary head coach of the UCLA Bruins men's teams. Between the years 1964 and 1975, Wooden's teams won a remarkable 10 national titles in 12 years, creating a standard for winning and achievement in sports competition. If Wooden created the standard, Coach Auriemma's women's basketball program at UConn lifted it to loftier heights. In 2010, his team set a record with 90 consecutive wins, a mark that surpassed Wooden's UCLA men's team, which had won 88 straight games. Although records are made to be broken, Coach Wooden's legacy as one of the great architects of a sports dynasty remains intact, forever making him basketball royalty. That the UConn women's basketball program dethroned these landmark achievements upset conventions of what female athletes are expected to do. During our interview, I asked Shaughnessy if Coach Auriemma and his teams had gotten enough respect from the media for all of their successes, like breaking records held by Coach Wooden's UCLA teams. He replied, "Yes, I do. Same sentence as John Wooden. That's good coverage."[68] By contrast, while on route to breaking the NCAA record for consecutive wins, Coach Auriemma chided that his team was only receiving greater media coverage because they were chasing the UCLA men's team record.[69]

Auriemma's statement underscores the gender inequalities in sports media coverage that have plagued his team and women's basketball in general. On the other hand, Shaughnessy seemed to give credence to Coach Auriemma's view by asserting their mere mentioning in the same sentence as Wooden was enough of an indicator of being respected by the media. But would the media coverage have been the same had UConn broken an NCAA women's team record, with a woman as head coach? When Auriemma's team eclipsed the University of Tennessee's Lady Vols and their legendary head coach Pat

Summitt in the number of NCAA national championship titles, the media coverage was far less than the attention accorded to their surpassing Wooden's teams. In an interesting irony, just as the sun was setting on Wooden's majestic run in the mid-1970s, Title IX legislation, first passed in 1972, was poised to reshape the dynamics of gender representation in sports competition. Its effect would catapult a new era of women's achievements through sports, culminating in the eventual rise of the UConn women's basketball dynasty.

THE GENESIS OF A DYNASTY

UConn hired Auriemma to be head coach of their women's basketball team in 1985. Despite the fact that Auriemma had no prior head coaching experience, the university's decision paid off. After going 12–15 in his first season, Auriemma's UConn teams have not since had a losing record, including six seasons when they were undefeated. Such achievements are especially impressive since prior to his arrival, the UConn women's basketball program had only one winning season in their history. Now they have a history of making history, with transcendent milestones in abundance. While en route to breaking the UCLA men's basketball record for most consecutive wins with 90 in 2010, they broke their own record of 71 straight wins that year. In 2010, they also became the first NCAA women's basketball team to win 78 straight games.[70] The same year, while hosting the team after their second straight National Championship win, President Barack Obama lauded them as the best team in any sport, irrespective of sex.[71] During my interview with Shaughnessy, I asked if he agreed with President Obama that the Huskies women's team was the best in all of sports. Even he conceded, "I'm not going to dispute it. They'd be in that conversation."[72] Being in the conversation would be a given, but does their body of work make the case for them indisputably?

In 2012–2013, the Huskies women's team set a record for most consecutive appearances in the NCAA Final Four, with six. In 2015, when the team returned for another visit to the White House, after their 10th National Championship, President Barack Obama highlighted the team's successes in the classroom. Five years prior, the president noted, Coach Auriemma's UConn teams had a 100 percent graduation rate over the previous 25 years.[73] These outstanding outcomes illustrated Coach Auriemma's success in developing a high standard of student athlete in major Division I sports. The president added that, between the years 2011 and 2015, every player on the team who persisted for four years graduated.[74] Obama further lauded the team for receiving an award for the highest average GPA of any women's team in their conference. Several of Auriemma's UConn players have been academic All-Americans. As if those achievements were not enough, the team is renowned for their charity work, including participating in holiday food drives for the less fortunate during Thanksgiving and spending time visiting the elderly and attending Christmas parties for terminally ill children. These sorts of character-building experiences are not designed to generate media coverage. But it would seem these human interest stories would be covered in the sports reporting media to a greater extent given that such strong character traits tend to translate into greater performances on the basketball court. With a commitment to academic success, and service to the least fortunate in our society, it is easier to understand why the UConn women's basketball program has redefined what it means to be a student-athlete and a champion. For a women's basketball program to win its first National Championship in 1995, and their more recent in 2016, with an outstanding track record of graduating players underscores a system of success for Coach Auriemma that is unmatched. More than 20 years of consistently churning out successful results speaks to the quality of female athletes that have been recruited at UConn. According to Auriemma, "They [female players] came because we recruited the right kind of kids, kids who loved what they were doing, had a great personality. We won an awful lot. And as it got bigger and bigger, then more people wanted to be involved."[75]

At the time Title IX was enacted, no one in the male-dominated sports reporting media could have imagined that a women's basketball team would achieve such prominence in building a model intercollegiate athletics program that would surpass the men's basketball game while setting new standards for what it means to be a student-athlete. Most cynics would have dismissed it as a stretch between folly and fairy tale. But the true story of UConn's emergence as a national powerhouse is no myth. Their ascension to the lofty status of dynasty through dominance is reminiscent of the Aesop classic fable *The Tortoise and the Hare*.[76] The latter does much to encapsulate the story of the men's basketball game, being very much akin to the hare, with speed, agility, and a measure of superior physical dominance and athleticism, all of which was magnified by the male-dominated sports reporting media. By contrast, the women's basketball game was more like the undervalued, underwhelming, uneventful tortoise, and as such was seen as no match for the men's basketball game, all of which became a metaphor for the gradual, but undeniable, change in sex participation in sports competition brought on by the Title IX law of 1972. The landmark legislation was the centerpiece that allowed the UConn women's basketball team to break records and shatter glass ceilings in sports achievements.

TITLE IX AND ITS IMPACT ON UCONN'S WOMEN'S BASKETBALL PROGRAM

The emergence of the UConn women's basketball team as the flagship sports program in the NCAA, irrespective of sex, is attributable to the advent of Title IX legislation passed by Congress in 1972.[77] It is interesting to observe that Title IX was created to establish better equality between men's and women's sports competition in educational institutions that receive federal funding. Yet, within the realm of winning percentages and championships, UConn's women's team has no equals, irrespective of sex, breaking records of the best women's and men's teams. In winning their ninth National Championship in 2013–2014, Coach Auriemma's UConn team surpassed legendary head coach Summitt and her University of Tennessee women's basketball program of the 1990s and 2000s for most national championships, with eight. As noted previously, Auriemma would eclipse the record for most NCAA national titles held by Wooden's UCLA Bruins of the 1960s and 1970s. Just as Wooden's program became the model of the NCAA men's game, so too was Summitt's program the prototype for women's basketball. Amazingly, Auriemma's UConn basketball program exceeded both of the aforementioned basketball dynasties, men's and women's alike, to become the most successful in the history of major NCAA sports. Hence, their women's basketball program has more than fulfilled the ambitions held by the framers of Title IX, which was designed to engender greater equality between male and female sports competition. The UConn program has scaled new heights in emerging as the premier program in all of NCAA sports. Most importantly, their successes are expected to have a positive effect on the participation levels of girls, who have tended to shy away from sports in deference to boys. Through patterns of gender socialization based on conventional attitudes that sports competition isn't ladylike, girls have had to play catch-up to the boys in levels of participation.

In measuring equality in gender participation, some Title IX cases have focused on better sports facilities for females. At the major NCAA Division I level, "facilities" is not cited as a major problem, but the lack of attendance at women's basketball games has been. Consequently, meager revenues are generated from their sport. A study of ticket prices of NCAA Division I men's and women's college basketball games revealed stark disparities in costs and perceived value of the respective team sports.[78] Ticket prices for the NCAA men's basketball game were higher than for the women's, which had the effect of devaluing their game. This, of course, may help to explain their low attendance. Title IX requires that institutions promote men's and women's sports equitably. Therefore, the disparate costs of tickets, which lead to less revenue for women's basketball, could become an issue of Title IX compliance in the future. For all of the good it portends, and the positive outcomes that have followed with greater participation of females in sports, Title IX is not without its critics.

The legislation has been blamed for fostering a separation of the sexes and a separate-but-equal institutional landscape, which reinforces "hierarchical differences" by sex that favors male participants in sports.[79] Title IX is also viewed as problematic given the sports contact exclusion clause in the legislation that has led to the segregation of the sexes.[80] While the idea of men and women competing together on the same basketball team or against each other seems hard to imagine today, the discussion has ensued. It is worth noting, however, that several NCAA major women's basketball programs scrimmage against male basketball players on campus.[81] The practice was pioneered in the 1970s by Coach Summitt. Other major universities that permit this more integrated competition include Notre Dame, Purdue University, Iowa State, and Louisiana Tech. The downside of these sex-integrated practices is the concession by most coaches that the male basketball players who would have played high school basketball and are seen as good enough to compete at the Division II or III level are sought because they are quicker, stronger, and more athletic than Division I women's basketball players. Hence, they can get their players better prepared for the national powerhouses by having their starters practice against men. Institutions like the University of Colorado decried the practice as limiting the team's ability to develop less talented scholarship players, who would have to watch their team's starters compete against men in practice rather than participate. Incidentally, UConn was the only other ranked college at the time that did not report using male practice squads, although they have had the occasion to use male practice players. Messner et al.[82] found that institutional sport has become "contested terrain" for gender relations and ideologies. Perhaps in no other social sphere has the debate about gender inequalities in sports been a more contested terrain than in the sports reporting media. That UConn women's basketball program has amassed such unprecedented success across gender-divided sports lines, yet still suffers inequalities in sports media coverage, is indicative of an ongoing problem.

GENDER INEQUITIES IN MEDIA COVERAGE: A DISCUSSION WITH SHAUGHNESSY

After UConn's women's team dismantled Mississippi State, 98–38, in the 2016 NCAA tournament, Shaughnessy decried their dominance as bad for the women's game, declaring it unwatchable.[83] Shaughnessy's comments created a firestorm of controversy.[84] During our interview, I asked if his controversial comments about the Huskies' dominance in the NCAA tournament were indicative of gender inequalities in sports media coverage. He completely disavowed the notion, stating, "My comments were about competition, not gender."[85] I reminded him that in 2010 he offered eerily similar criticisms of the UConn women's basketball team in a March column that appeared on SI.com, the online hub of *Sports Illustrated*. In the article titled "UConn Deserves Credit for Its Remarkable Run, But I Can't Watch," Shaughnessy stated, "ESPN has been force-feeding us women's basketball [college and professional] for more than a decade and it's a ratings dog. Men simply don't want to watch it and I don't blame them."[86] Shaughnessy's reference to "force-feeding" appeared very maternalistic, as if ESPN were akin to an obstinate mother forcing her children to consume their vegetables. I asked him to explain how his writings were not sexist, since they included references to both women's college and professional basketball. He replied, "I'm going [Bill] Belichick here; it is what it is. I didn't create this [sex typing in media coverage]. This is what exists. I could be wrong, but the numbers [television ratings] indicate that I am not."[87] Interestingly enough, Shaughnessy likened himself to Bill Belichick, head coach of the New England Patriots of the hierarchical male-dominated NFL. Belichick is renowned for his ambiguity and disinclination to own up to issues in sports culture that he may have created or contributed to. For example, when the "Spygate" videotaping scandal came to light in 2007, which resulted in his Patriots team being punished by the league for illegally recording their opponents, Belichick initially blamed the NFL. Shaughnessy may not have created the sex typing in sports reporting that leads to gendered allocations and inequalities in media coverage, as he stated, but he has contributed to them immensely. Derogatory references to UConn women's college basketball constitute sex typing 101. It magnifies the sex of the women as sports participants, which has the effect of diminishing their game as less meaningful. Shaughnessy was unrepentant in his view, asserting, "It goes both ways. I would rather watch the NBA rather than the WNBA."[88] He was adamant that his views were not about sex or gender but about covering sports based on the interest of his readers. But as a well-renowned columnist, he has the ability to alter the landscape of sports reporting, as he has demonstrated. Shaughnessy is a *New York Times* best-selling author of 12 books. Additionally, he was named Massachusetts Sportswriter of the Year 11 times; another nine times he was named one of the top 10 sports columnists in the nation by the Associated Press. During our discussion, he conceded to giving no more than 20 seconds of thought to his controversial tweet on the UConn women's team that went viral, which underscores his influence.[89] In an attempt to diminish the view that his statements were somehow sexist or contributing to gender inequalities, he likened the Huskies' dominant performance to the famous "Dream Team," the moniker bestowed upon the U.S. men's basketball team that captured the gold medal in the 1992 Olympics after obliterating their competitors. I asked Shaughnessy if he had levied similar criticisms in his columns on the Dream Team as he did the UConn women's team. He could not recall doing so.[90] The latter response is an indication of how gender inequalities in sports reporting persist, despite Shaughnessy's views to the contrary. When a male basketball team like the Dream Team dominates their competition, the male-dominated media finds a way to celebrate and tolerate their success. But when a women's basketball team does it, like the UConn Huskies, it is considered bad for the sport and unwatchable. As for the sport being watchable, Shaughnessy was correct in asserting that NCAA women's basketball has suffered from poor television ratings. According to him, his controversial tweet got so much media attention because ESPN needed ratings for their coverage of the NCAA women's tournament.[91] Higher ratings result in greater revenues that create greater profits for television networks. The lack thereof for ESPN with NCAA women's basketball is explicable by equity theory.

The perspective holds that the economic value of sports organizations, like NCAA men's and women's basketball teams, can be influenced by various cost factors, including financial donations to teams, the price of a game ticket, overall attendance at games, and ultimately the percentage of viewers watching on television. If for-profit networks like CBS and ESPN concluded that the value of the men's game is better than the women's because of greater television ratings and revenues, it can have a negative effect on the perceived value of the women's sport and the consumption habits of fans.

Shaughnessy's views were compelling because they seemed to reaffirm several pervasive problems associated with sports media coverage of women's college basketball. First, most journalists covering the sport are men, which reinforces a male-dominant hierarchy that makes the men's game appear more interesting than the women's. Despite comments that seem to demean UConn women's basketball team, Shaughnessy lauded their sport as more pure, less individualistic, and more fundamentally aligned with the way the game was designed.[92] But, when asked if UConn's men's basketball team would have been more heralded had they achieved as much as the women's basketball team, his response was revealing. First, he asserted that the men's basketball team would be just as much of a turn-off if they were winning by such large margins as the women's team (i.e., 40 points a game), but he conceded, "Yes, the men would get more attention; it would be heralded more because people tend to like men's sports more. UCLA's men's team was more popular than UConn's women's."[93] Shaughnessy's comments do much to reinforce a hierarchy of naming, where sex as an ascribed status gives men a superior status whereas women are given an inferior status based on perception. Labeling theory holds that individuals with social power, such as a nationally renowned sports columnist like Shaughnessy, can label others as they see fit. Such labeling can influence how others see those so labeled and ultimately influences their interaction. While his statements seem to fit the mold of the traditional male-dominated sports reporting media, in the for-profit industry, the issues of gender inequalities in coverage allocations is a wider social problem.

In fact, many not-for-profit media outlets, such as college newspapers, conference websites, and the NCAA itself, have been found to exacerbate inequalities in sports media coverage of the men's and women's games.[94] The greater concern here is that many for-profit media outlets get leads from not-for-profit NCAA-related sources. To better understand this phenomenon that plagues women's sports, the next section examines the role of both not-for-profit and for-profit media outlets (i.e., ESPN, CBS) in perpetuating inequalities in sports coverage of NCAA men's and women's basketball.

Not-for-Profit Media Outlets

The persistence of gender inequalities in sports media coverage of NCAA men's and women's sports competition continues despite the achievements of a sports dynasty like the UConn women's basketball team and requirements of the Title IX law, which necessitates that colleges receiving federal funding accord equal publicity to male and female sports teams to engender "equal fan support and media coverage."[95] Although one would reasonably expect media outlets associated with the NCAA, including campus newspapers and websites, to provide equitable media coverage in compliance with Title IX, the reality is they do not. For example, Milner and Braddock highlight that Emory University published an uncomplimentary and sexist account of a historic feat by Diana Nyad, an alumna of the college, who at 64 was the first known person to swim from Cuba to Florida without a shark cage.[96] The writer of the story questioned whether Nyad did all the work herself or whether she was unlawfully assisted. Milner and Braddock asserted that, had a male alumnus achieved the same, it is unlikely that this historic achievement would have been diminished in the same way. But what accounts for the disparities in media coverage of men's and women's basketball by not-for-profit sources associated with the NCAA and its member institutions? Such media outlets have featured men's sports like basketball to a greater extent than the women's game for no shortage of reasons, not the least among them is the view that the men's game is more popular, appealing, and interesting.[97] These inequalities are especially troublesome when considering several important factors. For one, it is presumed that more equitable coverage of women will influence a greater number of girls to participate in sports competition. Secondly, sports information directors (SIDs) on college campuses are expected to influence the content from not-for-profit media outlets and provide leads to for-profit media sources.[98] SIDs at NCAA colleges and universities are the gatekeepers of media content shared with the public. They are supposed to provide the pulse of what NCAA institutions stand for on the subject of gender equity in sports competition on college campuses, although this is not occurring enough. More experienced SIDs are more likely to uphold Title IX standards to a greater extent than have younger ones.[99]

Another issue with SIDs is the gendered division of labor that contributes to the unequal coverage allocations that favor men's sports. For example, SIDs for men's football and basketball tend to be men by margins of 88 percent and 86 percent respectively.[100] Conversely, women's sports like college basketball tend to have women as SIDs. Such a stratified division of labor is explicable by the gender schemata theory, which looks at the role of gender socialization in shaping our attitudes, behaviors, social roles, and placement in the occupational strata. Those who espouse such views that demarcate SIDs in such a way mistakenly perceive work opportunities distributed in this way as a natural process.[101] On the one hand, such a gendered occupational stratum by sex may seem congruent. However, since SIDs provide the leads to for-profit media outlets, where a male-dominated hierarchy exists, this may help to explain the unequal coverage and the view that women's sports are not as interesting as men's sports. This gendered division of labor is exacerbated by the fact that women SIDs, while being more inclined to highlight the value of women's sports, have to also tread lightly, to not "rock the boat."[102] In other words, even when women are employed as SIDs, they must still contend with a sports culture where "heteronormative gender roles" persist.[103]

The theory of gender stratification is also meaningful in explaining this phenomenon. The perspective examines how sports media as a social structure legitimizes and reinforces a male-dominated hierarchy that subordinates women.[104] To think that in the 21st century the issue of unequal sports media coverage of NCAA women's and men's sports is still a larger social problem begs the question "Who is more responsible for this unequal distribution of gender representation in sports reporting—the not-for-profit sources, such as the NCAA media outlets, which includes its member institutions, or for-profit sources, such as CBS and ESPN among others?" If not-for-profit media outlets are not providing equitable coverage of men's and women's major Division I basketball, how can for-profit media sources alter their conventions, which have favored men's sports?

For-Profit Media Outlets

There has been an evolution of mass media sports coverage of NCAA women's basketball from the 1990s to the present. This time period is supposedly an age of greater enlightenment, when there is greater acceptance of women's sports in our society. From the onset of the UConn women's basketball dynasty, which began in the 1990s, to the major achievements of women athletes during the 1996 Olympics, to the advent of the WNBA in 1997, these significant social markers paralleled the expansion of sport media coverage beyond the traditional platforms of television, radio, and print media, to greater use of the Internet. Yet, the question becomes, did the evolution of women's participation in sports, and the expansion of sports media coverage with newer technologies and platforms, result in more equal coverage of women's and men's sports? The answer, of course, is that neither media type has dramatically changed the unequal media coverage that still favors men's sports over women's.

Additionally, the sports reporting media coverage among for-profit outlets, in general, has not kept pace with the popularity and participation rates of women in sports. A problem magnified by the success, and yet relative unimportance, of the UConn women's basketball dynasty, given the disparate media coverage of the team's success. Since viewers and readers of sport consume more content from the men's game than the women's, gender-based coverage allocations follow. These coverage disparities occur in both the electronic and print media; however, television may be the media source most driven by gender-based consideration that favors men's sports.

Television Is Telling

Jonetta Weber and Robert Carini found that television sports coverage of female athletes has declined since 2004, and by 2009 it had dropped to the lowest level in 20 years.[105] In the case of ESPN, the network was cited for providing only nominal coverage of NCAA women's basketball while "lavishing huge amounts of air time" on the men's college basketball tournament. All of this is especially disconcerting since ESPN has the contract to broadcast the NCAA women's basketball. To further underscore this problem, in 2016 it was revealed that ESPN was broadcasting the first and second rounds of the NCAA women's basketball tournament using game announcers from the studio rather than courtside. The network conceded that the move helped save money by not having to place a production truck in a nearby lot or transport the broadcast talent. Realizing the inherent inequity, UConn's women's head coach Auriemma lamented, "I don't imagine that it's happening on the men's side at all."[106] The latter comment by the UConn head coach underscores the realization of gender inequalities in sports media coverage of women's and men's basketball in the for-profit media. I asked Shaughnessy if the aforementioned revelation of ESPN attempting to save money at the expense of better coverage of the NCAA women's basketball, in concert with Coach Auriemma's lamenting the problem, "vindicated" him. He replied, "No! Because they [ESPN] are spending money on what people watch [men's sports]. It reflects more the interest [of viewers]. It's their problem. They overpaid."[107] Shaughnessy's latter comment brings to mind the import of equity theory, which holds that the perceived value of a sporting event, based on cost factors like ticket pricing and revenue-generating potential, can influence the amount of public interest accorded to NCAA women's basketball. Such a concession by ESPN, which asserted the money saved would be reinvested in the production of broadcasts of later tournament rounds, gave credence to the overall view that for-profit media outlets provide inequitable coverage of women's sports based on perceived value. There is a prevailing realization by the likes of ESPN that NCAA women's basketball is not profitable while men's basketball is a financial boon. On March 29, 2016, I conducted a simple Google search using the terms "NCAA games today." I clicked on ESPN's online link and it brought up the men's tournament schedule.[108] The primary focus accorded to the men's tournament schedule was especially noteworthy, since ESPN has the license to broadcast the women's tournament. Perhaps, ESPN conceded that with over 15 million visitors to their site it would be better to highlight the more popular and profitable men's tournament, which amounted to another unfortunate concession on their part. Studies have shown that while ESPN has provided greater coverage to the NCAA men's basketball tournament on its main Web page, during the regular season, there has been more equitable coverage provided to the men's and women's sports' respective Web pages on ESPN.com. Consequently, men's sport receives greater proportionate coverage because they are featured on the network's main page and again on their individual page. To better understand these gender disparities in media coverage, one needs only to follow the money.

It has been estimated that 90 percent of the NCAA's revenues from sports come from the three-week men's basketball tournament in March. Equity theory would explain that this differential in value is owing to the women's game being devalued relative to factors like profitability. Given the disparities in media coverage, it is hardly surprising that ratings for NCAA women's basketball games have been poor. Shaughnessy and I discussed his March 2016 column, "UConn Women Are Too Dominant for Their Own Good,"[109] which followed his controversial remarks after the Huskies' 98–38 victory over Mississippi State. In the column, he stated, "Sports don't grow in popularity unless people watch it on TV."[110] When asked if his comments, which caused a national stir, made people less interested in watching the NCAA women's 2016 tournament, he replied, "No, people decide independent of what we [media] say. They make up their own minds."[111] But the theory of limited effects asserts otherwise. The perspective holds that the more informed people are about a topic, the less likely they are to be influenced by the media.[112] Because NCAA women's basketball and the UConn women's team have not received the equitable media coverage they deserve, the general public seems less knowledgeable and unappreciative. Consequently, they seem less likely to watch NCAA women's basketball, and the success of the UConn women's team has been cited as a factor. On the other hand, to some extent, Shaughnessy has a point—fans watch what they prefer, independent of the media. Milner and Braddock note that Super Bowl XLVIII, which featured the Seattle Seahawks versus the Denver Broncos, broke the record for the most watched television program in history despite the Seahawks' 22–0 lead at halftime and their ultimate win at 48–3.[113] Conversely, UConn gets widely criticized for blowing out teams in their national title games. In an interesting irony, in 2016, Las Vegas book makers had greater odds that an earthquake would strike during the Super Bowl than that UConn would lose the women's National Championship.[114] When I asked Shaughnessy about these odds, he replied, "Vegas gave such a probability because they care about such things because it costs them money."[115] The Dan Shaughnessys of the sports reporting media realize it is the readers of sporting news and television viewers that create readership and ratings, respectively, which brings greater revenue. Because women's sports have been written about less, and broadcast even less, their revenue-generating potential is seen as a nullity. Indeed, women's sports have been very unprofitable, even for NCAA institutions with great women's sports teams like the UConn women's basketball program. Other forms of electronic media among for-profit outlets, including the Internet, have continuously provided greater coverage to NCAA men's basketball over women's basketball. Such disparities have been observable among sources like ESPN.com and CBS's *SportsLine*, despite the growing number of women browsing the Internet. These disparities are also pronounced in print media, with such industry stalwarts as *Sports Illustrated*.

Sports Illustrated has been described as a "litmus test" of sports media coverage of women athletes.[116] *SI* is among the most popular sports magazines, with upward of 21 million weekly readers, 8 in 10 of whom are men, with a circulation of over 3 million. Not only were men more likely to appear on the cover of the popular sports magazine, but when women did appear on the cover, they were more often in complementary, nonathletic roles, like supportive spouse or mother of an athlete. Another problem identified in the coverage accorded to the UConn women's basketball team is that the male-dominated sports reporting media tend to report on female athletes in individual sports like tennis and golf rather than team sports like basketball. Interestingly enough, in my discussion with Shaughnessy he scoffed at the notion that he was in any way sexist. He added that media journalists like himself cover women's sports like tennis, golf, the World Cup, and the Olympics.[117] Perhaps not surprisingly, Shaughnessy's views align with research findings that show that women playing individual sports—tennis, golf, and skiing—receive better media coverage, as do those competing in sports considered more feminine, like volleyball and soccer, which are commonly featured during the Olympics. The idea that men would prefer to see women competing in sports that they perceive as more congruent with social constructs of what is more feminine has been established.[118] Additionally, the sports reporting media tend to provide better coverage of women's sports that are seen as promoting heterosexuality.

The former refers to suggestive and provocative poses in photos on magazine covers and in articles. It has also been observed that for-profit media outlets attempt to accentuate heterosexual normalcy in female athletes by profiling them as wives, girlfriends, and mothers. Conversely, team sports like basketball can run counter to social conventions of what a feminine athlete should look like. Hence, the media coverage is not as good.

CONCLUSION AND RECOMMENDATIONS

In the 44 years since Title IX was passed, there has been some observable progress, but inequities persist. The positive outcomes include greater participation in sports competition among girls and women in both high school and college. Yet, the quality and quantity of media coverage has not kept pace with the quality and quantity of their participation in sports. The success of the UConn women's basketball team represents the embodiment of what Title IX has sought to achieve. The Huskies women's basketball team has become the most successful sports dynasty in the history of the NCAA. Yet, it is their dynasty and dominance that makes them a compelling case study of gender inequalities that are rampant in sports media coverage. Despite their success, which includes the most National Championships in basketball with 11, and holding the mark for the most consecutive wins, they are still undervalued and largely underappreciated. Aside from Shaughnessy's derogatory comments about their dominance being a problem for their sport, it was also revealed that ESPN was saving money in the first two rounds of the 2016 NCAA national tournament by using game announcers from the studio rather than on location.

Perhaps not so coincidentally, no shortage of research on gendered allocations in media coverage have studied and analyzed both the NCAA women's and men's basketball tournaments, since both are hosted in March. The results show that in the last 30 years, women's sports in general, and NCAA women's basketball in particular, has continued to suffer unequal coverage from both not-for-profit and for-profit media sources. Be it NCAA news, campus newspapers, and even major conference websites, all have provided greater proportionate coverage to men's basketball over women's basketball. Moreover, for-profit sources like ESPN and CBS have also provided greater media coverage to NCAA men's basketball over the women's game. Print media sources like *Sports Illustrated* have also contributed to unequal coverage by according greater article and front cover space to men's sports over women's sports. That both for-profit and not-for-profit sources are contributing to such unequal media coverage is a cause for great concern.

As for potential solutions to improve the situation, colleges and universities must do a better job of ensuring full compliance with Title IX legislation. Specifically, these institutions need to ensure equal publicity and promotions of women's and men's sports, which is a requirement of the legislation. Studies cited in this chapter show that the NCAA news and its website, as well as campus newspapers, have provided greater coverage to men's sports over women's, including basketball. Additionally, sports information directors who are younger and less experienced have been cited for not upholding their Title IX obligations as much as older directors. Moreover, a gendered division of labor among SIDs, where men are more likely to be assigned to men's sports and women SIDs assigned to women's sports, may be contributing to the problem of unequal coverage. Since SIDs provide leads to the mainstream media, some in for-profit media may not be as considerate of leads provided by women SIDs, especially since the mainstream media sources are generally dominated by men. Therefore, it would be more advantageous to reduce the gendered division of labor among SIDs so that women and men could work with sports teams irrespective of sex, to reduce gendered allocations in media coverage. College and universities might also consider increasing the ticket prices to NCAA women's basketball games. Research cited in this chapter shows that when the ticket prices of NCAA women's basketball games were increased in a study, it had the effect of increasing the perceived value of the team and their sport. Such a change may have the effect of increasing game attendance, especially if the SIDs do a better job of promoting women's basketball teams. The NCAA needs to also examine the impacts of changes implemented to improve attendance, such as scheduling women's basketball games during the weekend and allowing top-rated teams to host the opening rounds of the national tournament. If these changes improve attendance at games, the association should find ways to expand these initiatives. Another suggestion to improve attendance and ratings of the NCAA women's tournament might involve hosting their Final Four in the same city as the men's basketball tournament.

Lastly, both for-profit and not-for-profit media outlets could use better training on the benefits of gender equality in sports reporting and commentaries. Reducing gender typing and sex typing during broadcasts could be achieved through better training for writers and television commentators. In addition, more women should be hired and empowered to effect changes in these male-dominated industries. It would also be beneficial to train people in the for-profit media outlets on the requirements of Title IX, since they are covering NCAA women's and men's basketball. While the for-profit media sources are not bound by Title IX like the not-for-profit sources, they are providing media coverage of the NCAA's member institutions and should better reflect their institutional objectives.

NOTES

1. Dan Shaughnessy, "UConn Deserves Credit for Its Remarkable Run, But I Can't Watch," *Sports Illustrated*, last modified March 15, 2010, http://www.si.com/more-sports/2010/03/15/uconn-women.

2. Administration of Barack Obama, "Remarks Honoring the NCAA Women's Basketball Champion University of Connecticut Huskies," September 15, 2015.

3. Michael A. Messner et al., "Separating the Men from the Girls": The Gendered Language of Television Sports," *Gender & Society* 7, no. 1 (1993): 121–37.

4. Edward (Ted) M. Kian et al., "ESPN—The Women's Sports Network? A Content Analysis of Internet Coverage of March Madness," *Journal of Broadcasting & Electronic Media* 53, no. 3 (2009): 477–95.

5. James R. Hallmark and Richard N. Armstrong, "Gender Equity in Televised Sports: A Comparative Analysis of Men's and Women's NCAA Division I Basketball Championship Broadcasts, 1991–1995," *Journal of Broadcasting & Electronic Media* 43, no. 2 (1999): 222–35.

6. Ibid., 223.

7. Ibid.

8. Ibid.

9. Equity & Excellence in Education, "Keeping Score: A Report Regarding Connecticut Secondary Schools and Title IX's Mandate for Gender Equity in Athletics," *Equity and Excellence in Education* 31, no. 3 (1998): 37–45.

10. Hallmark and Armstrong, *Journal of Broadcasting & Media*, 223.

11. Ibid.

12. Marie Hardin et al., "Ambivalence on the Front Lines? Attitudes toward Title IX and Women's Sports among Division I Sports Information Directors," *International Review for the Sociology of Sport* 49, no. 1 (2014): 42–64.

13. Ibid., 47.

14. Adrienne Milner and Jomills Braddock III, *Sex Segregation in Sports: Why Separate Is Not Equal* (Santa Barbara, CA: Praeger, 2016).

15. Hallmark and Armstrong, *Journal of Broadcasting & Media*, 223.

16. Messner et al., "Separating the Men from the Girls," 127.

17. Amy Jones and Jennifer Greer, "You Don't Look Like an Athlete: The Effects of Feminine Appearance on Audience Perceptions of Female Athletes and Women's Sports," *Journal of Sport Behavior* 34, no. 4 (2011): 358–77.

18. Messner et al., "Separating the Men from the Girls," 126.

19. Milner and Braddock, *Sex Segregation*, 12.

20. Messner et al., "Separating the Men from the Girls," 125.

21. Ibid.

22. Ibid., 126–27.

23. Coyte Cooper, "BCS Conference Coverage: An Investigation of the Gender Coverage Provided on Intercollegiate Athletic Websites within a Major NCAA Conference," *Women in Sport & Physical Activity Journal* 18, no. 1 (2009): 18–23.

24. James Bowman, "Why Women's College Basketball Might Be Stuck in the Red," *Swish Appeal*, last modified November 12, 2013, http://swishappeal.com/2013/11/12/5090384/ncaa-womens-college-basketball-profit.

25. Milner and Braddock, *Sex Segregation*, 81.

26. Hardin et al., "Ambivalence on the Front Lines," 45; Andrew Bucholtz, "Ratings Rise for NCAA Women's Tournament 46% from Last Year," *Awful Announcing*, last modified March 24, 2016, http://awfulannouncing.com/2016/ratings-rise-ncaa-womens-tournament-46-last-year.html.

27. Mary G. McDonald, "The Marketing of Women's National Basketball Association and the Making of Postfeminism," *International Review for the Sociology of Sport* 35, no. 1 (2000): 35–41.

28. Kian et al., "ESPN—The Women's Sports Network?," 491.

29. Michelle R. Hebl et al., "Paying the Way: The Ticket to Gender Equality in Sports," *Sex Roles* 51, no. 3/4 (2004): 227–35.

30. Hebl et al., "Paying the Way," 227.

31. Ibid.

32. Jere Longman, "A Push to Invigorate Women's Basketball," *New York Times*, last modified June 17, 2013, http://www.nytimes.com/2013/06/18/sports/ncaabasketball/official-offers-ways-to-invigorate-womens-basketball.html.

33. Jennifer Swann, "March Madness Exposes How Little Viewers Care about Women's Sports," *Take Part*, last modified March 29, 2015, http://www.takepart.com/article/2015/03/29/college-basketball.

34. Michelle L. Redmond et al., "Website Coverage of NCAA Basketball: Are Women Getting Equal Playing Time?," *Women in Sport & Physical Activity Journal* 18, no. 1 (2009): 78–90.

35. Michael A. Messner and Cheryl Cooky, "Gender in Televised Sports: News and Highlights Shows, 1989–2000," Center for Feminist Research, University of Southern California (2010), 1–35.

36. Bucholtz, "Ratings Rise for NCAA Women's Tournament," 1.

37. Dan Shaughnessy, interview by Kenneth N. Robinson, via telephone conversation, September 5, 2016.

38. Bucholtz, "Ratings Rise for NCAA Women's Tournament," 1.

39. Kian et al., "ESPN—The Women's Sports Network," 478.

40. Bowman, "Why Women's Basketball," 2.

41. Ibid.

42. Ibid., 3.

43. Ibid.

44. Milner and Braddock, *Sex Segregation*, 17.

45. Ibid., 96.

46. Ibid., 97.

47. Diana Kendall, *Social Problems in a Diverse Society*, 8th ed. (Upper Saddle River, NJ: Pearson, 2010).

48. Messner et al., "Separating the Men from the Girls," 127.

49. Milner and Braddock, *Sex Segregation*, 3.

50. Shaughnessy, interview by Kenneth N. Robinson, telephone interview, September 5, 2016.

51. Jones and Greer, "You Don't Look Like an Athlete," 359.

52. Ibid., 360.

53. Ibid.

54. Messner et al., "Separating the Men from the Girls," 126.

55. Jones and Greer, "You Don't Look Like an Athlete," 370.

56. Shaughnessy, interview with Kenneth N. Robinson, Question 2, September 5, 2016.

57. Dan Shaughnessy, interview by Kenneth N. Robinson, July 8, 2016.

58. Shaughnessy interview, Question 3, September 5, 2016.

59. Jonetta D. Weber and Robert M. Carini, "Where Are the Female Athletes in Sports Illustrated? A Content Analysis of Covers (2000–2011)," *International Review for the Sociology of Sport* 48, no. 2 (2012): 196–203.

60. McDonald, "The Marketing of the Women's National Basketball Association," 43.

61. Messner et al., "Separating the Men from the Girls," 128.

62. Shaughnessy, interview with Robinson, Question 1, September 5, 2016.

63. Messner et al., "Separating the Men from the Girls," 121.

64. Shaughnessy, interview with Robinson, Question 1, September 5, 2016.

65. Messner et al., "Separating the Men from the Girls," 121.

66. Ibid., 132.

67. Shaughnessy, interview with Robinson, Question 18, July 8, 2016.

68. Shaughnessy, interview with Robinson, Question 6, July 8, 2016.

69. Weber and Carini, "Where Are the Female Athletes," 197.

70. Congressional Hearing Transcript Database, "Remarks by President Barack Obama at a Meeting with the 2010 NCAA Women's Basketball Champions, The University of Connecticut," May 20, 2010.

71. Ibid.

72. Shaughnessy, interview with Robinson, Question 7, July 8, 2016.

73. Congressional Hearing Transcript Database, "Remarks by President Barack Obama," 1.

74. Administration of Barack Obama, "Remarks Honoring the NCAA Women's Basketball Champion," 2.

75. National Public Radio, "University of Connecticut Has Both Their Men's and Women's Basketball Teams in the NCAA Final Four," 2004, http://www.npr.org/.

76. Aesop, *The Tortoise and the Hare* (1668).

77. Equity & Excellence in Education, "Keeping Score," 37.

78. Hebl et al., "Paying the Way," 227.

79. Hardin et al., "Ambivalence on the Front Lines," 47.

80. Milner and Braddock, *Sex Segregation*, 6.

81. Welch Suggs, "For Top Women Women's Basketball Players, the Ideal Practice Includes Men," *The Chronicle of Higher Education* 47, no. 28 (March 23, 2011).

82. Messner et al., "Separating the Men from the Girls," 122.

83. Charles Curtis, "Geno Auriemma to Columnist Who Says UConn Is Bad for the Women's Game: 'Don't Watch,'" *USA Today*, last modified March 27, 2016, http://ftw.usatoday.com/2016/03/geno-auriemma-uconn-dan-shaughnessy-ncaa-tournament.

84. Jon Keller, "Dan Shaughnessy Is Wrong on UConn Women's Basketball," *CBS Boston*, March 29, 2016, http://boston.cbslocal.com/2016/03/2-dan-shaughnessy-uconn-womens-basketball-geno-auriemma; Jeff Jacobs, "Props for Getting the Country Talking about Women's Hoops," *Hartford Courant*, 2016, http://www.courant.com/sports/uconn-womens-basketball/hc-jacobs-column; Emmett Knowlton, "Geno Auriemma Compares UConn to Tiger Woods in Defense of Criticism That His Team Is Ruining Women's Basketball," *Business Insider*, March 28, 2016, http://www.businessinsider.com/geno-auriemma-rips-dan-shaughnessy-uconn-women; Kels Dayton, "UConn Women Are Dominant, Awesome and Boring at the Same Time," *Sportz Edge*, last modified March 29, 2016, http://sportzedge.com/2016/03/29/uconn-women-are-dominant-awesome-and-boring.

85. Shaughnessy, interview with Robinson, Question 12, July 8, 2016.

86. Shaughnessy, "UConn Deserves Credit for Its Remarkable Run," 1.

87. Shaughnessy, interview with Robinson, Question 5, September 5, 2016.

88. Shaughnessy, interview with Robinson, Question 5, July 8, 2016.

89. Shaughnessy, interview with Robinson, Question 10, July 8, 2016.

90. Shaughnessy, interview with Robinson, Question 3, July 8, 2016.

91. Shaughnessy, interview with Robinson, Question 10, July 8, 2016.

92. Shaughnessy, interview with Robinson, Question 3, July 8, 2016.

93. Shaughnessy, interview with Robinson, Question 7, July 8, 2016.

94. Cooper, "BCS Conference Coverage," 1.

95. Equity & Excellence in Education, "Keeping Score," 43.

96. Milner and Braddock, *Sex Segregation*, 9.

97. Cooper, "BCS Conference Coverage," 2.

98. Hardin et al., "Ambivalence on the Front Lines," 43.

99. Ibid., 51.

100. Ibid., 46.

101. Jones and Greer, "You Don't Look Like an Athlete," 360.

102. Hardin et al., "Ambivalence on the Front Lines," 45.

103. Ibid.

104. Messner et al., "Separating Girls from the Boys," 132.

105. Weber and Carini, "Where Are the Female Athletes," 197.

106. Bucholtz, "Ratings Rise for NCAA Women's Tournament," 1.

107. Shaughnessy, interview with Robinson, Question 8, July 8, 2016.

108. *ESPN*, accessed March 29, 2016 at 2:30PM, http://www.espn.com.

109. Dan Shaughnessy, "UConn Women Are Too Dominant for Their Own Good," *Boston Globe*, last modified March 28, 2016,https://www.bostonglobe.com/sports/2016/03/28/uconn-women-are-too-dominant-for-their-own-good/sltP6Ypys4C6x0UKSngnzK/story.html .

110. Ibid., 7.

111. Shaughnessy, interview with Robinson, Question 6, September 5, 2016.

112. Kendall, *Social Problems*.

113. Milner and Braddock, *Sex Segregation*, 109.

114. Ryan Chatelain, "UConn Women May Be Great, But Nobody Is Watching," *CBS New York*, last modified April 7, 2016, http://newyork.cbslocal.com/2016/04/07/uconn-womens-basketball-ncaa-womens-tournament-tv-ratings/.

115. Shaughnessy, interview with Robinson, Question 9, September 5, 2016.

116. Weber and Carini, "Where Are the Female Athletes," 197.

117. Shaughnessy, interview with Robinson, Question 4, July 8, 2016.

118. Jones and Greer, "You Don't Look Like an Athlete," 359.

8

Turf Wars: Safety, Sexism, and the 2015 Women's World Cup

Meredith Marie Schertzinger

Soccer is considered the most popular sport in the world.[1] In 2007, FIFA (Fédération Internationale de Football Association) completed the Big Count, an attempt to calculate the number of people who played soccer worldwide, and identified 270 million, which equates to roughly 4 percent of the world's population.[2] This number, however, has vastly increased since 2007, considering the growing popularity of soccer and the number of recreational players who were not involved in the initial survey. Due to the popularity of the sport, most people assume there is equality among sexes, especially since soccer is one of the most popular sports played by women in the United States.[3] Unfortunately, great strides still need to be made for such assumptions to become reality.

Being a soccer player and continuing to compete at the collegiate level, I am aware of the unspoken understanding that soccer should be played on grass. Growing up in the Midwest, I played most games on turf, but I played any major event, such as my high school state championship game and all college showcases, on grass. This implied rule holds true for any high-caliber soccer game—male or female, high school, college, or professional level—and any breach of this silent contract would cause uproar among participants, coaches, and fans alike. Prior to the announcement that the Women's 2015 World Cup (June 6 to July 5) would be played on turf, any person familiar with soccer would confidently have said that there was no way the World Cup, the most elite event in soccer, would ever be played on turf. No World Cup game in the history of men's or women's soccer had ever been played on turf because of the negative physical and tactical changes to which players must adapt.[4] High-level coaches and players were furious when the announcement was made. Those not participating even went to the extreme of not watching or becoming less invested in the tournament because the game would be altered so drastically. The soccer players competing did not settle for the turf without a fight against FIFA for making this decision. In a counterargument, FIFA used machinery diagnostics and scholarly studies to support its position that turf is equal to grass on all accounts. Ironically, this increasingly revealed FIFA's desperate attempt to hide behind the data and convince the world that this decision was not solely based on gender discrimination. At best, the lack of interest in the players' and coaches' opinions on surface preference and lack of financial compensation for the teams who succeeded in the Women's World Cup reflects a shocking lack of communication between the organization and its players. In the worst-case scenario, FIFA's decision provides evidence of the organization's minimal respect for the greatest women in soccer, demonstrated by the poor follow-through in treating men and women equally in soccer.

FIFA's official policy position on nondiscrimination states, "discrimination of any kind against a country, private person or group of people on account of ethnic origin, gender, language, religion, politics or any other reason is strictly prohibited and punishable by suspension or expulsion,"[5] a statement that specifically references gender discrimination as unjust and unethical. Yet FIFA clearly ignored this rule when making the steadfast decision to use turf for the 2015 Women's World Cup, an idea never implemented for any World Cup in history. Women countered this absurdity by filing a civil lawsuit with the Human Rights Tribunal in Ontario, lashing out at FIFA's blatant discrimination with the power of 80 signatures from international women competing in the World Cup.[6] FIFA responded with threats of suspension and fines if the women continued pressing the issue, an act that caused these women to file a harassment lawsuit as well.[7] Female players have noted that the men would likely have gone on strike, refusing to play until grass was provided;[8] the vast availability of global opportunities to showcase their play would allow for this option. Unfortunately for women, these global opportunities are few and far between, and at the World Cup, the pinnacle stage they have to display their strength and abilities, FIFA and the CSA (Canadian Soccer Association) refused to budge on the playing surface decision, asserting that no such discrimination had occurred or ever would occur.[9] As a result, the lawsuits were dropped and the U.S. women competed in the games and won,[10] inspiring young girls around the nation. However, this victory also created the ultimate platform to expose the discrimination that lies within the soccer community.

FIFA has created an advanced, third-generation turf that they argue is as good as grass. This "Football Turf" was developed to mirror natural grass and create equality in field surfaces around the world. For a turf field to receive a certificate indicating it is FIFA Recommended 1 Star or 2 Star, three "basic" criteria must be met: durability, ball/surface interaction, and player/surface interaction.[11] The highest-level fields, such as those used for the World Cup, must comply with the stricter 2 Star Recommended protocol. The parameters are tested by machinery designed to simulate what a player would experience on the field, such as shock absorption, bounce and speed of the ball, and slip and rotational resistance.[12] Other claimed benefits of the turf include multipurpose use, unlimited playing hours, no abandonment of games due to weather, and low maintenance cost once it is installed.[13] FIFA claimed the manufacturing of this synthetic grass would benefit countries that struggle with climate issues as well as the inability to afford the upkeep of natural grass facilities. That being said, the men's 2018 World Cup will be played in Russia and the 2022 World Cup in Qatar.[14] Both locations experience vast extremes in climate, making both ideal candidates for the installment of FIFA Recommended 2 Star turf.[15] However, the men will play both tournaments on grass. In contrast, Canada, where the controversial 2015 Women's World Cup was located, has a moderate climate, making it an ideal candidate for grass, especially compared to Russia and Qatar, yet the game was played on turf.[16] This further supports female players' reason for calling FIFA discriminatory in the organization's choice to mandate a turf field in 2015.

Fear of turf burns changes the way players execute certain types of slide tackles and defense maneuvers, which is one of the leading reasons soccer players dislike turf fields. To be qualified as FIFA Recommended 2 Star turf, a surface that supposedly eliminates concern for turf burns, machines must test friction and skin abrasion. These machines rub a "special silicone elastomer,"[17] which simulates skin, across the turf at high speeds. The damage to the silicone and friction between the surface and "skin" must fall into specific parameters to keep the burns players receive to a minimum in order to receive 2 Star certification.[18] Unfortunately, the machine was unable to erase the numerous turf burns received during the 2015 Women's World Cup. Players posted images of their bloody post-game shins in frustration.[19] As a soccer player myself, I tend to avoid slide tackles if possible when I play on turf fields. The pain and annoyance received from the burns following the game presents too great a risk to justify constantly sliding on the surface. These horrific burns are not the only form of burning that occurs on turf fields. Because the turf at the games was unable to regulate temperature as it should, field temperatures reached sweltering levels, from 120°F to 129°F, while air temperature in neighboring cities only measured around 80°F.[20] Australian national team player Michelle Heyman said that walking on this turf is "like walking on hot coals with your skin ripping and slowly cracking, constantly . . . you wouldn't want to see the bottom of our feet after a game. They just turn white. The skin is all ripped off. It's pretty disgusting."[21] These injuries are not additive but multiplicative, and to no one's surprise, the women had to deal with more adversities than benefits on the intelligent 2 Star turf. FIFA believed they potentially had an identical pitch to natural grass, but they needed a set of guinea pigs to confirm their theories, and they chose the top women in the world as their subjects.[22]

Following the manufacturing of FIFA's "football turf," many studies have been done in support of its effectiveness, both to give FIFA more confidence in their decision and to provide facts to obscure the truth behind such a potentially dangerous decision. *The British Journal of Sports Medicine* ran three studies comparing injuries on the 2 Star turf versus grass in a training setting, a match setting, and a prospective two-cohort study.[23] All three studies found coinciding results supporting the notion that, statistically, the turf was identical to the grass. Specifically, the studies focused on a match setting with United States NCAA (National Collegiate Athletic Association) collegiate soccer players, and found that injury caused by player-to-surface contact did not differ for either women or men between turf or grass.[24] On paper, the studies show that turf is just as safe, if not safer, than grass in regards to injuries sustained during a match or training. However, causation is not taken into consideration. These numerical values cannot show the reviewer players' mind-set as they compete on the different surfaces. Many players play more hesitantly on turf due to fear of injury, which could be a reason for the apparent decrease in injury. Other research findings regarding playing surface have noted a variation in injury patterns, specifically in ankle injuries. In two separate studies, one examining elite Swedish women players and the other a U-17 (under 17) women's U.S. team, researchers noted a significantly higher rate of ankle ligament damage on turf surfaces.[25] Given these findings on injuries, it is plausible that the players' style of defending and attacking changes significantly on turf versus grass. Moreover, the players themselves feel the turf takes a greater toll on their bodies than grass and they require more recovery time between games, which these players are, of course, not provided.[26] Clearly, there are a considerable number of confounding variables that could have contributed to the results found in the FIFA-supported studies, but they were not taken into account. FIFA merely chose to obtain the statistics that were in support of turf without any investigation of causation, creating the appearance that the updated 2 Star turfs had been developed and enhanced to the point that they could arguably be superior to grass in regards to safety.

As mentioned previously, a negative perception continues to surround the use of artificial surfaces in soccer. In an interview with National Public Radio (NPR), World Cup U.S. player Heather O'Reilly voiced the athletes' concerns for physical damage as well as the psychological changes that occur due to playing on turf:

> You know, slide tackling on grass—you know, you get up, you shake the grass off, get the dirt off. On turf, unfortunately, a little layer of

> your skin comes up with every slide tackle, so you get turf burns. Those diving headers that are so exciting on the world stage aren't going to happen on artificial turf because you can get injured. So it changes the game quite a bit. One, on the injury side. Two, it changes the game just on the soccer end. The ball just moves quite a bit faster on turf so, you know, it's out of bounds a lot, there's a lot of throw-ins, things like that. And it's also quite a bit more bouncy. It doesn't roll as easily as it may on grass, and it just loses the rhythm of the game and the fluidity of the game.[27]

Many of O'Reilly's fellow teammates echo her comments. Abby Wambach, famous for her high level of aggression within the opposing goal box, described the turf field situation as a "nightmare."[28] Wambach further commented that she would second-guess making a slide tackle or diving header, knowing she would receive bloody knees, elbows, or hip bones.[29] Statistically, the turf field may be comparable to grass, but no matter how many ways FIFA presents the information, players and coaches will continue to alter their tactics when playing a game on turf. These alterations are necessary when there is no other option, but it is atrocious for the best soccer players and coaches in the world to have to take into account all the fears and obstacles that come with turf during such an elite event as the World Cup.

Upon a visual review of the World Cup games physical performance statistics summary, it appears that there was a change in tactical style of play in comparison to the previous 2011 Women's World Cup.[30] For example, the success rate of passes decreased from 74 percent in 2011 to 72 percent in 2015, and an adjustment of play is seen in the increase of short passes from 211.5 to 231.7.[31] Statistical analysis still needs to be done to confirm this argument, but a simple conversation with players and coaches makes it evident that tactical alterations were in fact made. Several attempts have been initiated to better understand the players' perceptions of turf. In one questionnaire given to male Major League Soccer (MLS) players, 94 percent felt artificial turf would increase the risk of sustaining an injury, create greater surface stiffness and friction, and cause larger metabolic cost on the individual's body.[32] This study may not have involved female soccer players, but there is no doubt that both men and women are in agreement regarding the potential role of cognitive expectations on style of play. Moreover, early on in the decision-making process, FIFA could have surveyed the competing players and coaches to assess their valuable opinions on a subject that directly affects them. Additionally, a study from Sweden involving both male and female elite-club–level players analyzed movement and playing style on a turf field. Results supported O'Reilly's statement, as fewer slide tackles were noted in addition to an increase in shorter passes on the turf field, thereby corroborating the idea that turf causes alterations from the typical style of play.[33] Until the impact of player expectations on style of play is rigorously assessed, the lack of attention to this important element remains a crucial confounding factor in any reported results. Given this, the strength of the athletes' vocal protests should far outweigh any statistics FIFA was able to provide, but, sadly, the women's voices fell flat to the members of FIFA and CSA.

In addition to players' opinions, some studies have found evidence to support the players' physiological concerns about playing on turf. For example, one study examined male soccer players' heart rate and blood lactate levels on three varying surfaces (treadmill, natural grass, and 2 Star turf) at varying speeds.[34] The turf surface variable resulted in higher numerical values at all speeds for heart rate and blood lactate concentrations than the natural grass variable.[35] This evidence coincides with the perception that turf is more taxing on the body. Returning to the study evaluating the games throughout the 2015 World Cup as a whole, visual comparison between the 2011 and 2015 numbers seem to support this argument as well. The overall distance of high-intensity runs decreased from 301.6 m in 2011 to 298.4 m in 2015.[36] Furthermore, the average rest time between a high-intensity run increased from 4:47 to 4:55.[37] No measures of statistical significance between the values are presented, but upon visual review, it appears the numerical values added when players used turf influenced the players' overall performance. Unfortunately, more studies and more player opinions regarding this matter need to be pursued for FIFA to admit that turf will never meet the standard of grass. Each study alludes to a need to investigate this matter further to support the players' perceptions, but the funding has not been provided to do so, allowing FIFA to remain unscathed in its decision to use turf.

The turf war is not seen solely in the world of soccer. This battle spans a variety of sports, and with each sport there is a united negative opinion of turf. The universally negative outlook provides women's soccer greater credence, given that they are not the only sport that has dealt with turf frustration. For example, Major League Baseball had a period of experimentation with artificial turf in the 1960s.[38] At first, players with turf stadiums saw benefits in the new style of play created by the turf.[39] However, this optimism quickly faded when lingering injuries were detected from the punishing fields. Many players attribute their knee operations, back injuries, and reduction in career length to the turf. For example, Hall of Famer Andre Dawson played 11 big league seasons at Montreal's Olympic turf stadium, which resulted in 12 knee operations and a shortened career.[40] Dawson further commented that he would be shocked if one could find a big league player who enjoyed turf.[41] In concordance with Dawson, Terry Pendleton, former Cardinals player of seven seasons, commented one morning that he wondered "what the hell is going on with my back and knees," immediately blaming the turf for the pain and fatigue.[42] Terry Pendleton played 75 percent of his career games on artificial turf and had three knee operations.[43] Pendleton's fellow Braves coach Kevin Seitzer played five years on the Kansas City's Royals' speed carpet turf, enduring five knee operations in the process.[44] That baseball players suffer from the same unforgiving nature of turf that soccer players experience further supports the female soccer players' opinion. However, unlike women's soccer, Major League Baseball has listened to the players' voiced concerns. Now only two teams, the Toronto Blue Jays and Tampa Bay Rays, maintain turf fields, and both are making strides to completely eliminate turf from Major League Baseball.[45] As a result of the negative image, including the increased risk of injury, that surrounds turf, the Toronto Blue Jays and Tampa Bay Rays often struggle to recruit players.[46] The Blue Jays have worked with a leading agricultural school, University of Guelph in Ontario, to achieve the organization's goal of installing a grass outfield by 2018.[47] This past 2016 season, the organization moved one step closer by converting the base path to dirt.[48] They hope to achieve their goal of a grass stadium in a few years after further research has been completed. Studies have not been deemed necessary for statistical support in regards to injury increase and turf because the players' beliefs and observations are viewed with a high level of respect. Major league baseball did not request scientific analysis and data to support the players' thoughts. The organization simply understood that the players' health was a priority and that the top baseball players in the world deserve to play on a safe and well-maintained surface.

The National Football League has also experienced turf issues. More scientific studies have been completed in regards to football injuries sustained on turf compared to baseball. The NFL has the funds to do research and make adjustments to facilities for the benefit of players' health, but alterations have not been made for the complete elimination of turf, as in baseball. However, unlike FIFA, the NFL does everything in their power to put the Super Bowl game on the highest quality of grass.[49] This shows a level of respect for the players' wishes and once again makes it hard to understand why FIFA was unwilling to provide grass for even the championship game. Football players also agree with soccer and baseball players that turf creates weariness and injury. A 2010 player survey found that 69.4 percent of players prefer grass compared to 14.3 percent who prefer an artificial surface.[50] The numbers were overwhelming; 82.4 percent believed the turf contributed to injury, 89.1 percent believed it added to soreness and fatigue, and 89.7 percent believed it resulted in a shorter career.[51] Statistical evidence has been found to support the argument that more injuries occur on turf in comparison to grass. *The American Journal of Sports Medicine* did a systematic review of the knee and ankle sprains in the 2000 and 2009 seasons.[52] The observed injury rate of knee and ankle sprains on turf was 22 percent higher, and ACL sprains 67 percent higher, than the number sustained on grass, and the differences observed were found to be statistically significant.[53] This study continues to add support for the women's case to have the World Cup on grass. Even though these results are from a different sport, they still show that there is a greater risk presented from the turf surface. A systematic review was completed on the current literature studying the risk of ACL injuries on grass and synthetic turf.[54] Four studies conducted with American football cohorts on early-generation turf surfaces, and modern third-generation turf, consisting of 753 ACL injuries, found an increased risk for ACL injuries on turf.[55] Until more definitive scientific research is done for women's soccer, it is the players' opinions versus the organization's decisions; but should the players' bodies not be more valued and treated with a greater level of respect?

Consistent with the players' disapproval across sports, it has come to light that artificial turf, specifically the infill used, is having a devastating effect on goalkeepers nationally. In 2009, a monumental discovery by Amy Griffin, associate head coach for the women's soccer program at the University of Washington, catalyzed the call for additional research when two goalkeepers Griffin knew were diagnosed with non-Hodgkin's lymphoma, a disease that Griffin suspected may have been caused by close contact with synthetic turf material.[56] One of the goalkeepers with whom Griffin is associated spoke on this issue, stating that she believed the issue to be specific to the black pellets that emerge from turf.[57] As a soccer player from Ohio, I played on many indoor and outdoor turf facilities where turf pellets were a constant nuisance. My car floor was scattered with them from my shoes and clothes post-practice, and I often left a trail in my house when I returned home. For goalkeepers, this nuisance is even worse. Goalkeepers must continually dive on the turf, sending pellets into their hair, nose, mouth, and even in their turf-caused skin scrapes. No one thought anything of this situation until Amy Griffin identified 38 American soccer players (34 goalkeepers) who are now diagnosed with forms of blood cancers, such as leukemia and lymphoma.[58] Since NBC's interview with Amy Griffin in October 2014, 203 cases of athletes have now been documented—159 soccer players and 97 goalkeepers.[59] These pellets, called crumb rubber, come from old tires and are the main ingredient for the turf infill, which is composed of mercury, lead, benzene, and arsenic.[60] This can be a toxic combination, especially when the turf is hot during the summer. There are alternative infills, such as cork and coconut fiber, that could be used if comprehensive studies confirm the tire crumb does in fact pose a great health risk.[61] Thankfully, it does appear answers will be provided in the future. After years of silence from the EPA, the government has required the completion of a comprehensive study to determine the potential risk of turf usage.[62] There is no way FIFA could have been ignorant of the health risk turf was presenting.

Yet FIFA chose to remain steadfast in their position that turf is the future and to test their theory at the Women's World Cup.

FIFA continued to present extensive research to justify the decision to play the 2015 World Cup on turf, but the gender discrimination behind such a decision is far too apparent to hide. Ironically, FIFA openly admits in the "future steps" section of *FIFA Quality Concept for Football Turf*, "[FIFA] will always prefer a perfectly manicured grass pitch to an artificial surface,"[63] but in 2015 they chose to hold the most elite soccer competition in the world on turf. Additionally, CSA president Victor Montagliani made the biased comment that if Canada were able to pull off the Women's World Cup, then Canada would be in a good position to host "the big World Cup,"[64] referring to the men's World Cup, years later. This further emphasizes that many wrongly consider women's soccer illegitimate in comparison to men's, a belief that would support FIFA's choice to use the Women's World Cup as a trial run for a turf field. Interestingly enough, even though FIFA remains obsessed with the idea of turf, the France Football Federation, as well as the Korea Football Association, greatly opposes such a decision and confirmed that natural grass will be used in the 2019 Women's World Cup.[65] France received the bid and looks forward to returning the game to the standard and quality that the women deserve. FIFA secretary general Jerome Valcke assured Abbey Wambach that the World Cup would never be played on turf again. As a voice for women's soccer, Wambach responded, "That's a win . . . for me, that's progress."[66]

Against all odds, a positive outcome did arise from the decision to use turf. By providing a clear visual example of field inequality, this debate created the ideal platform to advance the need for change not only on the field but off the field as well. Following the 2015 World Cup, five women from the U.S. national team filed a wage-discrimination complaint with the Equal Employment Opportunity Commission, providing copious amounts of evidence of their unequal wages in comparison to male soccer players.[67] For example, the women received $2 million in earnings while the U.S. men's team, which was eliminated in the sweet 16, took home $9 million.[68] Carli Lloyd, a 12-year member of the U.S. women's team, wrote an essay for the *New York Times* providing further evidence. Lloyd gave a powerful example about the type of World Cup bonuses the men and women receive, explaining that if she were a male U.S. soccer player who had won the World Cup, she would have made $390,000; however, as a woman, she made only $75,000.[69] Furthermore, the men receive $69,000 for merely making the World Cup roster, while the women made only $15,000.[70] The pay inequalities continue like this across the board, since the men, unlike the women, receive bonuses for wins and extra travel money while on the road.

The women have had enough and are ready to forge a change. The argument that is often used to rationalize this pay gap is that women do not receive the same media attention that the men obtain. This counterargument has been shown to be flawed given that the 2015 Women's World Cup championship was the most viewed soccer match in American history. Indeed, the match reached 26.7 million viewers, a viewership that exceeded both the NBA finals and World Series.[71] In addition, following the women's soccer team's notable success, the U.S. Soccer Federation predicts they will make $5 million in profits next year, while the men are predicted to lose $1 million.[72] The women's team is on the rise and has the ammunition to power through this fight.

The women of the U.S. national team filed a gender discrimination complaint not only to highlight the discrimination in soccer but also to emphasize the national need for gender equality across careers. The Senate passed this resolution without debate in the hopes that change for women's soccer would initiate change across the board for all women in the workforce.[73] It does appear that there is a light at the end of this tunnel. The soccer organizations have been called out on their discriminatory actions and now have the opportunity to correct what they have done wrong for so many years. Thankfully, changes are slowly beginning to take effect. Within FIFA, President Joseph Blatter, whose sexism is well documented, resigned and has been replaced by Gianni Infantino, who commented, "The future of soccer belongs to women."[74] FIFA executive member Moya Dodd is also taking a stand and has pushed for a policy mandating that 16.2 percent of the executive FIFA positions must be filled by women.[75] These changes could portend a monumental movement toward gender equality and could provide hope and inspiration for the young girls who look up to these women and aspire to fill their shoes one day. The U.S. soccer team refuses to stop fighting until things are finally equal for those girls of the future. As our nation continues to progress toward gender equality, it is necessary to provide women everywhere with opportunities equal to men's. Using the upcoming Olympic Games and future events as a platform, U.S. national player Becky Sauerbrunn has stated that the U.S. national team is wholeheartedly inspired to continue to provide the strength and belief in the women's program. She commented, "I would like to leave a legacy where we have left the generations below us, whether they want to be soccer players or doctors, to follow that path and believe in it, and fight any obstacles that get in [their] way because all things are possible."[76] This battle may have ignited over the decision to host the 2015 Women's World Cup on turf, but it has evolved into a global symbol and movement for gender equality.

NOTES

1. Robert Wood, "The World's Most Popular Sports," *Topend Sports*, accessed July 5, 2016, http://www.topendsports.com/world/lists/popular-sport/index.htm.

2. "FIFA The Big Count 2006," Fédération Internationale De Football Association, last modified May 31, 2007, http://www.fifa.com/mm/document/fifafacts/bcoffsurv/bigcount.statspackage_7024.pdf.

3. Ibid.

4. Laken Litman, "Alex Morgan on Why Artificial Turf Is Tough for Players," *USA Today*, last modified October 15, 2014, http://www.usatoday.com/story/sports/soccer/2014/10/15/alex-morgan-us-women-artificial-turf-world-cup/17295011/.

5. "Sustainability—Diversity and Anti-Discrimination—FIFA.com," Fédération Internationale De Football Association, accessed November 15, 2015, http://www.fifa.com/sustainability/anti-discrimination.html.

6. Elizabeth Mitchell, "Soccer Wars," *Daily News*, last modified March 30, 2016, http://interactive.nydailynews.com/2016/03/how-us-soccer-mistreats-world-cup-winning-womens-national-team/.

7. Ibid.

8. Sophie Vick, "FIFA: The World Cup Should Be Played on Grass," *Coworker.org*, accessed June 3, 2016, https://www.coworker.org/petitions/fifa-the-world-cup-should-be-played-on-natural-grass.

9. Juliet Macur, "Inaction and Inequality on Women's World Cup Turf Issue," *New York Times*, last modified December 4, 2014, http://www.nytimes.com/2014/12/05/sports/soccer/inaction-and-inequality-on-womens-world-cup-turf-issue.html.

10. Mitchell, "Soccer Wars."

11. Fédération Internationale De Football Association, "FIFA Quality Concept for Football Turf," *FIFA* (2015): 23, accessed June 10, 2016, http://www.fifa.com/mm/document/afdeveloping/pitchequip/fqc_football_turf_folder_342.pdf.

12. Ibid., 29.

13. Ibid., 6–10.

14. FIFA Fact Sheet, "Overview of All the FIFA World Cup Host Countries 1930–2022," *FIFA*, http://www.fifa.com/mm/document/fifafacts/mencompovw/51/99/03/133485-factsheet-fifahostcountriesoverview1930-2022.pdf.

15. The website https://weatherspark.com was used for info on both Qatar and Russia.

16. "Average Annual Temperatures for Canadian Cities," *Current Results*, accessed July 6, 2016, https://www.currentresults.com/Weather/Canada/Cities/temperature-annual-average.php.

17. FIFA, "FIFA Quality Concept," 35.

18. Ibid.

19. Alexandria Greco, "Female Soccer Players File Discrimination Suit Over Women's World Cup," *CBS News*, last modified October 1, 2014, http://www.cbsnews.com/news/female-soccer-players-file-discrimination-suit-over-womens-world-cup/.

20. Kevin Baxter, "Players Try Not to Sweat It Over Hot Artificial Turf at World Cup," *LA Times*, last modified June 10, 2015, http://www.latimes.com/sports/soccer/la-sp-usa-soccer-notes-20150611-story.html.

21. Rebecca Rushton, "Matildas Highlight Issue of Heat Transfer from Synthetic Pitches at the 2015 Women's World Cup (Canada)," *Blister Prevention*, accessed June 30, 2016, http://www.blisterprevention.com.au/blister-blog/heat-transfer-synthetic-pitches-world-cup.

22. Greco, "Female Discrimination World Cup."

23. J. Ekstrand, T. Timpka, and M. Hägglund, "Risk of Injury in Elite Football Played on Artificial Turf versus Natural Grass: A Prospective Two-Cohort Study," *British Journal of Sports Medicine* 40, no. 12 (2006): 975–80.

24. Colin W. Fuller, Randall W. Dick, Jill Corlette, and Rosemary Schmalz, "Comparison of the Incidence, Nature and Cause of Injuries Sustained on Grass and New Generation Artificial Turf by Male and Female Football Players. Part 1: Match Injuries," *British Journal of Sports Medicine* 41 (2007): 20–26.

25. J. Ekstrand, M. Hägglund, and C. W. Fuller, "Comparison of Injuries Sustained on Artificial Turf and Grass by Male and Female Elite Football Players," *Scandinavian Journal of Medicine and Science in Sports* 21 (2011): 824–32.

26. Justin M. Wright and David Webner, "Playing Field Issues in Sports Medicine," *American College of Sports Medicine* 9 (2010): 129–33.

27. Rachel Martin, "Soccer Players Sue Over Proposed Turf Field for Women's World Cup," *NPR*, last modified October 2, 2014, http://www.npr.org/2014/10/02/353312770/soccer-players-sue-over-proposed-turf-field-for-womens-world-cup.

28. Monica Alba, "U.S. Soccer Star Abby Wambach: Playing on Turf a 'Nightmare,'" *NBC News*, last modified June 9, 2015, http://www.nbcnews.com/storyline/artificial-turf-debate/us-soccer-star-abby-wambach-playing-turf-nightmare-n371906.

29. Ibid.

30. "FIFA Women's World Cup Prozone Study," *FIFA.com*, last modified November 13, 2015, http://resources.fifa.com/mm/document/tournament/competition/02/73/25/69/fifa_womens_world_cup_prozone_study_final_en_neutral.pdf.

31. Ibid.

32. Constantine Poulos, John Gallucci, William H. Gage, Joseph Baker, Sebastian Buitrago, and Alison K. Macpherson. "The Perceptions of Professional Soccer Players on the Risk of Injury from Competition and Training on Natural Grass and 3rd Generation Artificial Turf," *BMC Sports Science, Medicine and Rehabilitation* 6, no. 1 (2014): 1.

33. Helena Andersson, "Elite Football on Artificial Turf versus Natural Grass: Movement Patterns, Standards, and Player Impressions," *Journal of Sports Science* 26, no. 2 (2008): 113–22.

34. Rocco Di Michelle, Anastasio Di Renzo, Sandro Ammazzalorso, and Franco Merni, "Comparison of Physiological Responses to an Incremental Running Test on Treadmill, Natural Grass, and Synthetic Turf in Young Soccer Player," *Journal of Strength and Conditioning Research* (2009): 1–7.

35. Ibid.

36. FIFA, "Prozone Study."

37. Ibid.

38. Ryan McMorrow, "Why Astro-turf no longer Belongs in Baseball," *Baseball Essential*, last modified December 21, 2014, http://www.baseballessential.com/news/2014/12/21/why-astro-turf-no-longer-belongs-in-baseball/.

39. Kevin Baxter, "When It Comes to Grass Baseball No Longer Fakes It," *LA Times*, last modified September 13, 2013, http://www.latimes.com/sports/la-sp-0912-baseball-astro-turf-20130912-story.html.

40. Ibid.
41. Ibid.
42. David Waldstein, "Toronto Blue Jays Take a Big Step: All-Dirt Basepaths," *New York Times*, last modified March 12, 2016, http://www.nytimes.com/2016/03/13/sports/baseball/toronto-blue-jays-take-a-big-step-all-dirt-basepaths.html?_r=0.
43. Ibid.
44. Ibid.
45. McMorrow, "Why Astro-turf No Longer Belongs in Baseball."
46. Ibid.
47. Walstein, "Toronto Blue Jays Take a Big Step: All-Dirt Basepaths."
48. Ibid.
49. Ken Belson, "Cue the New Sod: N.F.L. Plays Super Bowl on Its Own Turf," *New York Times*, last modified February 2, 2016, http://www.nytimes.com/2016/02/03/sports/football/super-bowl-50-nfl-turf-levi-stadium.html?_r=0.
50. Ron Hall, "NFL Players Say Grass Still Best," *Landscape Management*, last modified February 2, 2011, http://landscapemanagement.net/nfl-players-say-grass-still-best/.
51. Ibid.
52. Elliot Hershman, "An Analysis of Specific Lower Extremity Injury Rates on Grass and Field Turf Playing Surfaces in National Football League Games," *American Journal of Sports Medicine*, September 12, 2012, http://www.drlintner.com/wp-content/uploads/2012/09/Hershman-Turf-NFL-AJSM-Paper2.pdf.
53. Ibid.
54. G. C. Balaz, "Risk of Anterior Cruciate Ligament Injury in Athletes on Synthetic Playing Surfaces: A Systematic Review," *American Journal of Sports Medicine* 43, no. 7 (July 2015): 1798–804, http://www.ncbi.nlm.nih.gov/pubmed/25164575.
55. Ibid.
56. Hannah, Rappleye, "How Safe Is the Artificial Turf Your Child Plays On?," *NBC News*, last modified October 8, 2014, http://www.nbcnews.com/storyline/artificial-turf-debate/how-safe-artificial-turf-your-child-plays-n220166.
57. Ibid.
58. Ibid.
59. Nancy Alderman, "State Underplays Dangers of Synthetic Turf Fields," *EHHI*, last modified February 21, 2016, http://www.ehhi.org/turf/state_underplays2016.shtml.
60. Rappleye, "How Safe Artificial Turf Child Plays On."
61. Ibid.
62. Mike Ozanian, "Professor Identifies Cancer-Causing Chemicals in Artificial Turf," *Forbes*, last modified March 28, 2016, http://www.forbes.com/sites/mikeozanian/2015/10/26/epa-ignores-congress-and-nbc-queries-about-cancer-and-artifical-turf/#336231334538.
63. FIFA, "FIFA Quality Concept," 99.
64. Hampton Dellinger, "The Grass Ceiling: How to Conquer Inequality in Women's Soccer," *The Atlantic*, last modified July 5, 2015, http://www.theatlantic.com/entertainment/archive/2015/07/womens-soccer-world-cup-fifa-lawsuit/397592/.
65. Neil Davidson. "Turf for Canada, Grass for 2019 World Cup," *The Leader*, last modified November 6, 2014, http://www.surreyleader.com/national/sport/281852101.html.

66. Sophie Vick, "FIFA: The World Cup Should Be Played on Grass."

67. Andrew Das, "Top Female Players Accuse U.S. Soccer of Wage Discrimination," *New York Times*, last modified March 31, 2016, http://www.nytimes.com/2016/04/01/sports/soccer/uswnt-us-women-carli-lloyd-alex-morgan-hope-solo-complain.html?_r=0.

68. Andrew Das, "Pay Disparity in U.S.? It's Complicated," *New York Times*, last modified April 21, 2016, http://www.nytimes.com/2016/04/22/sports/soccer/usmnt-uswnt-soccer-equal-pay.html.

69. Carli Lloyd, "Carli Lloyd: Why I'm Fighting for Equal Pay," *New York Times*, last modified April 10, 2016, http://www.nytimes.com/2016/04/11/sports/soccer/carli-lloyd-why-im-fighting-for-equal-pay.html.

70. Ibid.

71. Richard Sandomir, "Women's World Cup Final Was Most-Watched Soccer Game in United States History," *New York Times*, last modified July 6, 2015, http://www.nytimes.com/2015/07/07/sports/soccer/womens-world-cup-final-was-most-watched-soccer-game-in-united-states-history.html.

72. Das, "Pay Disparity in U.S.?"

73. Travis Waldron, "Senate Passes Equal Pay Resolution for U.S. Women's Team Soccer Stars," *Huffington Post*, last modified May 26, 2016, http://www.huffingtonpost.com/entry/womens-soccer-equal-pay-senate_us_57472042e4b0dacf7ad42b01.

74. Mitchell, "Soccer Wars."

75. Ibid.

76. Ibid.

9

Invisible Pelotons: Women's Cycling and the Boundaries of Professionalism

Diana Tracy Cohen

INTRODUCTION

The start of a professional cycling race is quite a spectacle. Athletes anxiously roll their front tires to the edge of the starting line, their bodies poised for action. Competitors delicately measure the distance to the white start line on the road, pressing as close as possible without crossing it. The starting gun disrupts the nervous silence. Hundreds of sharp clicks fill the air—the unmistakable sound of riders pressing their cycling shoes into clipless pedal systems. A rainbow of colored jerseys quickly passes by, too fast to pick out any single rider in the crowded blur of athletes. This is the opening ritual that I have come to anticipate over my many years of observing races. Strangely, the start of the 2013 Tour of Languedoc Roussillon race looked nothing like this familiar scene. With only a few minutes before the start of the race, the professional women's field came to a standstill just behind the starting line. Given the race's significance in the annual racing calendar, the scene was extraordinary. Even with precious team ranking points at stake, not a single rider was perched upon her bike. Instead, athletes sat on the hot concrete, hands firmly propping up their delicate carbon machines as the shocking reality of the situation set in. The women were staging a sit-down protest in response to a race that had descended into managerial chaos. A political statement was being made—*treat us like professional athletes*.

For the casual racing fan, this scene was confusing. The contrast between expectations and reality could not be further apart. Where were the bodies in motion? What explained the dearth of racing sights and sounds? Where was the action? For those more fully entrenched in professional cycling culture, there was more activity than meets the eye. What appeared on its face to be inaction was, in reality, a critical turning point. Women are often treated like second-class citizens in their own sport, making this a moment of collective resistance that elicited conflicting emotions—disappointment and empowerment, sadness and hope. Allies for the athletes were proud to see the women taking a stand. At the same time, these same allies questioned how the sport had reached a point that necessitated such a protest.

The unrest leading up to this protest was no secret among those in the professional cycling world. Initially, the 2013 Tour of Languedoc Roussillon, an important race for earning points toward international rankings, was cancelled less than a week before the race—long after teams had committed time and allocated precious funds for traveling to the remote event location in France. The race director blamed a last-minute withdrawal of essential sponsorship commitments. With squads already at the venues, team managers found themselves in a precarious situation. Was it worth spending additional time and money to wait for a potential new sponsor? Additionally, race organizers had yet to pay local police their due deposit, meaning that safety precautions typically expected at a professional race—such as closing the course to vehicular traffic—could no longer be guaranteed.

Even if a new sponsor were to emerge, would the safety of the athletes be in jeopardy? With team managers angered and athletes no longer enthused about competing, several squads returned to their respective countries. Leaving was viewed as a resounding statement of disapproval to race organizers all over the world. Professional Dutch rider Iris Slappendel, representing one of the teams that withdrew from the competition, captured the sadness of the situation in the following tweet: "For the sake of women's cycling, it's sad, but after a day of uncertainty we decided to leave and not start tomorrow. #RaboLivGiant #Languedoc."[1] Thanks to the acquisition of a last-minute sponsor, the race was reinstated mere hours before the starting gun was originally scheduled to go off. Athletes remaining at the venue organized the starting-line sit-down protest to bring visibility to what they regarded as "inhumane treatment."

The title of this chapter—"Invisible Pelotons"—holds deep social significance. One can think of a cycling peloton as the main grouping in a bike race. It is best defined as the physical location in which most of the athletes are situated, with the pack providing protection and a sense of "weness" in a niche sport landscape. Given the size of the grouping, pelotons should be highly visible to the sport's key stakeholders, such as governing bodies, the media, current and potential sponsors, and spectators. My work challenges this notion of visibility, arguing that many of these athletes are caught between the elite amateur and professional athletic worlds—a space that I refer to as the *professional-amateur margin*. In addition to introducing the professional-amateur margin concept, I identify three policies within cycling that trap elite women in this space. These policies are deeply rooted in gendered politics, providing disparate opportunities for men and women. I argue that cycling's governing bodies are complicit in the undervaluing of women's athletic efforts, perpetuating gendered hierarchies within the professional ranks. Finally, I suggest that professionalism in the sport is intimately linked to hegemonic masculine practices, with these practices being feverously protected by cycling's own policies. This chapter untangles these concerns, identifying the social and political realities that push elite female racers to the fringe of their own sporting world.

THEORETICAL UNDERPINNINGS

Sport, Power, and Gender Relations

Before immersing ourselves into the lives of female professional cyclists, it is valuable to contextualize this research and highlight the powerful and privileged place that sport holds in society. Each individual sporting context has its own unique culture, yet common undercurrents are shared. This is because sport serves as a mirror to the society in which it is embedded.[2] Racism, materialism, classism, homophobia, and sexism, among others, are prominent norms and values displayed in sport.[3] Vital to this study of female cyclists, sport also plays a critical role in both the establishment and perpetuation of gendered social norms. Lance Armstrong has become a household name, but few people have been exposed to the other Armstrong of cycling—Kristin. Kristin Armstrong is one of the most dominant athletes in professional cycling history. She is a four-time Olympian, winning gold medals at the individual time trial in both the 2008 and 2012 Games. Her highly decorated career also includes two world time-trial championships and first-place finishes in numerous world tours; yet, as a woman, she is an unknown even among many self-proclaimed cycling enthusiasts. This lack of familiarity is not incidental. It is a consequence of the larger power structure in sporting culture—a culture that both reflects and perpetuates deep-rooted sexism and patriarchal relations of power.

Sport and Gendered Practices

Many studies in the early sociology of sport literature describe how the institution of sport has become a central site for the production of gender.[4] It is a space for people to interact with others and demonstrate gendered bodily practices.[5] Athletes who embrace hegemonic masculine practices, such as violence or physical domination, are idolized, as are the sports in which they participate. A prime example from the cycling world is Lance Armstrong, a well-known name even before his performance-enhancing drug scandal. His widespread fame stemmed from sheer domination of opponents. He was believed to have won the Tour de France a record seven consecutive times (1999–2005), until the titles were stripped in 2012. As a cancer survivor, he was viewed as a true Ironman—someone who achieved world-class success while overcoming a crippling disease. Prior to his performance-enhancing drug usage confession, his nickname within cycling circles was "The Boss," reflective of his masculine domination in the profession. This athletic prowess resulted in highly lucrative sponsorship contracts and widespread positive media attention.

The valuing of gendered practices is not limited to those demonstrated by particular individuals; society also celebrates specific types of athletic competition. These spheres of competition are feverishly protected, serving as "reserved domains" for masculine play.[6] In sport, this power and influence is closely associated with spaces where we see the production of hegemonic masculinity, such as the football field.[7] By engaging in "manhood acts," actions that reaffirm one's status as a biological male, men perpetuate their dominance using the world's most celebrated sporting arenas.[8] Competing in cycling's most prestigious multistage tours is a prime example. Riding for 3,535 kilometers (2,196.5 miles) across 21 stages, as riders did in the 2016 Tour de France, brings credibility to the presentation of a masculine self.[9] It is not coincidental that, despite their continued lobbying efforts, elite women are prohibited from entering many of cycling's grand tours—including the full edition of Le Tour. Women conquering an identical athletic feat would invalidate the treasured "manhood act" label that participation in Le Tour represents. As my analysis reveals, cycling's own governing bodies cocoon the sport's most treasured manhood acts via gendered policies on the distance that athletes can ride, the amount of consecutive days athletes can ride, and the number of athletes permitted on a team.

Through the gendering of sport practices, political and social hierarchies develop. Having a golden standard of masculinity, known as hegemonic masculinity, serves as critical informant of these hierarchical developments. This is because, most fundamentally, not all masculinities are treated as equal.[10] In order to create a hegemonic standard, society must have subordinate masculinities for comparison.[11] Femininity, and all who embrace it, are viewed as subordinate. The result of this gendered hierarchy is that women, as well as certain men, face oppression and powerlessness.[12] As Mary Louise Adams denotes in her sharp analysis of figure skating, sport is particularly powerful in perpetuating the social devaluing of effeminacy.[13] My work exposes how professional female cyclists, sidelined in the cycling world, are overtly effeminized. Numerous study participants described how their own governing body treats their athletic efforts as "a hobby," with their races characterized as a "sideshow to the real race"—that is, the event featuring their male counterparts. This reality pushes professional women, both physically and emotionally, to the fringe of their own sport.

Situating Women in Sport

Given the intricate connection between sport, masculinity, and power, history leaves women in a very precarious situation. With sport historically viewed as a male domain—an institution designed for men by men—where do women fit in? Understanding the growth of females in sport is not as simple as saying "add women and stir." With the rise of feminist scholarship, we now have a more holistic picture of how the influx of women into sporting environments has shaped the reproduction of this historically male institution. In an effort pioneered by the contributors of Michael Messner and Donald Sabo's edited volume, we benefit from a more varied and comprehensive awareness about systems of power and domination.[14]

One of the greatest insights recognized through the advent of such literature is that although women have successfully breached many men's sports, they have done so in a particular way. This reflects the notion that there are certain social norms surrounding sport and women's place in it—a fact that leads to the gendering of athleticism and competition. This is where the social construction of "men's sports" and "girls' sports" becomes critical. Feminine, or "girls' sports," are ones that focus on qualities such as balance, flexibility, and agility.[15] Labeling activities as "manly sports" or "girls' sports" reaffirms connections between masculine practices (those activities seen in "manly sports") and nonmasculine practices (those seen in "girls' sports"). In perpetuating a culture of difference, feminine characteristics—be they demonstrated by men or women—are devalued.

Different versions of the same game also reinforce gendered expectations. These expectations are evident in the way that each respective version is played and allow for the protection of privileged spaces where gendered practices unfold. For instance, Nancy Theberge discusses critical distinctions between men's and women's versions of ice hockey: Men are permitted to check and women are not.[16] Descriptions of women's hockey accentuate finesse over physicality. The very definition of finesse, to do something in a subtle and delicate manner, is often associated with less desirable forms of sport. By contrast, descriptions of men's games emphasize athletic qualities often revered in sport, such as violence, aggression, and excessive physical contact. It is not that women are incapable of checking, fighting, or boarding; rather, these activities are not deemed socially acceptable when performed by women. By prohibiting actions such as fighting and checking, punishable with harsh and decisive penalties, these manhood acts are reserved exclusively for the men's version of the game. Throughout this chapter, I demonstrate how these gendered constructions of difference manifest in cycling. I articulate how the sport's governing policies create two very different professional landscapes—men's cycling and women's cycling—with the former being politically privileged. Drawing on three specific sport policies, I show how the boundaries of professionalism in cycling are closely guarded via gendered policies, with women being pushed to the margins.

METHODOLOGY

Interviews

Study informants and recruitment

Cycling is a multibillion-dollar industry that includes many different entities—professional teams, sport-governing bodies, local shops, gear and nutrition manufacturers, media outlets, and, of course, athletes. From a period lasting from January 2011 through July 2016, I conducted 45 in-depth interviews that lasted between 45 and 140 minutes. Study participants were selected based on their ability to illuminate the main research foci. I asked questions about habits in training and racing, views toward cycling's governing body, women's involvement in professional cycling, and related topics. Individuals interviewed included amateur and professional competitors, bike shop owners, race directors, sport-governing body representatives, professional team managers, and both former and current professional team employees. Both men and women were interviewed, with sensitivity toward racial and ethnic sample diversity. More specifically, six men and 39 women were interviewed, with five study participants being racial minorities. Pseudonyms were used throughout this work to protect the identity of study participants.

Study participants were recruited in one of three ways. First, they were recruited on location at various cycling events. These events included a mixture of elite "invitation only" races and smaller "open field" competitions. Second, participants were recruited via the Internet. I targeted select Facebook groups and online discussion forums that I knew to be frequented by professional athletes. Facebook organization pages such as those for the Women's Cycling Association and various professional teams were also fruitful resources. A recruitment posting was issued making a call for participants. Individuals then expressed their interest in participating in the study by sending me an e-mail. The Internet turned out to be a rich recruiting source, giving my research visibility to professional athletes, coaches, and team directors all over the world. Finally, participants were recruited through snowball sampling. Women's cycling can be described as a small and relatively tight-knit community. This is particularly true within the professional ranks. After the conclusion of each interview, I asked participants if they knew of any other individuals who might inform the study. Snowball sampling was particularly valuable at the start of the project. Professional athletes helped to put me in touch with other members of their squad, as well as their coaches and team employees. As a recreational cyclist, I also drew on two personal contacts, both of whom were competitive racers, to help with initial connections.

Observations

This work is supplemented by personal observations of athletes in their native environments. This included watching pre- and postrace routines as well as interactions with other athletes, fans, and members of the press. These opportunities gave me the chance to see team dynamics as they unfolded. I was also able to observe valuable details about each venue. This included watching the behaviors of spectators, sponsors, race directors, officials, race announcers, and others in the cycling environment. In some instances, these observations provided invaluable opportunities to see both male and female competitors operating in the same sporting contexts. At the third stage of the 2014 Tour of Utah, the men and women utilized the same race venue. The courses themselves were not identical; however, the race set-up allowed me to draw insightful comparisons. For example, I was able to observe the parking areas for both the men's and women's squads. The differences in team vehicles were revealing. The men's teams used beautiful RVs. The women's teams used pick-up trucks and unmarked personal vehicles. Not a single RV was present on the women's side of the parking lot. Of additional value was the ability to observe the conclusion of the men's and women's races. Approximately 45 minutes separated the finish of the two fields. This time gap allowed for me to not just observe but *feel* each race as it unfolded. I took detailed notes of the spectators' reactions, the tone and language used by announcers, and the media attention for both the men and women.

Attending events also allowed me to conduct interviews on location. Although shorter, these interviews gave me a chance to capture participants' body language. I noted important nonverbal cues, such as the crossing of arms and shaking of heads. More critically, I could see the participant reacting to his or her sport environment in real time. Interviewing professional athletes just before the historic running of an inaugural women's tour is not something that can be replicated. I had the opportunity to ask competitors how they were feeling minutes before this historic event. Some women were overcome with excitement and nervousness. Lisa, a seasoned competitor, relayed: "I am not usually nervous before a competition, but today I am. I am a part of history. I want to race well and make this event a success." These authentic and uninhibited emotions may not have been fully captured had the interview been conducted at a later point in time.

Analytical Approach

Analysis of the in-depth interviews and observations utilized a grounded theory approach.[17] As opposed to exploring specific hypotheses, grounded theory allows researchers to investigate topics without any preconceptions.[18] It is through this process that the key themes presented in the analysis were revealed. Data was subject to multiple rounds of coding. An initial round of open coding gave me a general sense of the themes that were prevalent in the data.[19] These codes served as the basis for the emergence of more sophisticated concepts. I reviewed and collapsed concepts until key themes, or categories, emerged. Open coding of the interview transcripts was crucial for the illumination of repeating concepts. Each paragraph was coded with important notations, including what the respondent is talking about, adjectives that describe the phenomenon, and the like. Memos were also kept on the side for additional information. Aa an integral part of grounded theory analysis, I also wrote interview notes at the conclusion of each interview.[20] Memos were broken down into three categories—theoretical, methodological, and personal. Careful crafting of these memos allowed me to maintain an up-to-date "audit trail" of key decisions regarding the project.[21] Using the coding notes and memos together, findings were sorted into common themes and concepts.

ANALYSIS

The Professional-Amateur Margin

Women of the professional peloton are seemingly invisible within their own sporting world—as are the issues they face. Part of this invisibility stems from the fact that women often find themselves in a space of professional ambiguity. Many described a life where they are trapped in the gray area between elite amateur and professional-level athletic status. Using grounded theory analysis, I identify this ambiguous place as the *professional-amateur margin*.

I define this area as a space where athletes race as professionals but are treated as amateurs by key sport stakeholders (namely race directors, the media, sponsors, and elite decision-makers in their own sport). It is a space where the expectations and realities pertaining to professional athletic life diverge. Specific to my study, this margin does not recognize female cyclists for the professional athletes they are; their unique skills and attributes are not celebrated.

What leads athletes to fall within the professional-amateur margin? To answer this question, we must dissect the structural and cultural characteristics, as well as policies, of each particular sporting environment. To thoroughly do so for the sport of cycling requires a book-length analysis. For the purposes of this chapter, I limit the scope to the three most prominently discussed policies that emerged from my interviews. I argue that all three policies have a significant role in anchoring women to the professional-amateur margin. Throughout my analysis, I detail how these policies of the sport perpetuate gendered differences in elite riders, with women being treated as "lesser." The three policies are as follows:

1. *Minimum wage policy*—the international governing body of cycling offers a guaranteed minimum wage to men but not to women. In a society where money and athletic professionalism are often viewed as synonymous, the inability of most female cyclists to support themselves through cycling undermines their professional status.
2. *Professional license policy*—USA Cycling offers a professional license for men but not for women. On the international level, teams, not individual athletes, are eligible for a professional license. Women are denied the "rite of passage" of formally earning a professional license, an important ritual that helps legitimize their status as professional athletes.
3. *Race distance and duration policy*—the international governing body of cycling has different distance and duration limits for men and women. The limits placed on women resemble those currently applied to junior riders, classifying professional women's athletic abilities commensurate to that of young boys.

For many of my study participants, falling in the professional-amateur margin leads to difficult emotional conundrums. On the one hand, many athletes spoke with a resounding sense of gratitude for the opportunity to ride at a highly competitive level. However, beneath the surface of this gratitude was a desire for greater equality in opportunity. Respondents yearned for a guaranteed minimum wage, dedicated racing spaces, the opportunity to race in some of the world's largest tours, and a greater voice in the sport's governing body—all aspects of the sport that they saw their male counterparts as having. I argue that the construction of two distinct sporting landscapes reaffirms a hierarchy where men are seen (and treated) as more important than women and where masculine acts are protected.[22] The tide may be turning slowly, but professional cycling still reflects and perpetuates society's system of female oppression and powerlessness.[23]

Cycling's Minimum Wage Policy

Defining the sporting "professional"

What constitutes being a "professional?" *Dictionary.com* suggests that a professional is someone who follows an occupation "as a means of livelihood or for gain."[24] *Merriam-Webster* specifies the word "sport" in their definition, proposing that a professional is someone who is "paid to participate in a sport or activity."[25] Social construction of the term "professional" usually aligns with a perception of monetary payoff. This is particularly true in sport, where the inking of hyperinflated contracts makes headlines on a weekly basis. Payment is a primary reason in society for idolizing the social status of the professional athlete. The potential for money and fame, all in exchange for playing a "game," produces a job that many fantasize about.

The women of the peloton offer a significant challenge to the cultural conception of the term "professional." According to the rules of Union Cycliste International (UCI, cycling's international governing body), whereas a minimum salary is required for male professional riders, teams are under no obligation to offer equivalent compensation to female athletes. As a result, very few women in the professional peloton earn a livable wage from racing. Andrea described receiving the equivalent of $3,107 for her first professional contract. Furthermore, while she had her race entry fees and travel costs covered by the team, several riding-related expenses were not paid. She expanded upon these sentiments:

> The most recent salary I have been offered is somewhere in the range of about $5,000, so I don't really consider that to be a salary. It doesn't cover really food, let alone lodging and the health insurance to cover your, I don't know, deductible fees for a [bike] crash that you'll probably be in. So that's not a substantial income to really cover all the expenses. Many people end up having to rely on parents or spouses when cycling on that level.

According to an Ernst & Young study released in 2012, some top-level professional male cyclists earn more than $3 million a year, with estimated male salaries averaging just below $300,000 for those elite athletes. By comparison, top-level female professional cyclists earn an average of $22,413.[26] Those professionals, one prominent cycling reporter suggests, are "the lucky ones."[27] Put another way, the "lucky" female athletes make $16,809 less than the guaranteed minimum salary for men riding on a UCI professional team—a figure that stood at $39,222 in 2012.[28] In reality, the salary discrepancy is even wider than that. The potential race winnings for women are often a fraction of that offered to their male counterparts, even when competing at the same venue. As a result, many elite female competitors resort to financing their own professional athletic career, often spending thousands of dollars per year to race.

Self-financing a professional career

Two pathways emerged as ways that female riders made financial ends meet. First, as mentioned by Andrea, numerous participants cited living with parents or being supported by a working spouse. This route often combined employment in a flexible part-time job, such as coaching or personal training. Leslie, a former world champion, explained:

> You need to have all your financial ducks in a row in order to last a long time in the women's cycling world. You have to have a husband you can live off of. You have to have parents that will let you live at home. You need someone else to help support you, or you need to have a job, like I luckily had, that will support you. And then maybe, I would say my career was 10 years. I think that was good. But wouldn't it be great if it was 20? Or even 25? I could actually have a retirement plan and get paid to do what I love to do.

Kristie echoed this sentiment: "My husband is the one who makes all of the money, and I make a little bit." Lisa, a highly decorated rider with an advanced professional degree, concurred: "I'm not going to lie; if it wasn't for the support of my family and husband, there's no way I'd be able to do what I'm doing. I would have to work full time." Lisa supplemented her income by working part time in a flexible job.

As a second pathway to financial sustainability, some athletes attempt to juggle professional racing with full-time careers. These study participants served as nurses, professors, property managers, and doctors, among other occupations. With many women coming to professional racing later in life, they had already established trajectories toward high-powered careers. This is evidenced by the fact that the majority of study participants held advanced degrees. Brianna described this phenomenon in saying, "I think it's the reason the women's peloton is a lot older in the U.S. than in other countries—and much more highly educated. Almost every woman I know that I race against who's over 22 has at least a bachelor's degree. Tons of us have advanced degrees. There are a few with doctoral degrees." Lucy elaborated on the reasoning for this late-to-sport phenomenon, describing how "most of the women will have come to cycling late simply because they've had to focus on things like careers and education because there is no long-term financial future in cycling for them."

Men were viewed as having the opportunity to earn a sustainable income as professionals, but women were not. This lack of opportunity injected what many study participants described as a type of "realism" into their career trajectories and their relationship with sport. Victoria painted a vivid picture:

> There are a lot more opportunities for men. There's also a lot more incentive to going the distance for men; there's a lot more money to be made. Women's cycling is growing, but not at the rate I believe it should, simply because of money. It takes a metric shit ton of time and sacrifice for not a lot a payout. So most women have a job on the side or are going to school on the side. With training, racing, working, schooling, there's not much time left. Because of this, the numbers are smaller on the women's side, simply because not everyone can afford the lifestyle. For men, there are more men because they are able to make the money and be able to commit.

Throughout my interviews, this sentiment was resounding. The dearth of financial opportunity, perpetuated by the absence of a guaranteed minimum wage, severely hinders women's pursuit of a racing career. Employee rights are systematically denied to women, socially constructing a gendered "reserve domain" in cycling.[29]

Earning the "Professional" Title

Whereas the international cycling governing body is responsible for the sport's minimum wage policy, the gendering of opportunity is equally evident on a regional scale. Each country has its own cycling governing body. Within the United States, this entity is known as USA Cycling. USA Cycling establishes rider categories and determines licensing structure within the country. Compounding the challenges for elite women seeking professional recognition are the different licensing structures dictated for professional men and women by USA Cycling's governing body. Many study participants lamented specifically the fact that USA Cycling does not offer a professional license to women. Such contradiction in licensing practices plays a substantial role in trapping women in the professional-amateur margin. This is because, most fundamentally, such a gendered policy reaffirms the existence of separate landscapes in the world of cycling, where women are viewed as "lesser."

With no professional designation for women, USA Cycling denies female American racers an important "rite of passage" that their male counterparts enjoy. Further, the inability to obtain this particular title means that reaching the "professional" distinction becomes more of an amorphous phenomenon for elite women. When asked whether they classified themselves as professionals, many study participants struggled to answer. The question was met with long pauses, drawn-out "ums," and multiple changing of positions. With the absence of an official designation, study participants were challenged to recognize what defined a female cycling professional. Numerous study participants referenced reaching "that level," without actually defining what that threshold meant. In describing what she thought constituted a professional, Susan pointed to reaching a "competitive level":

> I don't think necessarily you have to be paid to be a pro . . . I think once you are at that competitive level, once you are at that top level. There is no further to go, so you are a pro. Women's racing in the States, you actually don't have a pro license, only an international pro license. So if you are in the U.S., you don't have to carry a license. Only the men do, which is something most people don't realize as well. So, technically my license doesn't say pro, but I am racing with these pro women whose [international team] license does say pro, and I'm just as competitive. So, I think once you are actually at that top competitive level, you can't go any further.

Mike, an avid cyclist and women's cycling supporter, also echoed the focus on competitive achievement level. When asked how he defined the word "professional," he replied:

> When you make it to the level. I mean, I think when you are racing at this level, you are a professional. I think a lot of people define professional as getting paid for it, but if you are racing and putting in time, an athlete like this, it's an all-day lifestyle. I mean, we hosted a couple of riders [for an upcoming race] and we got in late Sunday night and there was bananas, yogurt, oatmeal, and my wife was like, oh, look at this food, you eat so healthy, I mean, that's their life.

Looking at the highest level of the sport, the international sphere, obtaining a professional license is similarly elusive. At the international (UCI) level, teams, not individual athletes, are awarded a "professional" designation. In 2016, 40 teams held the UCI professional designation—27 from Europe, 2 from Asia, 10 from the Americas, and 1 from Oceania. Kendra described how teams were required to pay the UCI $30,000 to be awarded this designation, a fee that she identified as "a major expense for most female team budgets. It's money going in the wrong direction." Instead of being spent on athlete development, that $30,000 is paid directly to the UCI. The ability for teams to buy the designation comes at a steep cost.

Race Duration and Distance Policies

Finally, study participants also attributed reduced race duration and distance policies for marginalizing women cyclists. The rules of cycling's international governing body stipulate that female athletes are limited in race distances (number of kilometers cycled per day), race length (number of consecutive days that an event can last), and the number of athletes who can ride on a team.[30] With women's squads featuring fewer athletes than men's teams, each individual rider is responsible for doing more work during a race. Fewer athletes are available to assist with pace setting. The consequences of this is that each cyclist is responsible for setting the team's riding tempo for longer durations of time, accelerating the level of fatigue each athlete is subjected to. Additionally, the race distance and duration limits placed on women resemble those currently applied to junior riders, classifying women's athletic abilities commensurate to that of young boys. These antiquated policies make women ineligible to compete in most of cycling's major tours held around the world, including the full course of the Tour de France.

Study participants described the UCI race duration and distance limitations as "silly," "stupid," and "antiquated," among other adjectives. Further, numerous athletes described the feeling of being denied professional challenges due to these policies. When asked if she felt that women could complete the full Tour de France route, Veronica elaborated:

> I think that women have the capability to do it. I think that the hard thing is the day after day [riding], but why not give the women the professional challenge? If properly trained, I know there's a lot of women that have that capability. And so why limit? Why not give us a chance?

Several study participants mentioned a small group of women who ride the full Tour de France route in advance of the men's arrival. Charlotte explained:

> For the past couple of years there's been a small group who've ridden the exact route of the Tour de France. The same exact route, the same days, not racing, but have done it the day before or the day after or something like that. Yeah, and like eight women that have done it and completed it. But the thing is, you couldn't just up and do it. All of the racing would have to be made longer and harder so that you would be ready for it. Because the racing isn't that long and hard, it would be too much to make that jump—for anyone. You need to prepare, but it could be done.

When asked to explain why the UCI has the current riding limits on women, Debbie felt that "they don't think that the women are tough enough." She went on to say, "We can handle it. We train so hard, and so many days are spent training that could pay off in a longer race, so hopefully these limitations go away very soon." Debbie's sentiments show that professional women's training efforts would be on display in longer races. Training for (and racing in) events of longer distance would help advance their professional craft. Instead, because they aren't "tough enough," these elite athletes are treated like amateur junior male riders. The "manhood act" of riding farther, and across more days, is reserved for male professionals.[31]

DISCUSSION

Study participants described a lifestyle of continually negotiating the professional margin. Cycling's governing bodies, sponsors (particularly those that back out of financial commitments), media outlets, and race directors are instrumental in preserving the existence of such spaces. It is troubling when the sport's governing body substantially delegitimizes the effort of particular athletes and furthers the dual landscapes in the professional cycling world—"women's racing" and "men's racing." These realities reaffirm what Theberge refers to as "patriarchal relations of power."[32] Her analysis of the ice hockey context thoughtfully untangles inequalities in the distribution of resources (namely ice time) as well as the philosophies of hockey's provincial and country-wide governing bodies. My deconstruction of professional female cycling adds to this understanding of gendered institutions in sport. Similar to the athletes interviewed in Theberge's study, my participants talk about complex webs of resistance and discrimination. They face governing bodies that are separatists, keeping women on the fringe of the sport. The organizational structures that surround them present an unwillingness to challenge the power of men. In that vein, I suggest that the professional-amateur margin can be viewed as a form of "moving boundary of resistance." This means that as women make incremental progress in breaking down boundaries in some areas, they face increased resistance in others. That results in painfully slow net change, with women struggling to break out of the margins of the sport.

Of most concern regarding the presence of two distinct landscapes in cycling is that it reflects and perpetuates a binary view of gender and power. The emphasis on labeling "men's cycling" versus "women's cycling" reinforces social and physical distinctions between men and women, and thus, these gender-centered labels must be avoided in favor of more neutral language. Such labels lend credence to long-standing sex disparities within the sport's most important bodies, resulting in the misguided and false narrative that men compete in the sport of cycling while women participate in subordinate and less competitive races as a hobby. The formal regulation of competition based on these erroneous narratives allows for the exclusion of women from many of cycling's biggest events. Furthermore, such harmful narratives preclude some women from embracing their identity as professional athletes. In a world where we often see ourselves as we *think* others see us, it is no wonder these elite athletes struggle to call themselves professionals.[33]

NOTES

1. Iris Slappendel [@irisslappendel], Twitter post, May 17, 2013, 5:21 a.m., https://twitter.com/irisslappendel.
2. Jay Coakley, *Sports in Society: Issues and Controversies*, 10th ed. (New York: McGraw Hill, 2009); D. Stanley Eitzen and George Harvey Sage, *Sociology of North American Sport*, 8th ed. (Boulder, CO: Paradigm Publishers, 2009).
3. Eitzen and Sage, *Sociology of North American Sport*.
4. For example, see the following: Michael A. Messner and Donald F. Sabo, *Sport, Men, and the Gender Order: Critical Feminist Perspectives* (Champaign, IL: Human Kinetics Publishers, 1990).
5. Matthew Atencio, Becky Beal, and Charles Wilson, "The Distinction of Risk: Urban Skateboarding, Street Habitus and the Construction of Hierarchical Gender Relations," *Qualitative Research in Sport and Exercise* 1 (2009): 3–20; Susan Birrell, "Approaching Mt. Everest: On Intertextuality and the Past as Narrative," *Journal of Sport History* 34 (2007): 1–22; Nick Ford and David Brown, *Surfing and Social Theory: Experience, Embodiment and Narrative of the Dream Glide* (London: Routledge, 2006); Jason Laurendeau and Nancy Sharara, "Women Could Be Every Bit as Good as Guys: Reproductive and Resistant Agency in Two 'Action' Sports," *Journal of Sport and Social Issues* 32 (2008): 24–47; Holly Thorpe, "Jibbing the Gender Order: Females in the Snowboarding Culture," *Sport in Society* 8 (2005): 76–100; and Gordon Waitt, "Killing Waves: Surfing, Space and Gender," *Social and Cultural Geography* 9 (2008): 75–94.
6. Andrew Chadwick, *The Hybrid Media System: Politics and Power* (New York: Oxford University Press, 2013); Chadwick introduces the concept of reserved domains in the context of media; however, its application to sport is valuable.
7. Douglas Hartmann, "The Sanctity of Sunday Football: Why Men Love Sports," in *Sociological Perspectives on Sport: The Games Outside the Games*, eds. David Karen and Robert E. Washington (New York: Routledge, 2015), 123–29.
8. Douglas Schrock and Michael Schwalbe, "Men, Masculinity, and Manhood Acts," *Annual Review of Sociology* 35 (2009): 277–95.
9. Details of the 2014 Tour route can be found here: http://www.letour.com/le-tour/2016/us/overall-route.html.
10. Michael Kimmel, "Masculinities," in *Men and Masculinities: A Social, Cultural, and Historical Encyclopedia*, Vol. II, eds. M. Kimmel and A. Aronson (Santa Barbara, CA: ABC-CLIO, 2004).

11. Raewyn W. Connell, *Gender and Power: Society, the Person, and Sexual Politics* (Stanford, CA: Stanford University Press, 1987).

12. Kimmel, "Masculinities."

13. Mary Louise Adams, *Artistic Impressions: Figure Skating, Masculinity, and the Limits of Sport* (Toronto: University of Toronto Press, 2011).

14. Messner and Sabo, *Sport, Men, and the Gender Order.*

15. Adams, *Artistic Impressions.*

16. Nancy Theberge, *Higher Goals: Women's Ice Hockey and the Politics of Gender* (New York: SUNY Press, 2000).

17. Barney G. Glaser and Anselm Strauss, *The Discovery of Grounded Theory: Strategies for Qualitative Research* (Chicago, IL: Aldine, 1967).

18. Anselm Strauss and Juliet Corbin, "Grounded Theory Methodology—An Overview," in *Handbook of Qualitative Research*, eds. N. K. Denzin and S. Lincoln (Thousand Oaks, CA: Sage Publications, 1994), 273–85; B. G. Glaser, *Emergence vs. Forcing: Basics of Grounded Theory Analysis* (Mill Valley, CA: Sociology Press, 1992).

19. Barney Glaser, *Theoretical Sensitivity: Advances in the Methodology of Grounded Theory* (Mill Valley, CA: Sociology Press, 1978); Anselm Strauss and Juliet Corbin, *Basics of Qualitative Research: Grounded Theory Procedures and Techniques* (Thousand Oaks, CA: Sage Publications, 1990); and Anselm Strauss and Juliet Corbin, *Basics of Qualitative Research: Techniques and Procedures for Developing Grounded Theory*, 2nd ed. (Thousand Oaks, CA: Sage Publications, 1998).

20. Anselm Strauss and Juliet Corbin, *Basics of Qualitative Research: Techniques and Procedures for Developing Grounded Theory*, 2nd ed. (Thousand Oaks, CA: Sage Publications, 1998).

21. Norman Denzin and Yvonna Lincoln, *Handbook of Qualitative Research* (Thousand Oaks, CA: Sage Publications, 2000); Kathy Charmaz, *Constructing Grounded Theory: A Practical Guide through Qualitative Analysis* (Thousand Oaks, CA: Sage, 2006).

22. For examples, see Adams, *Artistic Impressions*; Todd W. Crosset, *Outsiders in the Clubhouse: The World of Women's Professional Golf* (New York: State University of New York Press, 1995).

23. Adams, *Artistic Impressions*; Kimmel, "Masculinities."

24. "Professional," *Dictionary.com*, http://www.dictionary.com/browse/professional?s=ts.

25. "Professional," Merriam-Webster, http://www.merriam-webster.com/dictionary/professional.

26. Additional salary figures can be found in Pidd's 2014 article. See Helen Pidd, "Paying Minimum Wage to Pro Women Cyclists Could Backfire, Says UCI," *The Guardian*, November 14, 2014, https://www.theguardian.com/sport/2014/nov/14/women-cyclists-pay-minimum-wage-uci-brian-cookson.

27. Ibid.

28. All salary figures cited in this paragraph are reported in 2012 U.S. dollars and reflect 2012 UCI salary requirements.

29. Andrew Chadwick, *The Hybrid Media System: Politics and Power* (New York: Oxford University Press, 2013).

30. A full description of UCI's road racing regulations can be found here: http://www.uci.ch/mm/Document/News/Rulesandregulation/17/42/14/2-ROA-20160603-E_English.pdf.

31. Schrock and Schwalbe, "Men, Masculinity, and Manhood Acts."

32. Theberge, *Higher Goals*, 8.

33. Charles H. Cooley, *Human Nature and the Social Order* (New York: Scribner's, 1902).

10

Athlete Domestic Violence: Contaminating Acts and the Violation of Self-Boundaries

Helen Owton and Jacquelyn Allen-Collinson

INTRODUCTION

This chapter explores the under-researched area of athlete domestic violence (ADV). Currently, there do not seem to be any definitions offered for what athlete domestic violence entails, and we discuss below some of the issues surrounding domestic violence and what has been termed "intimate partner abuse and violence." First, Katherine Starr describes ADV as a situation in which an athlete (not just professional/elite) is in a (perceived) "relationship" with a coach, which can involve the athlete being of consenting age or not.[1] Regardless of age, because of the professional standards (e.g., the duty of care) required by a coach, developing a romantic/sexual relationship with an athlete is not appropriate because the coach holds structural power advantage over the athlete.[2] Secondly, we argue that ADV is where athletes find themselves in an abusive relationship with a partner where they experience "any incident or pattern of incidents of controlling, coercive, threatening behavior, violence or abuse between those aged 16 or over who are, or have been, intimate partners or family members regardless of gender or sexuality."[3] Abuse includes (but is not limited to) the following:

- Psychological
- Physical
- Sexual
- Financial
- Emotional

Given some of the definitional issues and complexities surrounding "domestic abuse,"[4] Starr further explains why an athlete might remain involved in an ongoing relationship despite the harm and abuse she is experiencing:

> The competing athlete has something at risk, for example, dreams of being an Olympian, a college scholarship, playing time or financial gain. There is a complex "hook" keeping the athlete engaged in a relationship even when abusive and unhealthy. The athlete has to make decisions for the family, the team and the coach. When speaking up about the abuse, the athlete could be subject to retaliation from the team if there is a perceived threat of their dreams being compromised as a result of the coach removal; the parents that sacrificed everything to make sure that the child-athlete's dreams are fulfilled or the coach that convinces the athlete that the only reason for her/his success is because of the "coach."[5]

Domestic abusive relationships are complex, and much research outside of sport and physical activities can facilitate understanding. As we have noted elsewhere,[6] what is deemed to constitute "domestic abuse" and "domestic violence" vary considerably, and at the level of terminology a panoply of terms exists. For some researchers, "violence" fails to evoke the intense emotional and psychological aspects of abuse, while descriptors such as "domestic" and "family" in relation to abuse/violence may obscure who actually initiates and/or perpetrates the abuse/violence and whether it is uni-, bi-, or multilateral. For our purposes here, "intimate partner abuse" (IPA) refers to any abusive act deemed to have the intention, or perceived intention, of generating fear, causing physical injury, intimidation, disorientation, denigration, or emotional or psychological pain to an intimate partner. "Intimate partner violence" (IPV) refers to any act deemed to have the intention or perceived intention of causing physical injury to an intimate partner. The term "intimate partner abuse and violence" (IPA&V) is often used, and "athlete domestic violence" (ADV) refers to an athlete in an intimate relationship with a coach where the athlete experiences these abusive acts, as defined above. In many cases, of course, these forms overlap and/or are perpetrated simultaneously.

As has been noted,[7] IPA&V is extremely complex, not only in terms of its dynamics but also in how it is presented and by/for whom. It can be extremely difficult, for example, to ascertain the incidence, prevalence, and nature of such abuse and violence due to methodological, reporting, and recording differences and lack of identification of whether the violence was unilaterally initiated or responsive/defensive. Some researchers have found IPA&V to be asymmetrical in terms of men's violence to women; on dimensions of frequency, severity, and consequences for the victim/survivor and their well-being;[8] and the greater likelihood of women being injured and repeatedly beaten by male partners. Additionally, some feminist theorists suggest that "domestic violence is the result of patriarchal ideology in which men are encouraged and expected to control their partners."[9] Gender symmetry and asymmetry debates continue, however, with the overall picture indicating that women and men, heterosexual, bisexual, lesbian, gay,[10] and trans,[11] across age, physical ability, and socioeconomic and ethnic background, perpetrate abuse and violence.

Maureen McHugh and Irene Hanson Frieze call for more in-depth, qualitative studies into experiences of abuse and violence.[12] In this chapter, we seek to address this research lacuna in a specific area, by focusing at the microlevel of a particular case of ADV. In the domain of sport, Michael Flood and Sue Dyson argue that increasing links have been made between sport and violence against women.[13] Research has, for example, highlighted a link between major football tournaments and an increase in domestic abuse[14] and IPA&V, which suggests that individuals with more traditional or conservative attitudes toward gender and sexuality, such as those attitudes often condoned and emphasized in sport, are also more likely to condone domestic violence and sexual assault.[15] While sport is often seen as an arena for children to learn what are deemed "positive" norms and values, the "darker side of sport" often remains undisclosed and under-researched.[16] While there have been breakthroughs for victims of child sexual abuse (CSA), with an increased number (71%) of reported cases of CSA in the UK,[17] domestic abuse in sport remains a taboo topic for many. A growing body of research[18] investigating abuse in sport, however, suggests that competitive sporting environments provide a unique sociocultural context that offers possibilities for sexual abuse and exploitation to take place. In sport, the specific danger is the amount of *power* invested in the coach.[19]

In the case of Bella (white, middle class, able-bodied), who was groomed and sexually abused from the age of 13 years,[20] it became evident that if the sexual abuse continues to develop as an intimate domestic relationship, then it becomes more complex and can develop into ADV. Here, Bella's story provides us with an under-researched perspective, *the perspective of the abused*, which we analyze theoretically via Goffman's interactionist framework, focusing in particular on his conceptualization of the "territories of the self."

THEORETICAL FRAMEWORK: TERRITORIES OF THE SELF

In Erving Goffman's work, the conceptualization of what he terms "territories of the self," exemplified in *Relations in Public*,[21] offers a powerful analytic tool for exploring aspects of IPA&V and ADV. Violation of these territories via various means, such as "contaminative acts," which Goffman includes among the mortification processes described in *Asylums*,[22] are highly pertinent to Bella's case. In *Relations in Public*, for example, Goffman argues for eight distinctive territories of the self, which are socioculturally and situationally contingent. Four of these are particularly salient in addressing IPA&V and ADV, and relate to (in Goffman's own terminology) (1) personal space, (2) the sheath, (3) possessional territory, and (4) information preserve. We describe these in detail below, and in relation to our findings we analyze how some of these territories were violated by Bella's abuser via three specific means of contamination: (1) violation of information preserve, (2) physical contamination, and (3) interpersonal contamination.

"Personal space," for Goffman, relates to "the space surrounding an individual, anywhere within which an entering other causes the individual to feel encroached upon."[23] This is a kind of spatial envelope surrounding an individual in her or his everyday life. The amount of space required by individual social actors is both culturally and situationally contingent, depending, for example, on cultural norms and the degree of familiarity, closeness, or intimacy of coparticipants in the particular interactional milieu. The violation or breaching of personal space represents the violation of societal expectations and an unwelcome intrusion into a person's self-boundaries. Such intrusions are a regular and frequent occurrence for many victims of IPA&V and for Bella in her experience of ADV.

"The sheath" is Goffman's term for a person's bodily surface and clothing. He highlights how different parts of our bodily sheath are accorded different degrees of sensitivity and also ritual respect, with the face and "private parts" generally warranting greatest concern and respect. Our skin is experienced as the outer boundary of the self, so that the touch of a person or objects that are unwelcome, or not invited to touch, can be experienced as an intrusion into the most intimate realm of personal space.

"Possessional territory" is defined by Goffman as "any set of objects that can be identified with the self and arrayed around the body wherever it is."[24] Those subjected to IPA&V or ADV often find their possessional territory violated, their possessions disrespected, damaged, or even destroyed.

"Information preserve" Goffman portrays as "the set of facts about himself [*sic*] to which an individual expects to control access while in the presence of others."[25] This information includes a person's "content of mind," her or his biographical information, and also contents of pockets, handbags, documents, letters, and so on.

All the above territories of the self may be subjected to violation (including within IPA&V and ADV), and Goffman describes three specific dimensions of contamination in his work *Asylums*. Here, he portrays a range of mortification practices imposed upon inmates of "total institutions," such as prisons or military organizations, and which involve contamination and contaminative acts of various kinds. As he argues, "on the outside [of a total institution] the individual can hold objects of self-feeling—such as his [*sic*] body, his immediate actions, his thoughts, and some possessions—clear of contact with alien and contaminating things."[26] In contrast, within total institutions, these territories of the self are subjected to surveillance and often to regular and routinized violation, including contamination. Goffman identifies three forms of contaminative exposure: (1) violation of information preserve, (2) physical contamination, and (3) interpersonal contamination. These forms of contamination emerged strongly in Bella's account of her relationship with her coach, who subsequently became her partner.

We now describe the research approach adopted in investigating and constructing Bella's account of being subjected to child sexual abuse as a young athlete—abuse that subsequently continued in an intimate domestic relationship.

COLLABORATIVE AUTOETHNOGRAPHY

Much research on sexual abuse in sport has been undertaken via traditional approaches (e.g., experimental, questionnaires) or via analytical cross-case analysis.[27] With this in mind, we respond to the call for more layered and in-depth accounts of ADV from Starr.[28] Given the nature of the existing relationship between the researchers and Bella, the sensitive topic, and the collaborative perspective of the research, Bella's case lends itself well to a process described by Cathy Zanker and Michael Gard as collaborative autoethnography.[29] Helen Owton engaged in a similar writing process to *community* autoethnography and *coconstructed* narratives, which views relationships and narratives as jointly authored, incomplete, and historically situated.[30] Care was taken to acknowledge and respect alterity and seek to preserve some intersubjective distance[31] between Bella and ourselves as researchers. Given this stance, critical reflexivity was crucial in this collaborative autoethnographic process which guarded against a "merge"[32] with Bella and her story and to address "relational ethics" that are heightened for autoethnographers.[33]

In the account that follows, we present Bella's story as extended narratives, seeking to preserve the integrity of her account and the identity of those involved, which is subsequently discussed and emplaced within our theoretical and conceptual framework. We seek to engage readers in the experiences of ADV so that they might react from the different positions they occupy. The selected representations are designed to stimulate and encourage multiple interpretations that invite and allow readers a greater interpretive open-ended freedom to form their own conclusions, so that they are better able to understand Bella's experiences as they transfer this understanding into their own lives.[34] To render the account more direct, we have chosen to write in the first person and begin with a poem based on Bella's narrative.

Masking

Years spent thinking,
Nobody believing,
Anything . . .
Nobody's policing,
Rogue's getting
away with anything.

It's been so easy for me,
To hide away what people don't see,
Habitual staging allowed me to be,
An expert at masking; acting happy
Nobody cares; me
care free.

Emotions, memories blocking,
Good compartmentalising.

A *BLURRING*,
this BLeeeeDING.

Flashbacks re-emerging.
Of pain and suffering,
Years hiding,
Easily masking.

How *stupid*! No use,
Memories embodied, always still there,
of abuse
no escape,
exposed, laid bare.

My Woman

"I think you should stop competing," he announces in the café where we've stopped for lunch with his boys. I burst out crying and he laughs.

"Jeez, I didn't realize you'd be all upset about it." He chuckles with his friends. I keep crying, so he changes his tack and puts his hand on my shoulder. "I just don't want *my woman* competing like that," he says, quiet but stern. "Do you understand? I just can't have *my woman* getting hurt, and what if you get your face mashed up. I couldn't have that."

I'm completely gutted. I was just getting good, *really* good, and I think I could have gone all the way. I don't understand at all. I feel thrown into a pit of unknown despair. I've been talked about as an upcoming star; the last competition I had, the world champion had congratulated me even though I had lost because it had been so tough.

I was just beginning to "come into my own" and was thriving on it. I had spent all this time, since the age of 12, getting to this point—it was flowing. I was in the zone now! Why stop? I'm completely confused. He obviously didn't anticipate how distressed I would be at this news. I'd never thought about how much I could get hurt; I just enjoyed it, enjoyed the skill, and I now feel that he's embedding a fear in me that means that if I did compete again and something painful happened to me then he'd just say, "I told you so."

"Obviously, you can still *teach*," he offers. This eases me a little, but I just feel so much loss and that so much meaning has just been taken away from me, so simply—just like that! At *his* word, *his* control. He continues the conversation and tells us all about examples of serious injuries.

"Remember this one guy who just fell and broke his neck and now he can't walk!" he says. "What if that happened to you? You could get seriously injured. You could get your *face* mashed. Now you're *my* woman—I just can't have that." I nod solemnly as I feel thankful for not being injured so far. He's obviously just trying to protect me, but I'm just so downhearted about it. I feel that he's taken away a part of me, a part of me that gave me strength. He's dangled the possibility of competing for England in front of me for years, and now he's taking it away. He used to be the one who told me that I needed to learn how to look after myself in case a stranger who would want to rape me should attack me. He said he would be angry with me if I didn't fight back, he'd said. He'd said that if I'd been attacked and I'd fought back then he'd be able to live with it, but if not . . .

Here, Ray seeks to exert ownership and control over Bella (aged 20 years), drawing on his power over her through sport, as her coach, to curtail her growing sense of power as an athlete, which he may find highly threatening. Sport can provide women and girls with a sense of control and power, and physical cultures and practices can be generative of relative freedom and personal empowerment.[35] While some sports can enable women to engage actively and assertively, challenge gender norms, and become empowered, this demonstration of (purportedly) "masculine" behavior can be threatening to others, particularly to an abuser who wants to have total power *over* an athlete.[36] While sport as a "hook" is a complex dynamic of power, the power Ray had over Bella through using sport as a "hook" renders her even more powerless as he takes the choice of sport away just when she feels that she is at the top of her game. By rendering her powerless, he can violate her sense of empowerment within herself that she may have gained via her involvement and growing competence in sport. Bella seemed to have a strong sporting identity, which meant that she may well have experienced threats to her sporting involvement as direct threats to her sense of self. Bella described how sport, which she experienced as a protective spatial envelope surrounding her in her everyday life, was contaminated by him. Subsequently, and perhaps not surprisingly, Bella now has an ambivalent and difficult relationship with sport. The next section considers Goffman's notion of violation of "informational preserve."

Throwing Money

We get ready for a night out and then head into town, to a local pub. Ray enjoys drinking, showing off, and parading round the busy pub with me "hanging" off his arm like a trophy. Then, toward the end of the evening, I get tapped on the shoulder.

"'Ello, Bella!" Nigel says.

I turn and hug him.

"Aw, hey! How are you?" I exclaim over the noise. I turn to see Ray glaring at me with a sinister, scary smile.

"Um . . . er, this is Nigel," I say to Ray.

"All right, mate!" he says, sternly shaking Nigel's hand strongly and arrogantly.

"Hey," Nigel says cheerfully, shaking Ray's hand, appearing oblivious to Ray's attempts to scare him. He turns back to me and tries to chat to me. I'm petrified that Ray will figure out that this is my friend that I slept with, so I try to play it cool and chat with him while maintaining a bit of a distance. But Nigel touches me, taps me affectionately like we used to when we were good friends. I've not seen him for a few months, since I left college.

"So, what are you up to?" I ask, sipping my drink.

"Oh, you know, I've been away for the summer sailing! It's been great fun!" he replies and brags about his adventures. We have a bit of a laugh, but I'm careful not to "flirt" too much; I've got *him* breathing down the back of my neck.

"Aw, it's great to see you, Bella!" he says, hugging me again. It feels warm, and it's nice to see an old friend. "Catch up again in a bit!"

He turns away and I look back at Ray, who seems to be waiting for me to finish.

"So, *who* was *that*?" he asks me accusingly.

"Um . . . er, you know, Nigel, a friend from college," I say nervously.

"Hmmm," he says, smirking. "You *fucked* him I bet."

I blush.

"I *knew* it!" he says, feeling and enjoying the power he now has over me. I hang my head shamefully, and I feel the warm joy of seeing Nigel seeping out of me.

"How could you fuck that?" he says, riling, his face getting redder. "He's not even athletic! Look at his fucking saggy arse!"

I hang my head in silence.

"That's *the* guy isn't it?" he continues.

I nod silently with my head still hanging to the floor. I sense his temper boiling more and more as he drinks more and more.

"You're a *fucking* slag!" he hisses quietly close to my ear.

"He's just a friend," I say, quickly looking up.

The night starts blurring, and the next thing I know I find myself outside with Ray shouting at me on the street. We're waiting for a taxi.

"You were fucking flirting with him! How do you think that makes *me* feel?" Ray shouts. "You made me look fucking stupid!"

"I wasn't, I, I, I didn't, I didn't mean . . . " I try to defend. "He's just a friend . . . " I turn to walk in the direction of anywhere but near him.

"That's fucking bollocks!" he shouts. "Yeah, that's right! *Fuck* off!"

I stop and turn. "I need some money to get a taxi," I say, changing my tone. "I want to go back to my mum's."

"*Fuck* off!" he shouts, coming toward me.

Scared, I turn and carry on, scampering away. There are fights starting outside the pub in the other direction.

"Here you go! You fucking *slag*!" he shouts from close behind. Suddenly I feel immense pitters of pain, like hard pieces of rock hitting the back of my head. *Clunk, clunk, clunk, clunk, clunk.*

"Owwwwwww!" I shriek, falling to the ground and wrapping my hands around the back of my head.

"That's all the money I got!" he shouts.

I look down, shrieking and sobbing, and see coins scattered on the pavement.

"Owwww!" I continue cowering on the pavement. As I start desperately scraping up the coins, he walks by and throws a five-pound note down at me.

"For *fuck's* sake!" Ray sighs sinisterly. "You're *pathetic*."

I watch the five-pound note float down beside me among the rest of the coins. He storms off down the hill toward the bed-sit and leaves me sitting on the cold pavement, scraping up the bits of shrapnel. Humiliated, I start thinking survival. I have the keys to the bed-sit as well, so I quickly run on ahead of him.

I run and run and run.

I get to the top of the hill where there's a phone box. I race to the phone box and use the coins to call my mum, but she doesn't answer. The street is dark, cold, and empty and a fearful shadow of fear consumes me. I collapse in the phone box. Then I look up and see him walking past me. I think quickly and irrationally.

"*Wait!*" I cry.

Frantically, I chase after him, feeling like I have no other option.

As outlined above, according to Goffman,[37] information preserve relates to personal information about the self (e.g., a person's "content of mind," her or his biographical information, and also contents of pockets, handbags, documents, letters, and so on, which a person wishes to keep private in the presence of certain others). Here, Ray violates Bella's information preserve vis-á-vis her prior relationship with Nigel, bringing this forcibly into a more public domain against her wishes. He then blows things out of proportion to use this information against Bella in order to generate fear, disorientation, and denigration and cause emotional and psychological distress and pain. Allied to this emotional distress and pain is the sudden physical pain of having objects thrown at her, pelting and damaging the protective "sheath" of her clothing and skin. Bella (aged 18 years) experienced this as an intrusion into the most guarded realm of her personal space. Goffman's work on vulnerability and danger analyzes in detail the violation of a range of personal territories. In *Relations in Public*, Goffman identifies that information and conversational preserve, decision-making turns, personal space, and claims to space as well as biographical details that we can usually choose to reveal or conceal according to the situation can be intruded upon.[38] In the above narrative, not only does Bella experience the violence of objects thrown at her body in a denigrating and hostile fashion, she also feels intensely an invasion of her personal space and information preserve.

My Baths

I feel a sense of physical and mental relief as I slip into my steaming hot bath. The weight of hypervigilance lifts as I lie back and exhale deeply. It is not long before *he* comes sneaking up on me to find out what I am up to. *He* struts in and sits importantly on the toilet with his newspaper. I analyze him and the horrid, tense feeling I have just felt by the interrupting presence of his grotesque, macho, hypermasculine aura. I suddenly think that he looks old, fat, and ugly, and it is this creature who has just rudely intruded on *my* bathing sanctuary to ruin it by making a stench; *his* stench, like a dog marking *his* territory.

These baths are *me* time, I get to have with *myself*, where I have recently been having thoughts about the frightening future I might continue to have with *him*. Hearing about my sister having children, and thinking about whether I'd like children, has made me think about what I was like as a child, what sort of parent I would like to be and what I would like for *my* children. I've been starting to feel depressed about it.

"It's weird, isn't it? I mean, you've known me since I was twelve. That's weird, isn't it?" I ask curiously. "You were my instructor, and you were married. That's wrong, isn't it?"

"*What*? Oh my god. Don't start that shit! How dare you make me feel like that! Me? A paedophile? I only came in for a crap!"

He washes his hands and checks himself in the mirror. I watch as I notice his cold blue eyes burn with anger. *He* then glares at me, tuts, shakes his head. "Twat," he snidely mutters. I jump as he storms past, and that angers him even more.

"Oh, don't flinch as if I'm some kind of wife beater!"

I go back to staring at my toes playing with the taps. I start feeling sad, but *I* don't get upset. I don't really feel anything. I wonder if he's always been that old, fat, and ugly. I wonder how I found myself here so far away from anyone with no friends, no family, and a lonely, superficial, fearful way of life with an abusive and violent "predator." He turned me against my family and my friends and won't allow me to have any friends here. I have nobody to talk to, to confide in, or to question about whether this is *normal*. He makes everything sound so *normal*. He makes me feel stupid for even *questioning*. He says he "tamed" me.

Yet, now I wonder how *normal* it is to get coins thrown at your head, to get spat at, to get criticized, ordered about, intimidated by scary stories of his violence, to fulfil all his sick sexual fantasies, and to get routinely raped.

Initially, I was so *flattered* by his attention, but I was so vulnerable and young and just didn't know; I just didn't recognize the signs. Bit by bit, things get so normalized. And I *needed* his attention. I *needed* to please him. I did *anything* for him. I *needed* a father figure . . . but just not one like him. I just *needed* to be loved. And now I think about how weird it is for a sports coach, a married man, to fancy a student half his age. I didn't realize he was abusing his duty of care. I felt *special.* He *told* me I was *special.*

I don't feel special now. I feel like I have been so used and abused . . . by *him*. *He* abused his position of power.

Escape feels too late now. I feel trapped. So trapped! I have nobody to talk to. It feels like there is no way out. Not now.

Here, at the age of 23 years, Bella's personal and private space of her bathroom and her own bathing privacy are invaded by Ray against her wishes. She experiences this invasion as an unwelcome intrusion into her own created sanctuary where she was attempting to construct boundaries of her private self. According to Goffman, in the general interaction order, "private parts" warrant greatest concern and respect from others,[39] which makes the above incident an invasion of the most intimate realm of personal space, particularly given that Bella is naked in her bath and thus devoid of the outer protective layer of the "sheath" in the form of clothing. Furthermore, not only is the invasion visual but also olfactory: Ray contaminates the pleasurable and safe olfactory space of Bella's bath with the stench of his bodily waste; he imposes his smell upon her, without permission, thus violating her bathing sanctuary and personal space. As noted above, Goffman portrays a range of modalities of violation, and these include the intrusion of bodily excreta and the odors of these, along with, for example, tainted breath and body odor.[40] Bella was thus subjected to the above excreta-contaminative experience, leaving her feeling defiled by Ray's imposition of his bodily waste and smells.

My Pussy

I try so hard to make him happy. I'm constantly trying to please him, but I find it hard to please his sexual needs. Sex is excruciatingly painful, and he won't take no for an answer. It's been getting worse and worse recently, and I have to wince and scream silently as he "has his way" with me. I feel so used and sore.

"Come on," he persists. He'll start with the whinging, then the sulks, then the physical pressure, going on and on and on . . . and I *always* dread waking up to the "morning poke." I've started jumping out of bed before he wakes up, and if I can be dressed beforehand then I'll be a bit safer. I think I have thrush; I have some cream, but nothing helps.

"If I put cream on my dick, then it'll help you," he says persuasively through a deeply embedded pressurizing voice. I believe everything he says—I always have, and who can I ask anyway? We've moved so far away from my family, and he's told me how unsupportive they are of me anyway. He always makes so much sense to me, so I start believing that he can make me better by having sex with me, even though I have to stop myself from crying with the pain.

After sex, he leans over and puts his hand between my legs, grabs it firmly and says, "This pussy is *mine*. It's mine."

Similarly, Goffman's notion of physical and interpersonal contamination can be applied here to understand Bella's IPA&V. As Goffman argues, the amount of space required by individual social actors is both culturally and situationally contingent, depending, for example, on cultural norms and the degree of familiarity, closeness, or intimacy of coparticipants in the particular interactional milieu.[41] Ray's claim over Bella's body, including her "private parts," represents the invasion of the most intimate realm of personal space. Bella experiences Ray's unwanted penetration of her as a violent act of physical contamination of her most intimate personal space[42] and a violation of her self-boundaries. As shown above and throughout Bella's account (aged between 18 and 24 years), such intrusions were a regular and frequent occurrence in her experience of ADV.

CLOSING POINTS

In his conceptualization of the territories of the self, Goffman explores how individuals hold rights (both legally enshrined and more informal) and expectations in regard to self-preserves. He argues that individuals should be wary against violations of territories of the self, which can be visibly fixed or geographical and some situational or idiographic.[43] From Bella's account, the following emerged as salient examples of invasions of territories and her personal space via:

- Violation of information preserve
- Physical contamination
- Interpersonal contamination

The implications of such violations and contaminative acts for Bella's identity and selfhood are highly deleterious and damaging, for, as Jacquelyn Allen-Collinson highlights, "routine and explicit disrespect for violation of such territory may thus be regarded in many ways as an assault on selfhood."[44] As previous accounts by Bella have shown,[45] these narratives invite an aesthetic reading in which readers become coparticipants in the creation of meanings and contribute their own questions, answers, and experiences to the story as they read and resonate with it. Indeed, we hope that readers experience the story as affecting one's own life and find in that effect a certain truth of one's life.[46] We note that while there are risks to this approach because it destabilizes readers' preconceived assumptions about gender and power and taboos in sport, we are in agreement with others[47] that the risk of *not* sharing these kinds of "hidden" narratives and reflecting on them seems to be a much greater risk to take. Like Kitrina Douglas and David Carless,[48] we hope the story reveals the complex and significant power dynamics in the relationships and in ways that uncover and explore taboo and silenced issues in sport. Lastly, we hope that readers and those working in sport settings share Bella's story with others, with the intention of promoting change and shaping policy in practice at the individual and institutional level. For example, recommendations for practice could include the need to discuss, explore, question, and examine intimate relationships between coaches and athletes more openly (e.g., child protection training). Given the considerable lack of knowledge in this specific field, we call for more qualitative research into ADV, to learn more about the prevalence of this phenomenon, to examine the relational dynamics, and to explore the effects of ADV in more depth.

NOTES

1. Katherine Starr, "Breaking Down Sexual Abuse in Sports," *Huffington Post*, last modified January 18, 2013, http://www.huffingtonpost.com/katherine-starr/breaking-down-sexual-abus_b_2500956.html.

2. Sandra Kirby, Lorraine Greaves, and Olena Hankivsky *The Dome of Silence: Sexual Harassment and Abuse in Sport* (London: Zed Books, 2000); Starr, "Breaking Down Abuse."

3. Home Office, "Domestic Violence and Abuse," *Gov.UK*, last modified March 8, 2016, https://www.gov.uk/guidance/domestic-violence-and-abuse.

4. Jacquelyn Allen-Collinson, "Intimate Intrusions Revisited: A Case of Intimate Partner Abuse and Violations of the Territories of the Self," *Qualitative Sociology Review* 1 (2009): 50–69; Jacquelyn Allen-Collinson, "Assault on Self: Intimate Partner Abuse and the Contestation of Identity," *Symbolic Interaction* 34 (2011): 108–27.

5. Starr, "Breaking Down Abuse."

6. Allen-Collinson, "Intimate Intrusions Revisited"; Allen-Collinson, "Assault on Self"; Jacquelyn Allen-Collinson, "A Marked Man: A Case of Female-Perpetrated Intimate Partner Abuse," *International Journal of Men's Health* 8 (2009): 22–40.

7. Allen Collinson, "Intimate Intrusions Revisited"; Stewart Palin-Davies, *Male Victims of Female-Perpetrated Domestic Violence* (Norwich, UK: School of Social Work and Psychosocial Studies, University of East Anglia, 2006).

8. Russell P. Dobash and R. Emerson Dobash, "Women's Violence to Men in Intimate Relationships," *British Journal of Criminology* 44 (2004): 324–49.

9. Wayne W. Bennett and Kären M. Hess, *Criminal Investigation*, 8th ed. (Andover, UK: Cengage Learning, 2006), 312.

10. David Island and Patrick Letellier, *Men Who Beat the Men Who Love Them* (New York: Harrington Park Press, 1991); Lettie L. Lockhart, Barbara W. White, Vicki Causby, and Alicia Isaac, "Letting Out the Secret: Violence in Lesbian

Relationships," *Journal of Interpersonal Violence* 9 (1994): 469–92; Claire M. Renzetti and Charles H. Miley, *Violence in Gay and Lesbian Domestic Partnerships* (New York: Haworth Press, 1996).

11. Nicola Brown, "Stories from Outside the Frame: Intimate Partner Abuse in Sexual-Minority Women's Relationships with Transsexual Men," *Feminism and Psychology* 17 (2007): 373–93.

12. Maureen C. McHugh and Irene Hanson Frieze, "Intimate Partner Violence: New Directions," in *Violence and Exploitation against Women and Girls* (Annals of the New York Academy of Sciences, Vol. 1087), eds. F. L. Denmark, H. H. Krauss, E. Halpern, and J. A. Sechzer (New York: New York Academy of Sciences, 2006), 121–41.

13. Michael Flood and Sue Dyson, "Sport, Athletes, and Violence against Women," *Australian Research Centre in Sex, Health and Society*, La Trobe University, republished in *NTV Journal* 4 (2007): 37–46.

14. Sandra Kirby, Brian Francis, and Rosalie O'Flaherty, "Can the FIFA World Cup Football (Soccer) Tournament Be Associated with an Increase in Domestic Abuse?" *Journal of Research in Crime and Delinquency* 51 (2014): 259–76.

15. Michael Flood and Bob Pease, "The Factors Influencing Community Attitudes in Relation to Violence against Women: A Critical Review of the Literature," *Trauma, Violence, & Abuse* 10, no. 2 (April 2009): 125–42.

16. Kitrina Douglas and David Carless, "Exploring Taboo Issues in Professional Sport through a Fictional Approach," *Reflective Practice* 10 (2009): 311–23.

17. Sandra Laville, "1,400 Investigated in Child Sex Abuse Inquiry, Including Politicians," *The Guardian*, last updated May 20, 2015, http://www.theguardian.com/uk-news/2015/may/20/1400-suspects-operation-hydrant-politician-and-celebrity-child-sex-abuse-inquiry.

18. Celia H. Brackenridge, *Spoilsports: Understanding and Preventing Sexual Exploitation in Sport* (London: Routledge, 2001); Joy D. Bringer, Celia H. Brackenridge, and Lynne H. Johnston, "Swimming Coaches' Perceptions of Sexual Exploitation in Sport: A Preliminary Model of Role Conflict and Role Ambiguity," *Sport Psychologist* 20 (2006): 465–79; Michael Burke, "Obeying Until It Hurts: Coach-Athlete Relationships," *Journal of the Philosophy of Sport* 28 (2001): 227–40; Kari Fasting and Celia H. Brackenridge, "Coaches, Sexual Harassment and Education," *Sport, Education and Society* 14 (2009): 21–35; Michael Hartill, "Concealment of Child Sexual Abuse in Sports," *Quest* 65 (2013): 241–54; Sylvie Parent, "Disclosure of Sexual Abuse in Sport Organizations: A Case Study," *Journal of Child Sexual Abuse* 20 (2011): 322–37.

19. Trisha Leahy, "Working with Adult Athlete Survivors of Sexual Abuse," in *Routledge Handbook of Applied Sport Psychology: A Comprehensive Guide for Students and Practitioners*, eds. Stephanie J. Hanrahan and Mark B. Andersen (London: Routledge, 2010), 303–12.

20. Helen Owton and Andrew C. Sparkes, "Sexual Abuse and the Grooming Process in Sport: Learning from Bella's Story," *Sport, Education and Society* (2015): 1–12; Helen Owton, *A Qualitative Case Study of Sexual Abuse in Sport* (Basingstoke, UK: Palgrave Macmillan, 2016).

21. Erving Goffman, *Relations in Public: Microstudies of the Public Order* (Harmondsworth, UK: Penguin, 1972), 50–87.

22. Erving Goffman, *Asylums. Essays on the Social Situation of Mental Patients and Other Inmates* (Harmondsworth, UK: Penguin, 1976), 31–40.

23. Goffman, *Relations in Public*, 52.

24. Ibid., 62.

25. Ibid., 63.

26. Goffman, *Asylums*, 31–32.

27. Daniel Rhind, Jamie McDermott, Emma Lambert, and Irena Koleva, "A Review of Safeguarding Cases in Sport," *Child Abuse Review* 24 (2015): 418–26; Celia H. Brackenridge and Kari Fasting, "The Grooming Process in Sport," *Auto/Biography: An International and Interdisciplinary Journal* 13 (2005): 33–52.

28. Starr, "Breaking Down Abuse."

29. Cathy Zanker and Michael Gard, "Fatness, Fitness, and the Moral Universe of Sport and Physical Activity," *Sociology of Sport Journal* 25 (2008): 48–65.

30. Carolyn Ellis, Tony E. Adams, and Arthur P. Bochner, "Autoethnography: An Overview," *Historical Social Research/Historische Sozialforschung* (2011): 273–90.

31. Jacquelyn Allen-Collinson, "Autoethnography: Situating Personal Sporting Narratives in Socio-Cultural Contexts," in *Qualitative Research on Sport and Physical Culture*, eds. Kevin Young and Michael Atkinson (Bingley, UK: Emerald Publishing, 2012), 191–212.

32. Brett Smith, Jacquelyn Allen-Collinson, Cassandra Phoenix, David Brown, and Andrew C. Sparkes, "Dialogue, Monologue, and Boundary Crossing within Research Encounters: A Performative Narrative Analysis," *International Journal of Sport and Exercise Psychology* 7 (2009): 342–59.

33. Carolyn Ellis, "Telling Secrets, Revealing Lives: Relational Ethics in Research with Intimate Others," *Qualitative Inquiry* 13 (2007): 3–29; Lydia Turner, "The Evocative Autoethnographic I," in *Contemporary British Autoethnography*, eds. Nigel P. Short, Lydia Turner, and Alec Grant (Berlin, Germany: Springer Science and Business Media, 2013), 213–29.

34. Frances Rapport and Andrew C. Sparkes, "Narrating the Holocaust: In Pursuit of Poetic Representations of Health," *Journal of Medical Humanities* 35 (2009): 27–34.

35. Jennifer Hargreaves and Patricia Vertinsky, *Physical Culture, Power, and the Body* (London: Routledge, 2007).

36. Brackenridge, *Spoilsports*; Vikki Krane, "We Can Be Athletic and Feminine, but Do We Want To? Challenging Hegemonic Femininity in Women's Sport," *Quest* 53 (2001): 115–33; Helen Owton, "Reinventing the Body-Self: Intense, Gendered and Heightened Sensorial Experiences of Women's Boxing Embodiment," in *Global Perspectives on Women in Combat Sport: Women Warriors Around the World*, eds. Alexander Channon and Christopher Matthews (Basingstoke, UK: Palgrave Macmillan, 2015), 221–36.

37. Erving Goffman, *Stigma: Notes on the Management of Spoiled Identity* (New York: Glencoe: The Free Press, 1963).

38. Goffman, *Relations in Public*.

39. Ibid.

40. Ibid., 72–73.

41. Goffman, *Relations in Public*.

42. Ibid.
43. Ibid.
44. Allen-Collinson, "Assault on Self," 123.
45. Owton and Sparkes, "Abuse and Grooming."
46. Ibid.
47. Allen-Collinson, "Assault on Self"; Jacquelyn Allen-Collinson, "A Sociology of Everyday Violence: Interactional Encounters in Intimate Partner Abuse," *Auto/Biography Yearbook 2015. The Annual Journal of the British Sociological Association Study Group on Auto/Biography* (2016): 14–27; Douglas and Carless, "Exploring Taboo Issues"; Owton, "Qualitative Study of Abuse"; Owton and Sparkes, "Abuse and Grooming."
48. Douglas and Carless, "Exploring Taboo Issues."

11

The Hierarchy within Women's Sports: NARPs, No-Bow Lesbos, and Horizontal Violence

Angie Henderson, Christine Nancy Ingoldsby, and Mark Shuey

Since the passage of Title IX in 1972, the past few decades have yielded significant increases in the percentage of girls participating in sport. Yet, women historically and still today struggle for equality in sport,[1] partly due to the stereotypes that others hold of female athletes, including the perceived incongruity between "athlete" and "woman."[2] Contemporary gender expectations in U.S. culture place dual pressure on female athletes wanting to excel at their sport yet also maintain a feminine persona that balances the masculine cue of athleticism.[3] Coined the "feminine apologetic" by Jan Felshin,[4] this phenomenon suggests that female athletes emphasize their feminine traits and roles in an attempt to apologize for their participation in sport. More recently, researchers Laurel Davis-Delano, April Pollock, and Jennifer Vose[5] found that a significant number of female athletes utilize the feminine apologetic to socially verify their heterosexuality and reaffirm their feminine roles within society. About half of female athletes engaged in a substantial amount of apologetic behavior in an attempt to adhere to normative gender constructs.

These trends are easily identified at the professional level as well, particularly among highly successful professional female athletes. In order to supplement the meager income of, for example, a professional soccer player, female athletes must succumb to hyperfeminized gender expectations in order to gain popularity and secure endorsement deals. This is illustrated on a routine Google search of professional soccer players Alex Morgan and Clint Dempsey. An Internet search of Alex Morgan immediately illustrated the importance of her body in that, within the first few links, there was a connection to her

2012 *Sports Illustrated* swimsuit portfolio. Furthermore, an image search of Alex Morgan revealed that four of the first five categories one could choose to narrow the search referred to her feminine roles: (1) a 2015 *Sports Illustrated* swimsuit shoot; (2) a 2012 *Sports Illustrated* swimsuit photo shoot; (3) her wedding; and (4) her engagement. In these shoots, her appearance is clearly designed to emphasize her sexuality and her femininity, not her participation in sport. In contrast, an Internet search of Clint Dempsey concentrated on his accomplishments in his sport; only two of the five categories emphasized parts of Dempsey's life unrelated to sport (family and tattoos). Interestingly, the first category that emerged was "wife," displaying an abundance of images of *his wife* in a bikini or hyperfeminine clothing. Examples similar to Morgan and Dempsey are countless—Jeff Gordon and Danica Patrick in car racing, Anna Kournikova and Roger Federer in tennis, and Elena Della Donne and Kobe Bryant in basketball—and it may exemplify that the litmus test for a female athlete is her sex appeal. Indeed, Mary Jo Kane and Heather Maxwell[6] found that a number of elite female athletes feel obligated to emphasize sex appeal to not only secure endorsement deals for themselves but also to help promote women's sport. Contemporary professional female athletes continually have to battle to be taken seriously for their efforts in sport, even when their list of accomplishments includes a World Cup championship, as is the case for the U.S. women's soccer team.

It is clear that hyperfeminine expectations are fairly universal for professional female athletes. However, this does not mean that all sports are created equal when it comes to managing the complex set of social expectations associated with being a female athlete. If all female athletes need to adhere to socially prescribed gender expectations in order to be considered "successful," how does, for instance, a tennis player differ from a swimmer in gendered performance? How do different sports navigate the hegemonic standards of femininity and manage the oppressive emphasis on appearance instead of athleticism? How does sport matter when it comes to resisting (or conforming to) the hyperfeminine standards set forth for contemporary female athletes? The present study examined these processes among collegiate female athletes as a way to manage the conflicting roles of "female" and "athlete."

LITERATURE REVIEW

While coverage of women in sport has increased since the passage of Title IX, the type of messaging that sport consumers receive about female athletes may look and sound different on the surface, but the general message has stayed constant: women and sport are sold by the sports media commercial complex as incongruent. Early messages focused on "the lesbian threat" by depicting female athletes as "muscular amazons"[7] to discourage female participation in sport and to utilize the lesbian label as a mechanism to intimidate, divide, and silence women in sport.[8] More recent research documents the trend in sports coverage of emphasizing femininity and heterosexuality and downplaying athleticism for sport consumers.[9] In recent years, the focus of the apologetic has shifted away from actual behaviors to a fixation on physical appearance. In fact, research has argued that "it is precisely because women no longer have to exhibit traditionally 'feminine' *personality* traits . . . that they must exhibit hyperfeminine *physical* traits."[10] Female athletes are expected to be strong and agile enough to do well in sport, but they must also be shapely, trim, and lean. Matthew Ezzell described the ideal for a modern female athlete as "heterosexyfit," a term that emphasizes three of the most important traits a female athlete must have if she wishes to conform to the ideal of mainstream society.[11] In order to be accepted, she must either be or appear to be heterosexual, which includes dressing and acting accordingly. The last component, *fit*, is accomplished by having some degree of muscle without going "overboard." Many female athletes worry about the plausibility of developing too much muscle to be considered desirable by what they think of as the majority of society, making it difficult to gauge the true potential of female athletes in general. Because of these messages at the macro level, female athletes often openly admit to overtly emphasizing femininity in order to actively "play nice" and maintain the status quo,[12] and some openly admit to sexualizing themselves because "sex sells."[13]

Studies on contemporary sportswomen have found much evidence of this feminine "apologetic," though it is not referred to as such consistently in the literature. What has remained consistent is the finding that these behaviors are performed for the benefit of others, for the sake of social inclusion rather than rejection. Pat Griffin dubbed it the "protective camouflage of feminine drag."[14] Davis-Delano, Pollack, and Vose linked societal stereotypes directly to the apologetic, finding three common fears that drive apologetic behavior: (1) the fear of being labeled as overly masculine, (2) the fear of being labeled as a lesbian (falsely or otherwise), and (3) the belief that female athletes are inferior to male athletes in regard to strength, speed, and toughness.[15]

However, it is also important to point out that scholars have argued that the acceptable level of muscular athletic build is highly dependent on the sport. Sports that require the use of force, attempts to physically subdue an opponent, and bodily contact would be acceptable for men and are therefore unacceptable for women.[16] Ann Colley et al. found that individual sports (e.g., tennis, golf, and gymnastics) were deemed more appropriate for women than team sports. In other words, the more congruent a sport is with how society is accustomed to viewing females, the more socially acceptable it is for women to play.[17] The societal gaze is accustomed to viewing women individually, focusing on their appearance (unimpeded by a bulky uniform), and performing in a nonthreatening way (in noncontact sports).

Each of these social prescriptions undoubtedly affects how modern sportswomen negotiate their dual identities. Further, the ways in which women exert agency in reaction to social conventions is highly dependent on context, and the present study argues that it is likely also dependent on sport. That is, how does sport dictate the ways in which sportswomen respond to notions of the "ideal" (feminized) female athlete? What processes emerge as a result of these negotiated identities? The purpose of the present study was to investigate how female athletes view and negotiate their identities as athletes, paying special attention to differences between sports as a predictor of just how feminine an apology can be.

METHODS

Sample

The participants in this study were female athletes from a National Collegiate Athletic Association (NCAA) Division I university in the western region, which participates in Division I athletics and annually enrolls about 10,000 undergraduate-level students and 2,000 graduate-level students. The university is mostly white (81%), while the rest of the students identify themselves as racial minorities.

A total of 52 female athletes participated in this study. Participants represented D-I athletes from golf, soccer, softball, swimming and diving, tennis, track and field, and volleyball. The athletes were primarily Caucasian, ages 18 to 20, with an overrepresentation of freshmen and sophomores.

Procedure

Approval from the researchers' institutional review board and permission from the Department of Athletics were secured in order to conduct this study. The investigators in this study attended team meetings to explain the purpose of the study and to recruit participants. Data were collected at seven focus groups—divided by sport—with two or three moderators present. While all sports were recruited to participate in the study, the final focus groups included track and field (N=10), swimming and diving (N=10), softball (N=7), golf (N=6), volleyball (N=8), soccer (N=6), and tennis (N=3). Focus groups lasted approximately an hour to 90 minutes.

Focus groups were selected as the methodology for a number of reasons. We were interested to learn how these women experienced their bodies in relation to their athletic and social identities. Group discussions with people who have similar experiences encourage self-disclosure and lessen anxiety that is often associated with individual interviews.[18] Group discussion can also encourage a more dynamic dialogue and free-flowing conversation by enabling the participants to respond to one another. The discussion was intended to flow as if it were a normal conversation, cued by previously prepared topics but able to take on a life of its own. Focus groups have been described as especially effective in feminist research, and group interactions about the female body yield a dialogue in which participants react to each other and freely express themselves. David Morgan suggested that focus groups are a viable alternative to interviews if the individuals are likely to discuss the topic in day-to-day life.[19] Molly George's ethnographic study of a Division I soccer team revealed that dialogue surrounding body and musculature is quite frequent among team members.[20] The advantages of focus groups are consistent with the essence of this research. These advantages indicate that when participants are able to formulate natural interactions, the discussion content can provide higher-quality data than individual interviews.

Phase I: Drawings

Before the focus group began, the moderators asked participants to draw an image that represented how society perceives female athletes. David Chambers developed the Draw-a-Scientist Test (DAST), from which he obtained data from elementary school students reflecting stereotypical images of scientists.[21] One explanation for employing this method was that children lacked the necessary skills to verbalize adequate information regarding their perceptions. The inclusion of drawing activities derived from the DAST has been useful in conducting focus groups by enabling a fun warm-up session, maintaining focus, lengthening the concentration period, and providing a different way for participants to express their ideas.[22] Although traditionally used in focus groups with young children, the idea was adapted here for this study's focus group with female athletes. This particular technique provided an icebreaker, a foundation for conversation prompts, and a means to achieve visual data portraying the athletes' perceptions before discussion began. It also allowed the researchers to become listeners while the participants explained the meaning and expertise behind their drawings. It is important to note here that of the 52 participants in this study, only 50 felt comfortable allowing us to analyze their drawing. Thus, the total N for the drawings is 50.

To initiate the focus group, each participant shared her drawing if she felt comfortable. The drawings often prompted laughter, conceivably adding to the rapport within the group. This approach also gave each individual a chance to interpret her drawing and share the thoughts behind it. The drawings usually sparked conversation and were used as a foundation for dialogue.

Phase 2: Focus Group Discussion

To further address the research questions, the moderators used a semistructured focus group guide to ensure that each focus group was addressed with similar questions. The questions were open-ended and used as a rough template to spark conversation. As the conversations evolved, the moderators inquired with follow-up questions only as needed. In order to allow the power to be shifted to the group members, the moderators made an effort to remain relatively uninvolved. Each focus group session lasted approximately an hour to 90 minutes. The discussions were audio recorded and later transcribed for analysis. The analysis led to the discovery of patterns and themes that challenged early assumptions. The reading and rereading of transcripts led to the emergence of broad classifications, further categorized as they related to the research questions.

Analysis

Themes that emerged from this study were grouped and presented using quotations from the female athlete participants. The themes related to the goals of this research sought to examine (1) how collegiate female athletes experience the dual identities associated with being a female athlete, and (2) how sport is related to the ways in which sportswomen respond to notions of the "ideal" (feminized) female athlete.

As the focus group interviews were conducted and transcribed, data were analyzed using thematic analysis. They were coded using a list of themes generated inductively from the raw obtained information and deductively from prior research.[23] Thematic categories were formed from the transcripts, and quotations were assigned to those categories as they related to the research questions.

RESULTS

In total, 52 female athletes participated in this study. The flexibility of the drawing activity yielded a collection of images—the majority of which were illustrations of female athletes—with a variety of meanings. Many of the athletes shared drawings of women within their own sport, while some described a more generic female athlete. A smaller portion of the athletes drew an athlete in a particular sport but one that was not their own. One of the most common themes we found in the data was a tendency to discuss feminizing appearance, either as a tactic to increase attendance at competition or as a way of "normalizing" the dual identity as a female athlete. Each of the seven focus groups involved a discussion of feminizing appearance that stemmed directly from the drawings the participants provided. However, the ways in which the comparison of feminine versus nonfeminine identities and behaviors emerged varied by sport yet held one consistency: the discussion centered on the practice of "othering" as a way to draw boundaries between the female athlete identity and the other. The "other" varied depending on the sport, but it was an important tactic used across all discussions.

It should also be noted that while the researchers categorize (as detailed below) the othering as a reaction to the oppressive standards of feminization, the participants did not always discuss the standards of femininity and beauty in negative terms; they *did* contribute to discussing the "other"—an out-group—in negative terms. In addition, when male athletes (or men in general) were discussed, the language used was not antagonistic in nature; participants would casually mention that male athletes get more (attention/budget/attendance at competition) and then proceed to discuss other groups (female peers) who they *did* describe in antagonistic terms. As a result, the data we present here are discussed in light of horizontal violence, where oppressed people or groups lash out or act in a hostile fashion toward their peers instead of their oppressors. Paulo Freire posits that this occurs when one group becomes marginalized by the dominant group and subsequently marginalizes another group with similar or less power.[24] Othering—an act of horizontal violence—came up in every focus group, though the "other" differed by sport. Therefore, while it was not the intention of this study to explore group dynamics between different sports, the results are presented in light of this concept. The themes are presented in turn below, beginning with the primary concepts of the feminine apologetic and being "othered" first. A discussion of horizontal violence among female athletes follows.

Primary Themes: The Feminine Apologetic and Being Othered First

The vast majority of drawings depicted a female athlete. Only one participant did not draw an actual female athlete but instead drew two fields, one with a male team and full stands and another with a female team and very few people in the stands. Fifty-eight percent of the drawings depicted big muscles on the female athletes, 20 percent depicted a female athlete as "bigger" than a comparison group of other females, and another 16 percent wrote the word "manly" next to their figures. Ten percent of the participants depicted feminine qualities in their drawings either textually or visually; those participants were tennis, track and field, or volleyball athletes.

One of the most consistent findings from the drawings was that female athletes compare themselves to an "other" group—either (1) male athletes, (2) other female athletes in a different sport, or (3) female nonathletes. Forty-two percent of the drawings had either textual or visual evidence that compared the female athlete depicted to an "other" group. That is, either the participants drew two figures/scenarios depicting a comparison, or they narrated their drawing with, for instance, "inferior to all male sports" as a descriptor of their picture. This is a key determinant of both the feminine apologetic and any resulting hierarchical "othering" performed by female athletes, because in order to participate in horizontal violence, one must be "othered" first. Several examples of this emerged in the focus groups; participants described this oppressive arrangement in the golf, tennis, softball, track and field, soccer, and volleyball focus groups.

The discussion for each focus group centered on these notions of "us" versus "them" as a way to describe societal perceptions of female athletes. One volleyball player described her drawing in this way:

> The picture I drew was showing that all the emphasis of importance is put on male athletes and they are put on higher pedestals automatically because they are male. I drew a female athlete on a small pedestal because even though we are athletes and in the same situations as the boys, we are less looked at.

The participants acknowledged how perceptions of female athletes are often based on the initial, unfair comparison to male athletes. A volleyball player specifically pointed out that being accepted and taken seriously as an athlete can sometimes be based on how well female athletes emphasize their sex appeal. This participant was quick to say that for her team, she knew that

> bench players [those who did not play often during matches] get full-on ready before games because . . . their biggest contribution to the team was to be eye candy for fans. They wouldn't sweat because they weren't playing, so . . . they would put on full makeup and completely do their hair because it was their job.

The volleyball team agreed that in order to get fans to come to games, it was important to have the bench players look as feminine as possible. Another quipped—referring to the volleyball players' uniform—"Spandex is an easy way to get people to games" but that it was even more important to go out on weekends and "look hot . . . because then girls think the boys will come support them because guys know what they *can* look like." These participants clearly understand the societal value of sex appeal when it comes to acceptance of female athletes. They also discussed the importance of being careful to make sure they did not outperform male athletes in the weight room; the men's gaze proved very important in the performance of femininity as an athlete:

> One spring, I had a high squat max of around 270, which is pretty high for a girl. Later I found out that [the strength coach] was making fun of boys who could not squat that much on the basketball and football teams. He used my name and would be like "Well, she can squat more than you, you [expletive]!" When I found out, I got super embarrassed because I don't want those boys to think I was manly! I thought they would make fun of me or be less attracted to me if I can squat more than them!

Similarly, some members from the track team explained how they often know the men's stats better than their own. One of the women described how she could rattle off the exact stats of a handful of male runners but did not even know the stats of her own teammates. She also explained how "the more successful you get, the more you kind of keep [accomplishments] quiet." When asked why this is, her response was, "You don't wanna be too badass for guys" because "success can be intimidating." More teammates expanded on this:

> [Track and field pole vaulter:] And I think sometimes, they think that we're almost, if we kind of brag about it, that we're better than them, and it makes them feel inferior . . . At my high school, I was probably bigger and stronger than some of the guys that did sports there. And I'm sure they felt kind of inferior to me, but I was never one to boast about it. . . . It's kind of like a respect thing.
>
> [Track and field sprinter:] When I ran in high school, I was really good on the girls' team. And when I'd win things, the boys would congratulate me on it when we got back. But then you always have the guys who are like "you can't run faster than me" or "you can't jump further than me" and it's always a comparison, every time I do something. That comes up all the time. So after a while, you don't even talk about it because it gets so annoying for guys to compare themselves to females. Because we have girls that can be faster but, naturally, guys are supposed to be faster. It's not something you should really compare.

Thus, a common theme was the struggle of being "othered" by a more powerful group (male athletes), while also understanding that outperforming that powerful group is unacceptable and threatening to a female athlete's sense of self.

Golf participants also compared themselves to male athletes, again emphasizing the importance of the male gaze to balance out the cue of playing "such a masculine sport." Golfers said they can wear sweats, but "you gotta wear a little bit of makeup" to make up for it. The participants also brought up how far behind they feel golf is when compared to other sports in terms of gender equality:

> Women have been allowed to play [other sports] a lot longer . . . golf, I would say, is . . . was not allowed for women for a long time. And there are still courses that will not allow women . . . the old saying is "gentlemen only, ladies forbidden"—that is what G-O-L-F stands for.

They went on to discuss the fairly recent controversy of allowing the first woman ever to play at Augusta National Golf Club[25] and how the status of golf as a profession makes it hard for them to feel like they are taken seriously. Because of this, an overarching theme to this focus group was golfers feeling inferior to their male counterparts and that they lacked respect and recognition as female athletes.

This finding was consistent throughout the focus groups. Interestingly, some participants described their events and being perceived as being less interesting and less fun to watch compared to men's sports. One runner explained that no matter the sport, women are overshadowed by men. She described how, while everyone might watch the National Basketball Association (NBA), "no one watches WNBA," the Women's National Basketball Association. Some of the participants mentioned that certain sports are able to garner more respect than others. For example, athletes in more competitive sports seemed to be more often recognized for their athleticism. A member of the softball team admitted that, as a softball player, she felt more respected as an athlete and was perceived by others to be more athletic compared to women from other sports. Athletes from golf, swimming, and tennis felt that their perceived lack of respect stemmed from the lack of understanding surrounding their sport. In another example, the golfers explained how golf is often considered "not a sport" and that the time and effort they put in is underestimated. One participant explained her perception that although male golfers may face some of the same stereotypes due to golf's noncontact nature, they still receive significantly more credibility than the women.

In sum, many participants cited instances of being "othered" simply because they held the status of Division I female athlete. They were aware of the perceived inferiority to male athletes and actively navigated around the rigid strictures of being successful at sport, but not *too* good, and certainly not outperforming their male counterparts. Physically, they also actively marked themselves as feminine in order to balance out the dual identity. The next section investigates how female athletes, as a result of being "othered" first, drew boundaries between their female athlete and nonathlete peers to construct a clear hierarchy between sports.

Horizontal Violence: NARPs and No-Bow Lesbos

Each team consistently compared themselves (as a group) to the other female sports teams on campus. However, two teams in particular—the swim and dive team and the softball team—aggressively drew boundaries as part of the feminine apologetic. These processes—criticizing those who also have limited power—is a quintessential example of horizontal violence. Each team participated in horizontal violence for different reasons, however. For the swim and dive team, the lack of time to perform femininity sparked discussion not only in their focus group but in other team focus groups as well. Indeed, three of the seven focus groups mentioned the swim and dive team as an example of a group they "felt sorry for" because they were so limited in how much they could emphasize femininity. A handful of participants brought up the swimmer's body—specifically the shoulders—and how "it must be hard . . . because you can't cover those big shoulders up." The swim and dive team was most often described as overly masculine in their appearance by athletes from other sports.

These sentiments were not lost on the swim and dive participants. The swimmers themselves described their inability and/or unwillingness to conform to the appearance-based expectations of other women, both in sport and not. They believed that most nonathletes who saw them in class every day thought of them as "lazy" or "gross" because they often wore sweatpants or had visibly unshaven legs. However, since their desire to fit in with female athletes outweighed their desire to be accepted by nonathletes, the swimming and diving team reactively othered female nonathletes, who they described in the opening minutes of the focus group as "NARPs"—nonathletic regular people: "I stay away from the NARPS . . . they're weird . . . I don't know, they just don't get it. They don't get why we do what we do."

When prompted to elaborate on characteristics of NARPs, they made no distinctions between different groups of nonathletes (e.g., sorority girls versus those who are heavily involved in academics) but instead lumped them all into one group, which they simply labeled as NARPs; in this way, the swimmers reacted to being othered by the athletes by accentuating the differences between athletes and nonathletes. The swim and dive team resented how much time the NARPs had to feminize: "The girls around campus that I see, they have their makeup, their sports bras and their yoga pants . . . they always have nice hair, or braids . . . we get in the pool, we can't like fix our hair between events . . . literally the only thing we can do is paint our nails."

Throughout the focus groups with the swim team, perhaps the most frequently mentioned complaint about their participation in sport was that it took up so much of their time, leaving little time for doing their hair or makeup. But while they teased the other female athletes and the nonathletes for "lik[ing] clothes and makeup," they also made it very clear that they themselves would behave in much the same way were there no time constraints imposed upon them. As one participant put it: "I mean, there was, like, a week span where . . . after [lifting] weights . . . I would go straighten my hair, and then get in the pool, dry my hair, go back, straighten it. It was so much effort. I mean, it's possible, but it's just not worth the extra time."

Spending the time to go back to their dorms to shower and make themselves "presentable" would mean cutting into time otherwise spent sleeping or eating, both of which eventually gained precedence over the desire to primp.

This is not to say that most of the swimmers did not try to maintain a feminine appearance when first arriving at the university. For part of the first semester, many of them would return to their dorms after practice in order to do their hair and/or makeup before heading to class or the dining hall. However, they did not immediately realize how much more demanding their schedules had become compared to high school, and while they tried to "keep up" for a while, spending time on their appearance eventually came to be seen as something that was "not a priority." Because of their highly regimented schedules, during the week when they have to juggle classes and practices, they are never afforded the luxury of having extra time to spend on their appearance. As they claimed, they wear sweatpants to class "every day," and their hair is usually up in a "dirty bun." They also do not wear makeup to class. The team had much to say about how this made them feel looked down on by others in the classroom. They believed the nonathletes saw *all* female athletes as "lazy" (for not putting time into their appearance) but that they themselves were especially seen in this way. The volleyball girls looked "cute" because "they have the bows" as well as the "nice hair" and "spankies." The track girls were described as "not normal" because they wore makeup and yoga pants. On the rare occasion they are able to put time into their appearance, they will often spend hours perfecting their look. Spending so much time on their appearance suggests that they are apologizing for the appearance they generally maintain throughout the school week, trying to prove to others that they can indeed be feminine.

However, even if the swimmers believed that most other female athletes on campus spent more time on their appearance than they did, they still saw the nonathletes as spending even *more* time on their appearance. The way the swimmers saw themselves as compared to the nonathletes becomes abundantly clear in the swimmers' drawings of female athletes, many of which contained both an athlete and a nonathlete. The nonathletes were drawn with voluptuous figures or otherwise "feminine" bodies, while the athletes were drawn with square-shaped bodies that often had disproportionately large body parts, especially shoulders. Most all the athletes in the drawings had their hair in a ponytail or bun, while the nonathletes were drawn with long hair worn down. In addition, the nonathletes were depicted with makeup, while the athletes were not. It is clear that the swim team saw physical presentation as one of the most decisive differences between athletes and nonathletes.

No-Bow Lesbo

Athletes from two sports—softball and golf—drew parallels between feminizing appearance as an effort to appear heterosexual. This was a central theme during the softball focus group; many of the participants discussed it. It is likely that a contributing factor to this is that softball is often seen as one of the more "masculine" sports as well as having a reputation for being the sport of choice for "butch women." The women on the softball team told of a multitude of unspoken rules that supposedly allude to players' sexuality, not just in their sport but in other sports as well. For instance, one participant said of female soccer players that "if they wear their hair up high, they're straight, but if they wear their hair low, they're les."

The idea that hair relates to one's sexuality recurred throughout the focus group discussions. For instance, the softball team had what they called a "dyke braid" (a combination of a ponytail and braid) and a fairly strict rule about hair bows. Supposedly, a heterosexual player should wear a bow in her hair in order to assure others that she is, indeed, heterosexual. Those caught violating this norm are labeled "no-bow lesbos," a term that, according to some on the team, is "pretty universal."

Another perhaps not-so-common idea in softball is that the number 00 is an indication of one's sexuality. Said one player: "When I was littler, I was double zero. Quit that number when I learned it was a *les* number. . . . The girls on my team [told me that], and then when I got to high school, there was a double zero, and it was the les."

It is not just softball that has these unspoken rules. A golf player told of her experience with wearing black shoes and stud earrings to practice in high school. She was apparently taken aside by her coach and told, "Do not wear black shoes . . . do not wear stud earrings, and wear a bow in your hair. And, like, wear makeup." These were, according to her coach, some ways in which to avoid receiving the label of "lesbian."

When asked to name which teams on campus were the most masculine or feminine, the swim team was mentioned by each of the other five focus groups as being very masculine, usually relating in some way to their physical appearance and/or their feminine presentation. (Interestingly, the swimmers themselves usually came to the conclusion that softball and the throwers on the track team were the most masculine.) Most often, the comments were about their build (broad shoulders, muscular thighs, etc.) or their self-presentation (not wearing makeup or "cute clothes" to class). The golf team, for example, talked about how the swimmers look "so bad, like all the time" because they "just don't put on makeup and don't try." The softball team, who play a sport that is perhaps most often labeled as a "lesbian sport," almost all agreed that the swimmers were the "least girly" team on campus because "their hair is always up, and they're always wearing sweats, and they have really big arms."

It should be noted that most of the "reasons" the other teams gave for labeling the swimmers as unfeminine have nothing to do with choice, unless one counts the option of choosing not to swim at all. Their arms must be muscular if they wish to swim well, and the muscles they must focus on lead to a broadening of the shoulders. Their hair and makeup are rarely done because of an extremely busy practice schedule that leaves little time to devote to their physical appearance. Also, unlike the other sports in campus, they cannot wear makeup during practice or competition, since they are continually in and out of the water.

In addition to being labeled as "masculine" for these overt reasons, the swimmers themselves pointed out something else that might contribute to the idea that swimmers are "masculine"—their eating habits. In many circles in U.S. society, it is expected that females not only monitor what *kinds* of foods they eat but also the *amount*. Since the swimmers participate in a sport that requires a lot of physical exertion, they have voracious appetites and could care little about trying to hide this. Though they themselves do not really care, this hardly escapes the notice of others. The amount of food that they eat gets pointed out to them "all the time" through comments such as, "Whoa . . . could you *eat* any more food?" or "Oh, did you bring enough food for the whole table?"

Comments such as this may not appear to be such a big deal at first, but they do seem to be a way for others to insult the swimmers for exhibiting such a counterfeminine behavior in public. Teasing comments such as this do not come exclusively from one sex, but the sentiment behind these comments is often different depending on the insulter's sex, at least as the swimmers themselves perceive it. As one teammate put it, when a comment is made "jokingly, I think it's the guys more," to which her teammate added, "I feel like the girls . . . get mad about it." Another added, "The girls get disgusted sometimes."

While their displays of femininity may be, in the eyes of some, a bit lacking, the swimmers themselves are well aware of the stereotypes that are held against them but can do little to change that, short of quitting the sport they love. Again, this is mostly because of their full schedules that leave little time for anything but practice, weight lifting, eating, and attending classes. Instead of devoting what little free time they have to "improving" their physical appearance, they choose to openly "reject" the idea of traditional femininity by scoffing at those who do spend time on their appearance. The best choice for them is to focus this energy on the nonathletes at school, or, as they like to refer to them, the NARPs. To hear the swim team talk, you would think that the term "NARP" was commonly used among all the teams on campus. Indeed, this is what the researchers intended to find in their subsequent focus groups. However, of the other participants, only some had heard the term and none could explain the acronym without first being prompted. The swimmers, however, seemed to regularly use the term, and most every teammate was familiar with it. Because the swim team was at "the bottom of the pack" among the sport teams on campus, they chose to focus most of their chagrin on a group *outside* the world of athletics, thus creating a ubiquitous category of students known as NARPs. (It should be noted here that this term was not created by the swim team but instead was an idea that sprung from the Internet.) Since the swimmers' status was mostly due to their appearance, they othered the NARPs on this exact basis—for feminizing themselves too much. While it is true they made fun of other teams for "being girly," they seemed to hold a particular antipathy for nonathletes.

Many of the swimmers drew both an athlete and a nonathlete in their drawings as a way to show how "different" they saw the two groups. The female athletes depicted (not always swimmers) were generally of a larger build, with sweatpants and ponytails. They did not draw any makeup on the athletes either. However, those who drew NARPs drew them with skirts or dresses and heavy makeup. One gave her NARP what she described as a "clearly . . . designer purse." Another drew her athlete, a swimmer, with lines indicative of a foul odor coming off of her. As she explained it, "she kinda smells a little bit." The NARP in her picture, however, "smell[ed] really good."

It makes sense that the swimmers should choose nonathletes as their main "other," especially since the identity of "athlete" is one of the most salient at this stage in their lives. By pointing out how different the nonathletes are from the athletes, they are symbolically likening themselves to the rest of the female athletes on campus. In addition, by saying the nonathletes spend too much time on their appearance, they are attempting to downplay the societal importance of attaining a feminine appearance.

DISCUSSION

Overall, the swimming and diving team was most consistently labeled as masculine in the focus groups. They were also aware that this was largely to do with their appearance. However, rather than call out the patriarchal system that holds them to such standards, they instead displace their aggression onto the nonathletes who do spend the time working toward that standard. The swim team itself was very aware of their status within the context of "female athletes," and because of this, they reactively othered the nonathletes on campus. If the swimmers themselves were made fun of (by other athletes) for not wearing makeup, then they would make it a point to act as if wearing makeup was cause for consternation. This not only lessens the feelings of the "importance" of wearing makeup, but it also serves to remind the other athletes that, while the other teams may see the swimmers as "different," they are still more similar to the swimmers than they are to the nonathletes.

The results give a glimpse into the complex relationships that exist among and between the female sport teams at a Division I school. While there is often little actual interaction between most of the teams, each team seemed to form fairly ubiquitous judgments of one another. Most of these judgments were based on gender constructs, with the most unpopular team (the swimming and diving team) on campus being consistently labeled the most "masculine." While the swim team was often scorned or scoffed at for not exhibiting enough femininity, the swimmers themselves openly scorned the female nonathletes who spent any significant amount of time before class preparing their hair and makeup. It is especially interesting to note that most of the swimmers themselves said that if they did they not have such busy schedules they would spend just as much time prepping for the day as what they considered to be the average for female NARPs. In this way, the swim team reactively othered the nonathletes. Since they understood that staying on the team meant sacrificing, among many things, their ability to present themselves as they might like, the swimmers mocked those who do spend any significant portion of their time on their appearance. Making fun of NARPs who spend time feminizing their appearance allowed the swimmers to define a clear boundary between athlete and "other," giving them a sense of camaraderie with the other athletes on campus.

The use of the focus group method, while invaluable in some ways, was also limiting to the study. Since the early interviews had no specific direction, a lack of uniformity in some of the questions is apparent throughout. However, this lack of uniformity gave the interviews an exploratory feel, wherein many strong themes emerged, including the link between acceptance and the adherence to gender roles. Unfortunately, none of the male teams were interviewed, so their feelings toward the swim team are merely speculation, but there was still plenty of evidence to show that the swimmers were not very highly regarded by the other female teams on campus. Naturally, there are many factors that play into this, and while this study seemed to suggest a link between the "amount" a female athlete apologizes to how accepted she is both by other female athletes as well as nonathletic females, the focus groups themselves were originally intended to find evidence of apologetic behavior in female sport teams, which may have affected the data.

Many of the other limits of this study had to do with the sample. Participants were recruited based on a convenience sample and were therefore from the same university in a smaller town in the West. The majority of the sport teams on this campus are Division I, which means it is likely these particular athletes experience a more intense training schedule and see sports as a more central part of their life than the average college athlete. Most participants were white, and most were freshmen or sophomores, so no data was gathered regarding the later experiences of college athletes. Since the study was originally intended to find evidence of apologetic behavior among female athletes, male athletes were not interviewed, and therefore the opinions of male athletes were all pure speculation on the part of the female athletes themselves. Similarly, no female or male nonathletes were interviewed, so it is not known if the athletes are correct in assuming that the majority of female nonathletes cast female athletes as "other" because of their self-presentation in class.

CONCLUSION

In the world of women's sport, othering is most frequently done on the basis of gender roles, either because one group (or team) is too feminine or else not feminine enough or outright masculine. In this way, one could say that each team's status is related to the degree to which the individuals on each team apologize. The most "unapologetic" team, the swimming and diving team, chose to reactively other a group outside the realm of athletics as a way to further reinforce the boundaries between athletes and nonathletes in an attempt to gain status merely on the basis of being an athlete. Since the swimmers were seen as being most incongruent with their gender role, they chose to mock a group who they saw as being consistently congruent with their role as "female."

The results of this study give us a better idea of the way complex and often contradictory emotions and behaviors combine to create social bonds as well as social barriers. The results offer evidence that the feminine apologetic is still a major part of many female athletes' lives and that othering can occur on the basis of gender roles. At the small university at which the data for this study was gathered, the swimming and diving team was most often labeled as masculine, and they were also the team most likely to receive negative comments. Being othered in this way by the rest of the athletes led the swimmers to reactively other the nonathletes. They focused their energy on making fun of the nonathletes for taking the time to feminize their appearance, which is the very thing that led to their being ostracized by nonswim/dive team female athletes. Campuses with similar issues as the ones described here may benefit from preventive education targeted at not only the athlete population but the entire population of women college students. For instance, more efforts to increase socialization between athletes and nonathletes may reduce othering and lead to an increased sociological imagination, or the ability to "walk in another's shoes." Campus initiatives targeted at bringing women together on the basis of similarities, as opposed to magnifying differences, could also help address these in/out-group dynamics. Indeed, in order to truly address what Freire described as horizontal violence, the oppressed groups need to build solidarity as opposed to conflict among themselves.[26] The first step to doing this is raising awareness about the processes that are occurring, which could be accomplished by a number of campus groups, including a women's resource center, the campus life offices, or the student affairs offices.

NOTES

1. Leslie Heywood and Shari L. Dworkin, *Built to Win: The Female Athlete as Cultural Icon*, Vol. V (Minneapolis: University of Minnesota Press, 2003); Mary Jo Kane, Nicole M. LaVoi, and Janet S. Fink, "Exploring Elite Female Athletes' Interpretations of Sport Media Images: A Window into the Construction of Social Identity and 'Selling Sex' in Women's Sports," *Communication & Sport* (2013): 1–30; Adrienne N. Milner and Jomills Henry Braddock II, *Sex Segregation in Sports: Why Separate Is Not Equal* (Santa Barbara, CA: ABC-CLIO, 2016); Steven J. Karau and Alice H. Eagly, "Invited Reaction: Gender, Social Roles, and the Emergence of Leaders," *Human Resource Development Quarterly* 10 (1999): 321–27.

2. Angela C. Henderson, Heidi Grappendorf, and Laura J. Burton, "Investigating Attractiveness in the Hiring Process of Female Athletes," *Gender in Management: An International Journal* 24 (2009): 156–77; Vikki Krane, Precilla Y. L. Choi, Shannon M. Baird, Christine M. Aimar, and Kerrie J. Kauer, "Living the Paradox: Female Athletes Negotiate Femininity and Muscularity," *Sex Roles* 50 (2004): 315–29.

3. Matthew B. Ezzell, "Barbie Dolls on the Pitch: Identity Work, Defensive Othering, and Inequality in Women's Rugby," *Social Problems* 56 (2009): 111–31; Michael A. Messner, *Taking the Field: Women, Men, and Sports* (Minneapolis: University of Minnesota Press, 2002).

4. Jan Felshin, "The Triple Option . . . For Women in Sport," *Quest* 21 (1974): 36–40.

5. Laurel R. Davis-Delano, April Pollock, and Jennifer Ellsworth Vose, "Apologetic Behavior Among Female Athletes: A New Questionnaire and Initial Results," *International Review for the Sociology of Sport* 44 (2009): 131–50.

6. Mary Jo Kane and Heather D. Maxwell, "Expanding the Boundaries of Sport Media Research: Using Critical Theory to Explore Consumer Responses to Representations of Women's Sports," *Journal of Sport Management* 25 (2011): 202–16.

7. Sylvia Klasovec, "The Sexual Politics of Women in Sport: A Survey on Lesbophobia," *Canadian Woman Studies* 15 (1995): 63–66.

8. Elaine M. Blinde and Diane E. Taub, "Women Athletes as Falsely Accused Deviants: Managing the Lesbian Stigma," *The Sociological Quarterly* 33 (1992): 521–33; Susan K. Cahn, *Coming on Strong: Gender and Sexuality in Twentieth-Century Women's Sport* (Cambridge, MA: Harvard University Press, 1995); Helen Lenskyj, "Female Sexuality and Women's Sport," *Women's Studies International Forum* 10 (1987): 381–86.

9. Elizabeth A. Daniels and Heidi Wartena, "Athlete or Sex Symbol: What Boys Think of Media Representations of Female Athletes," *Sex Roles* 65 (2011): 566–79; Julia Weber and Natalie Barker-Ruchti, "Bending, Flirting, Floating, Flying: A Critical Analysis of Female Figures in 1970s Gymnastics Photographs," *Sociology of Sport Journal* 29 (2012): 22–41.

10. Susan J. Douglas, *The Rise of Enlightened Sexism: How Pop Culture Took Us from Girl Power to Girls Gone Wild* (New York: Macmillan, 2010).

11. Ezzell, "Barbie Dolls on the Pitch," 112.

12. Molly George, "Making Sense of Muscle: The Body Experiences of Collegiate Women Athletes," *Sociological Inquiry* 75 (2005): 317–45.

13. Kane, LaVoi, and Fink, "Exploring Elite Female Athletes' Interpretations of Sport Media Images," 17.

14. Pat Griffin, "Changing the Game: Homophobia, Sexism, and Lesbians in Sport," *Quest* 44 (1992): 251–65.

15. Davis-Delano, Pollock, and Vose, "Apologetic Behavior Among Female Athletes," 146.

16. Sally R. Ross and Kimberly J. Shinew, "Perspectives of Women College Athletes on Sport and Gender," *Sex Roles* 58 (2008): 40–57.

17. Ann Colley, John Nash, Laurence O'Donnell, and Lesley Restorick, "Attitudes to the Female Sex Role and Sex-Typing of Physical Activities," *International Journal of Sport Psychology* 18 (1987): 19–29.

18. Esther Madriz, "Focus Groups in Feminist Research," *Handbook of Qualitative Research* 2 (2000): 835–50.

19. David L. Morgan, "Focus Groups," *Annual Review of Sociology* (1996): 129–52.

20. George, "Making Sense of Muscle," 339.

21. David Wade Chambers, "Stereotypic Images of the Scientist: The Draw-a-Scientist Test," *Science Education* 67 (1983): 255–65.

22. Faith Gibson, "Conducting Focus Groups with Children and Young People: Strategies for Success," *Journal of Research in Nursing* 12 (2007): 473–83.

23. Richard E. Boyatzis, *Transforming Qualitative Information: Thematic Analysis and Code Development* (Thousand Oaks, CA: Sage, 1998).

24. Paolo Freire, *Pedagogy of the Oppressed* (New York: Continuum Publishers, 1970).

25. Charles P. Charpentier, "An Unimproved Lie: Gender Discrimination Continues at Augusta National Golf Club," *Villanova Sports & Entertainment Law Journal* 11 (2004): 111.

26. Freire, *Pedagogy of the Oppressed*, 62.

12

Team USA: Gender Diversity and Team Success at the 2012 London Olympic Games

Christina Sanchez-Volatier, Jomills Henry Braddock II, Adrienne N. Milner, Ashley Beth Mikulyuk, and Marvin P. Dawkins

As sex segregation in most traditionally male-dominated organizations and institutions has declined, gender diversity has received growing research attention. Studies of gender diversity have often focused on whether diversity leads to organizational growth and productivity.[1] Recent empirical studies of gender diversity across a wide range of organizational and institutional contexts have produced mixed results.[2] Although many of these studies have found that gender diversity is positively associated with productivity and effectiveness in many different settings,[3] this relationship has not been studied in sport organizations. The present study breaks new ground in examining the impact of gender diversity on the performance of the U.S. Olympic team (Team USA) during the 2012 London Games. Specifically, we examine the relationship between Team USA's gender diversity and male–female overall medal winning success and success by type of sport.

The lack of research on this topic is a direct consequence of near-universal patterns of sex segregation in sports. Despite dramatic declines in sex segregation in most major social institutions, persistent sex segregation in sports[4] has made it virtually impossible to identify contexts in which to examine the effect of "true" gender diversity on team performance. To examine the effects of true gender diversity on performance would require that sport organizations allow teams (e.g., basketball, soccer) to vary in gender composition. However, in the United States, like other societies, a dominant gender ideology organizes most athletic competitions in ways that limit women and men to competition in same-sex sports, even in noncontact activities. Dominant gender ideology defines sports as a masculine domain and constrains or structures female participation opportunities in ways that reinforce male dominance.[5] For example, in high school sports like basketball and soccer, where comparable numbers of boys and girls participate, team competitions are virtually always sex segregated. In the rare instances of sports where mixed-sex teams are permitted, these mixed-sex teams generally do not compete against all-male or all-female single-sex teams.

In the modern era, however, national Olympic teams are becoming increasingly gender, as well as culturally, diverse.[6] Thus, Team USA serves as an interesting, and important, organizational context in which to examine the relationship between gender diversity and success in sports. It is important to note that although Olympic team members compete as individuals and/or as sport team participants (e.g., basketball), every American athlete is a part of Team USA, selected by the U.S. Olympic Committee solely for the purpose of competing against other national teams. Thus, Olympic athletes not only compete for themselves but for their countries. Indeed, earlier national polling data has shown that Americans are as likely to view the Olympics as a competition between nations (47%) as a competition between individual athletes (49%).[7] To the extent that every male and female athlete can contribute to the nation's overall medal count, Team USA can be considered to represent a true gender diverse team in competition against other national teams whose gender diversity may also vary.

SIGNIFICANCE OF THE OLYMPIC GAMES

In the United States, the Olympic Games are clearly the most closely followed international sports mega event. Other major international sports mega events, such as the Tour de France or World Cups in soccer, rugby, and cricket, draw very limited attention in the United States. The Olympic Games appeal to a large segment of the American population, including significant numbers of women. It also draws the attention of people who have a limited interest in sports. Indeed, during the Olympic Games, Americans avidly follow many sports—gymnastics, swimming, track and field—that are low in popularity. As John Nauright suggests, the symbolic power of the Olympic Games, and other international sports mega events, can evoke powerful imagery and elicit strong emotional responses among spectators.[8]

For the United States, like many other nations, the Olympic Games provide an international forum to not only demonstrate athletic prowess but to showcase an idealized image of a nation's character to a global audience.[9] In covering the Olympics, the American media explicitly emphasizes particular virtues of our national character by highlighting the significant progress toward gender parity in the composition of our Summer Olympic teams and the growing racial and ethnic diversity of our Winter Olympic teams.[10] In this way, the Olympic Games have served as a global stage on which to project particular aspects of *American exceptionalism*—the special character of the United States as a uniquely free nation based on democratic ideals and personal liberty.[11] Historically, it is not uncommon for other nations to use the Olympic Games and other international sports mega events (e.g., FIFA World Cup, Rugby World Cup, etc.) in similar ways. For example, Adolph Hitler viewed the 1936 Berlin Olympic Games as a platform to demonstrate the virtues of Germany's national character and commitment to Aryan superiority to the world. During the Cold War, both the United States and the Soviet Union sought to demonstrate the superiority of their national character in Olympic stadiums. More recently, in South Africa, even though rugby had traditionally been viewed as a symbol of Apartheid, for white and black South Africans alike, winning the World Rugby Championship in 2007 and hosting the World Football Championship in 2010 represented important symbolic milestones in the construction of a new form of national unity and racial reconciliation.[12]

It has also been argued that modern Olympic sports help maintain national unity and cohesion.[13] Jane Mower's recent comparative analysis found that a majority of people in 18 of the 20 countries studied indicated that national Olympic sports performances contribute to feelings of national pride.[14] Olympic success also influences international prestige.[15] Thus, an increasing number of countries explicitly invest in achieving a better position on the Olympic medal index. Historically, the former Soviet Union, and more recently China, have shown a willingness to spend vast sums of private and public money on international sports mega events as a way to promote their political and economic systems.[16]

WOMEN IN THE OLYMPIC GAMES

The father of the modern Olympics, Baron Pierre de Coubertin, did not believe that women should participate as Olympic athletes; instead he asserted that their only role in the games should be to "crown . . . the winner with garlands."[17] Though originally excluded from participation, women have competed in the Olympics since the Paris Games in 1900.[18] The first American female Olympian and medalist, Margaret Abbott, won the women's golf competition in the Paris Games.[19] Since that early period, female participation has grown slowly but significantly, especially over the last half-century. Between 1900 and 1960, women's Summer Olympic participation grew from less than 1 percent to 11.4 percent of all athletes. However, over the last half-century, since the 1964 Tokyo Games, women's participation has increased to nearly one-half (45 percent) of the total number of athletes in the 2012 London Games. For the first time, at the 2012 London Games, every participating country included at least one female athlete in its delegation.

During the Opening Ceremony in London, Jacques Rogge, the president of the International Olympic Committee, was warmly applauded when he described women's progress in the Olympic movement as "a major boost for gender equality." Indeed, the 2012 London Games has been heralded as the "Year of the Woman at the Olympics."[20] At the 2012 London Games, for the first time, Team USA included more women (268) than men (261). The International Olympic Committee has led a number of initiatives and reforms to promote gender equity, including applying pressure on Saudi Arabia to include women on their Olympic team for the first time at the 2012 London Games. Also for the first time, women competed in all 26 sports, including in traditionally male-dominated events like boxing, at the London Games. Overall, these patterns of growing female Olympic participation reflect a global trend toward increasing gender equity, including in sports. As sport has historically been viewed as masculine turf,[21] more equitable participation and increasing accomplishments by female athletes suggests that sports are experiencing gender diversification. Gender diversity in sports, as in other institutional contexts (e.g., labor market, military, politics, education, religion) is accompanied by both challenges and opportunities.

In the United States, Title IX—which mandated equal opportunities for women in educational programs that receive federal funds—has played a major role in laying the foundation for American women's Olympic success. Title IX led to more teams, greater support, and better facilities for females in both interscholastic and intercollegiate sports. According to Scott Blackmun, chief executive of the U.S. Olympic Committee, Title IX gave U.S. women more opportunities in sports before other nations did the same, laying a foundation that has yielded a trove of Olympic medals.[22] Overall, female Olympic *participation rates*—the proportion of Olympians who are female—have grown in tandem with increases in *participation opportunities*—the proportion of sports and events open to female athletes. Figure 12.1 shows over-time trends in both female Olympic participation opportunities (events open to female athletes) and female participation rates.

As the graph illustrates, 678 females (13%) competed in the 1964 Tokyo Olympics, and the female share of Olympic athletes has increased steadily in each Olympiad since. In the 2012 London Games, 4,688 women competed, making up 44.7 percent of all athletes. Likewise, the percentage of events that include women has also risen in each Olympics leading up to the 2012 London Olympic Games, where women competed in 46.4 percent of the 302 events. It is not surprising that the lines in Figure 12.1, representing

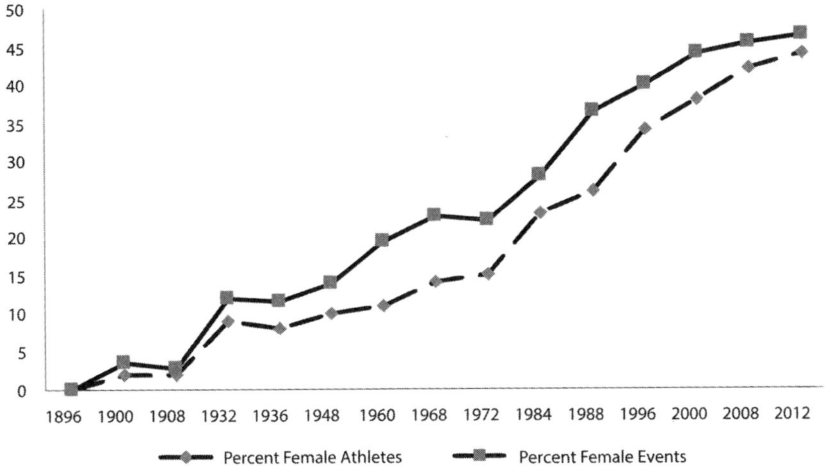

Figure 12.1

percentage of women's events and percentage of female athletes, are virtually parallel, given that female participation is contingent on opportunities available to women. The patterns shown here are quite similar to what has been found for girls' participation in high school sports. Nationally, Jomills Braddock II et al. found that, net of other factors, females' high school participation rates (i.e., ratio of male to female students participating in single-gender sports) across states is strongly related to participation opportunities (number of sports and sport teams open to females).[23]

In the Olympic Games, like high school and college sports, creating a level playing field for women's participation opportunities remains a challenge. For example, at many American high schools where girls and boys play basketball it is not uncommon for schools to offer both varsity and junior varsity basketball teams for boys while girls typically are provided only varsity basketball teams. Thus, even though both males and females are allowed to play high school basketball, boys often have twice the participation opportunities of girls in that sport. In the Olympics, women's participation opportunities are similarly constrained even though they are allowed to participate in the same number of sports. For example, at the 2012 London Games, some traditionally male sports (e.g., boxing and wrestling) in which women now compete offer more weight classes for males than females in these events. Thus, even though women have been recently permitted to compete in sports like boxing, because of the manner in which these competitions are structured they continue to offer a greater number of participation (and medaling) opportunities to males.

RESEARCH ON PRODUCTIVITY AND SPORT TEAM DIVERSITY

As previously noted, because of sex segregation in sport, the relationship between gender diversity and team performance has not been studied. Although many sports remain race-typed black sports (e.g., basketball), or white sports (e.g., golf), race-ethnic integration in sports has outpaced gender integration in sports. However, our review only located a few empirical studies that directly examine the relationship between ethnic diversity and performance in team sports contexts. Jessica Weiss and Paul Sommers examined the association between team racial composition and success among professional basketball teams and found that team racial diversity in the NBA appears to be neither an asset nor a liability to team performance (winning percentage).[24] Craig Bogar examined the association between racial composition and success among Atlantic Coastal Conference (ACC) men's and women's college basketball teams and found that (1) coaching diversity was unrelated to winning percentage; (2) among women's teams, diversity was positively, though not significantly, related to winning percentage; and (3) among men's teams, diversity was positively and significantly related to winning percentage.[25] Neither of these studies examined Olympic sports or the effects of gender diversity. Interestingly, although a number of studies,[26] largely by economists, have sought to identify social and demographic correlates of Olympic success (medal counts) across nations, gender typically has not been among the correlates examined. In the one recent study in which gender composition of Olympic teams was examined as a potentially important correlate of national teams' success (as measured by medals won), the results are ambiguous.[27] In a very complex set of analyses examining multiple models, each with alternative specifications, the authors found that the proportion of female athletes on national teams was positively and significantly correlated with medals won under some model specifications but not in others.[28]

METHODS

Data pertaining to U.S. athletes' participation rates and demographics for the 2012 London Olympic Games were gathered from the U.S. Olympic Team (Team USA) website. Data pertaining to U.S. medal counts was collected from the NBC website covering the London Olympics, from the official website of the 2012 London Olympic Games, and the Team USA website.[29] Because our analysis examines participation and success of individual athletes rather than national teams, we count medals awarded to each individual athlete. Thus, our analytic medal counts differ somewhat from official team medal counts. For example, both the men's and women's basketball teams earned gold medals. The official team medal count would be two U.S. gold medals. However, each of the 12 members of the men's and women's basketball teams was awarded gold medals, resulting in an individual count of 24 gold medals. A similar strategy was employed in track and field and swimming competitions where, for example, a four-person relay team earns a single national team medal, but each of the four swimmers or runners is counted as an individual medal winner. Similar procedures were followed for other team sports (e.g., soccer, volleyball, doubles tennis) in which individual athletes are awarded medals based on team success. Likewise, when an individual athlete wins medals in more than one event (swimming, track and field, gymnastics, etc.), each medal is counted.

We examine gender parity (equality or similarity) in Olympic participation and success using social indicators.[30] Comparisons of females' and males' participation and success can appear quite different in magnitude when different indices are used to present identical data. Suzanne Donovan and Christopher Cross describe three different indices for measuring parity.[31] A risk index could be calculated by dividing the number of females participating in the Olympics by the total number of high school and college female athletes in the school population. Thus, the risk index would represent the proportion of female Olympic participants. An odds ratio could be calculated by dividing the risk index for females by the risk index for males and would represent a comparative index of risk. If the risk index for a participation indicator is identical for males and females, the odds ratio will equal unity or 1.0. Odds ratios less than unity indicate that females are underrepresented relative to males while odds ratios greater than unity would indicate that females are overrepresented. Finally, a composition index would be calculated by dividing the number of females participating in Olympic athletics by the total number of athletes participating in the Olympics. This measure would represent the proportion of all Olympic athletes who are female. The composition index can produce misleading results because it does not control for baseline representation for gender subgroups. In this project, we calculate a parity index by dividing the proportion of female Olympic participants by the proportion of male participants. Because female and male athletes' baseline numbers are roughly equivalent, the parity index measure employed here approximates an odds ratio indicator. Parity, or unity, is represented by the value 1.0, such that values below 1.0 reflect underrepresentation and values above represent overrepresentation. Our descriptive analysis uses the parity index to assess male–female representation and performance in the 2012 London Olympic Games. In addition, we perform a simple bivariate OLS regression analysis to assess the strength of the relationship between female representation on Team USA and U.S. Olympic team success over time.

FINDINGS

Descriptive results are presented in Table 12.1 As indicated in the bottom panel of Table 12.1, Team USA had a slightly higher representation of female (51%) compared to male (49%) athletes.

The parity index (1.02) shows that females had a 2 percent greater presence among U.S. Olympic athletes. As noted earlier, this was the first time in Olympic history that Team USA was majority female. In this instance, female overrepresentation was due mainly to the failure of the U.S. men's soccer team to qualify. Results in the bottom panel of Table 12.1 also show that relative to their participation, female athletes accounted for a disproportionate share of total medals won by the U.S. Olympic Team in the 2012 London Games. Specifically, the parity index for Team USA medals won (1.78) indicates that female athletes (147) earned a 78 percent greater share of total team medals than their male (82) counterparts. This finding reveals a clear benefit of gender diversity to American success in the London 2012 Olympic Games. Indeed, the total medals won by American females was higher than the total number of medals won by all but five nations competing in the games.

Not only did Team USA women win more total medals than their male teammates, they won medals in a broader range of sports, including traditional male-dominated sports, such as boxing and wrestling. Team USA males earned medals in 12 sport categories (archery, basketball, diving, gymnastics, judo, rowing, shooting, swimming, taekwondo, tennis, track and field, and wrestling). In contrast, Team USA females earned medals in 17 sport categories (basketball, boxing, cycling, diving, fencing, gymnastics, judo, rowing, shooting, soccer, swimming, taekwondo, tennis, track and field, volleyball, water polo, and wrestling). Among all the specific sport categories where both males and females earned medals, females won a disproportionate share of Team USA medals in six sport categories: (gymnastics (1.80), judo (1.25), rowing (1.65), shooting (1.67), tennis (1.14), and wrestling (1.06), while their male teammates were overrepresented in just three sport categories: diving (1.47), swimming (1.13), and track and field (1.02). The results in Table 12.1 also show greater success of Team USA females compared to males even in traditional male-dominated or masculine-typed sports like boxing, judo, shooting, and wrestling.

The descriptive results presented thus far are based on comparisons of the performances of individual male and female athletes in the 2012 London Olympics. We turn next to an aggregate analysis of Team USA's success in 14 different Olympic Games between 1932 and 2012 to examine the strength of the association between gender diversity (female representation) and Team USA success over time. We perform bivariate OLS analyses regressing

Table 12.1 Participation and Success of U.S. Athletes in the 2012 London Olympics by Gender

Sport	Men			Women			Total	
	Athletes % (n)	Medals % (n)	Parity Index	Athletes % (n)	Medals % (n)	Parity Index	Athletes N	Medals N
Archery	50 (3)	100 (3)	2.00	50 (3)			6	3
Badminton	67 (2)			33 (1)			3	
Basketball	50 (12)	50 (12)	1.00	50 (12)	50 (12)	1.00	24	24
Boxing	75 (9)			25 (3)	100 (2)	4.00	12	2
Canoeing	71 (5)			29 (2)			7	
Cycling	50 (12)			50 (12)	100 (5)	2.00	24	5
Diving	45 (5)	67 (4)	1.47	55 (6)	33 (2)	0.61	11	6
Equestrian	54 (7)			46 (6)			13	
Fencing	50 (8)			50 (8)	100 (4)	2.00	16	4
Field Hockey				100 (18)			18	
Gymnastics	50 (6)	10 (1)	0.20	50 (6)	90 (9)	1.80	12	10
Judo	60 (3)	50 (2)	0.83	40 (2)	50 (2)	1.25	5	4
Pentathlon	33 (1)			67 (2)			3	
Rowing	55 (24)	25 (4)	0.46	45 (20)	75 (12)	1.65	44	16
Sailing	56 (9)			44 (7)			16	
Shooting	70 (14)	50 (2)	0.71	30 (6)	50 (2)	1.67	20	4
Soccer				100 (18)	100 (18)	1.00	18	18
Synchronize				100 (2)			2	
Table Tennis	25 (1)			75 (3)			4	
Taekwondo	50 (4)	50 (1)	1.00	50 (2)	50 (1)	1.00	6	2
Tennis	50 (6)	43 (3)	0.86	50 (6)	57 (4)	1.14	12	7
Track & Field	50 (63)	51 (22)	1.02	50 (62)	49 (21)	0.98	125	43
Trampoline	50 (1)			50 (1)			2	
Triathlon	40 (2)			60 (3)			5	
Volleyball	50 (16)			50 (16)	100 (16)	2.00	32	16
Water Polo	50 (13)			50 (13)	100 (13)	2.00	26	13
Weight Lifting	33 (1)			67 (2)			3	
Wrestling	76 (13)	75 (3)	0.98	24 (4)	25 (1)	1.06	17	4
Totals	100 (264)	100 (82)		100 (271)	100 (147)		535	226
Medals %		36			64			
Athletes %	49			51				
Overall Women/Men Participation Index			1.03					
Overall Women/Men Medal Parity Index			1.78					

(N in parentheses)

Olympic success on the gender composition (% female) of U.S. Olympic teams over time. Olympic success is measured in two ways: 1) medal count—total medals won by Team USA in each Olympics, and 2) medal prestige—a weighted medals index constructed as the sum of medal points—gold (three points), silver (two points), and bronze (one point)—earned by Team USA in each Olympic year. Table 12.2 reports the result of bivariate regression of Team USA percent female on Team USA medals count and medals prestige.

The results in the left panel of Table 12.2 show that percent female (b = .670, $p < .05$) is positively and significantly associated with the medals count index for Team USA. The significant F-statistic (6.470, $p < .05$) indicates a fairly good model fit. Thus, there is little chance that the observed correlations are due solely to random sampling error. The adjusted R^2 (.313) indicates that gender composition alone accounts for roughly one-third (31%) of the total variation in Team USA's medal count. The results in the right panel of Table 12.2 show that percent female is also positively and significantly associated (b = 1.245, $p < .05$) with the medals prestige index for Team USA. Higher scores on the medals prestige index reflect the status of medals (i.e., gold versus silver or bronze) earned. Thus, this finding suggests that Team USA earns higher-status awards when female athletes are well represented.

The significant F-statistic (5.872, $p < .05$) indicates a fairly good model fit. Again, there is little chance that the observed correlations are due solely to random sampling error. The adjusted R^2 (.289) indicates that gender composition alone accounts for roughly 29 percent of the total variation in Team USA's weighted medals index. Thus, for both measures of Olympic success (medals prestige index and medals count index), gender composition accounts for nearly one-third of the total variation in these outcomes for Team USA.

Figure 12.2a and 12.2b present graphic representations of the association of gender diversity and team success.

The results in Figure 12.2a display the relationship between Team USA percent female athletes and scores on the medals prestige index in 14 different

Table 12.2 Regression of Olympic Success Indicators on Team USA Gender Diversity

	Medals Count Index			Medals Prestige Index		
	b	ß	S.E.	b	ß	S.E.
Percent Women	0.670*	0.609	0.263	1.245*	0.59	0.514
Constant	72.921***		8.715	159.869***		17.002
Adj. R^2		0.313			0.289	
F-Statistic		6.470*			5.872*	

* = $p < .05$; ** = $p < .01$; *** = $p < .001$

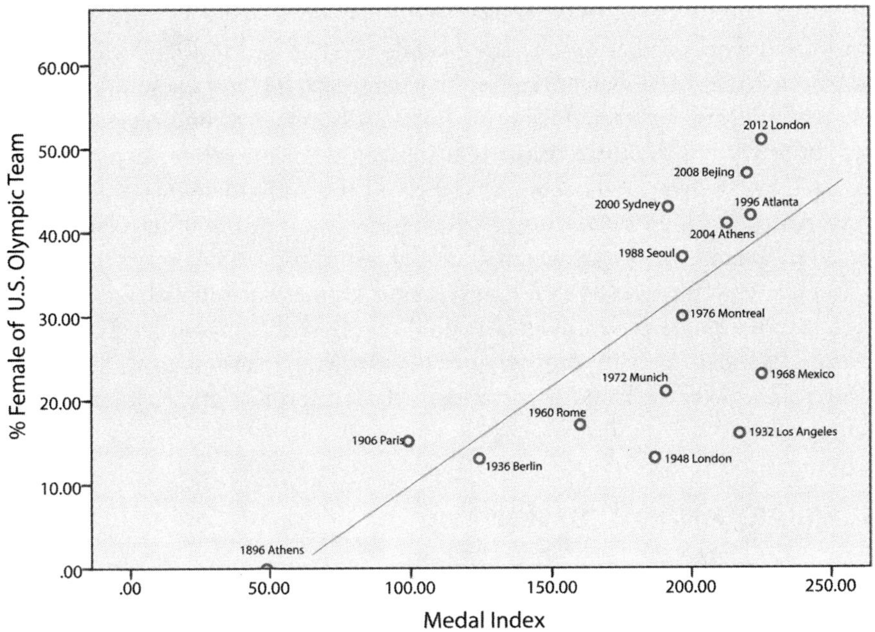

Figure 12.2a

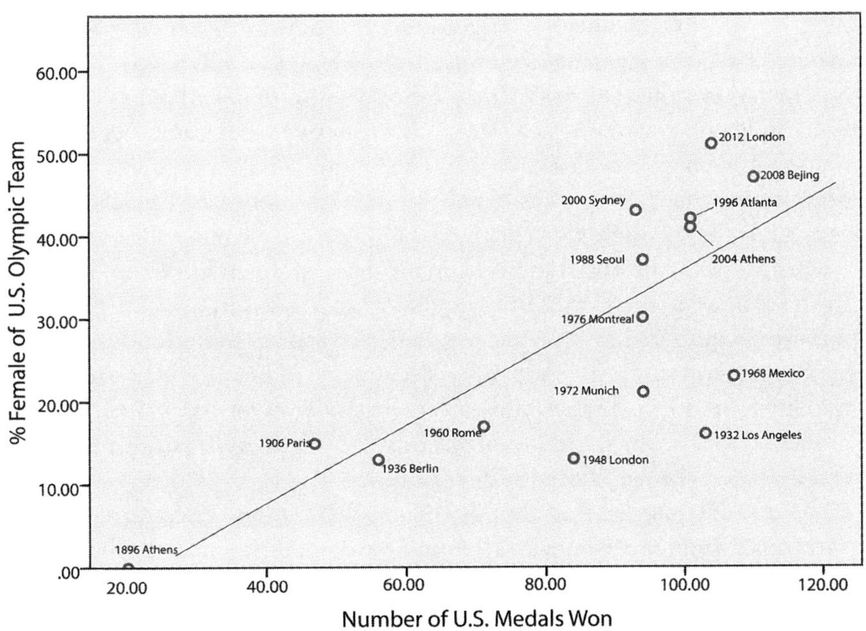

Figure 12.2b

Olympic Games between 1932 and 2012. Olympic success, shown on the horizontal axis, is measured by the medals prestige index. Gender diversity, on the vertical axis, is measured by the percent female of each U.S. Olympic team during the period examined. The solid vertical line represents the best approximation of the linear relationship between gender diversity and Team USA's Olympic success. As indicated, the relationship is strong and very positive. Likewise, the results in Figure 12.2b display the relationship between Team USA percent female athletes and the medals count index for Team USA in the same 14 different Olympic Games between 1932 and 2012. Again, Olympic success (medals count index) is shown on the horizontal axis and gender diversity on the vertical axis. This relationship is also quite strong and positive. In both instances, the scatterplots approximate linear relationships.

SUMMARY AND DISCUSSION

Assessing the costs and benefits of diversity has become an increasingly popular topic in the social sciences. However, few studies have focused on sport, and the handful of previous studies[32] that examine diversity and productivity in sport have mainly focused on racial diversity rather than gender diversity. In the one study in which gender diversity is the focus, Pravin Trivedi and David Zimmer's results were inconclusive.[33] The current study sought to add to this research literature by examining how gender diversity impacted both the performance of the U.S. Olympic Team in the 2012 London Games and the success of Team USA over an 80-year time period. Our results indicate that there is a strong and positive association between the number of women included on Team USA and medals won, supporting the notion that gender diversity is beneficial in sports contexts. Specifically, our descriptive results show that in the 2012 London Olympic Games, female athletes accounted for a disproportionate share of Team USA's total medals (78%) won, and female athletes were more successful in a broader range of sports (including traditionally male-dominated sports) than their male counterparts. In terms of how gender diversity impacted Team USA's success over time, bivariate OLS analyses indicate that gender diversity is positively and significantly associated with total medals earned as well as the prestige of medals earned (i.e., gold versus silver or bronze).

These results suggest that the U.S. National Olympic Committees should continue to promote women's Olympic participation since the benefits of gender diversity extend beyond individual female athletes. More specifically, this study shows that Team USA as a whole earns both a greater number and prominence of awards when female athletes are well represented. Furthermore, because the Olympics serve as an international arena to display national character, strength, unity, and pride, the United States benefits from female athletes' contributions to the nation's Olympic success—both in the number and the prestige of medals won by Team USA. Thus, it is clear that at the highest level of international sports mega events such as the Olympic Games, the United States benefits from gender diversity.

There are several explanations for why gender diversity may have a positive impact on Team USA's performance in both 2012 and over time. First, the sheer number of individuals on a team results in increased opportunity for success, and with no cap on how many athletes per country can participate in the Games, larger numbers of female athletes on Team USA results in more chances for the United States to earn medals. Secondly, because the United States is one of the few nations to promote women's athletics through collegiate scholarships, the growth in the number of women's Olympic events puts the United States at an advantage over other countries who have yet to encourage women culturally, and financially, to compete at the highest levels of sport. Lastly, the size of the United States, and therefore the amount of women in the country compared to many other nations, primes the United States to win more medals than those nations as there are more women to compete in diverse sports at the highest level.

Because these results are only applicable to the United States, future studies could extend this line of research to assess how gender diversity has affected the success of other nations. In addition, subsequent studies could include other measures of diversity, such as race, to examine their effects on the number and prestige of medals earned by the United States or other nations. Such research should also account for intersectionality in relation to diversity by focusing on how the representation of women (and men) of color impacts Olympic success.

NOTES

1. Sarah Fisher Ellison and Wallace P. Mullin, "Diversity, Social Goods Provision, and Performance in the Firm," *Journal of Economics & Management Strategy* 23 (2014): 465–81; Vivian Hunt, Dennis Layton, and Sara Prince, "Diversity Matters," *McKinsey & Company*, last modified November 24, 2014, http://odpowiedzialnybiznes.pl/wp-content/uploads/2015/04/Diversity-Matters.pdf.

2. Ellison and Mullin, "Diversity, Social Goods Provision, Performance."

3. Ibid.; Hunt, Layton, and Prince, "Diversity Matters."

4. Adrienne N. Milner and Jomills Henry Braddock II, *Sex Segregation in Sports: Why Separate Is Not Equal* (Santa Barbara, CA: Praeger, 2016).

5. Michael A. Messner, "Sports and Male Domination: The Female Athlete as Contested Ideological Terrain," *Sociology of Sport Journal* 5 (1988): 197–211.

6. Daniel K. N. Johnson and Ayfer Ali, "Coming to Play or Coming to Win: Participation and Success at the Olympic Games," Wellesley College Department of

Economics Working Paper, 2000–10 (2000); Jim Parry, "Sport and Olympism: Universals and Multiculturalism," *Journal of the Philosophy of Sport* 33 (2006): 188–204; Thomas M. Hunt, "Countering the Soviet Threat in the Olympic Medals Race: The Amateur Sports Act of 1978 and American Athletics Policy Reform," *The International Journal of the History of Sport* 24 (2007): 796–818.

7. U.S. News and World Report, "U.S. News & World Report/Bozell Worldwide Sports Poll," Bozell Worldwide (May 1996); The Tarrance Group, Lake Research, and KRC Research, "Roper Center for Public Opinion Research," Cornell University, Ithaca, NY, retrieved September 26, 2016, https://ropercenter.cornell.edu/.

8. John Nauright, "Selling Nations to the World through Sports: Mega-Events and Nation Branding as Global Diplomacy," *Public Diplomacy Magazine* (2013): 22–27.

9. Ibid.

10. Jackie Hogan, "Staging the Nation: Gendered and Ethnicized Discourses of National Identity in Olympic Opening Ceremonies," *Journal of Sport & Social Issues* 27 (2003): 100–23; Don Sabo, Sue Curry Jansen, Danny Tate, Margaret Carlisle Duncan, and Susan Leggett, "Televising International Sport: Race, Ethnicity, and Nationalistic Bias," *Journal of Sport & Social Issues* 20 (1996): 7–21; Andrew C. Billings, *Olympic Media: Inside the Biggest Show on Television* (New York: Routledge, 2008).

11. Steven W. Pope, "Rethinking Sport, Empire, and American Exceptionalism," *Sport History Review* 38 (2007): 92–120; Andrei S. Markovits and Steven L. Hellerman, "Women's Soccer in the United States: Yet Another American 'Exceptionalism,'" *Soccer & Society* 4 (2003): 14–29; Mark Dyreson, *Crafting Patriotism for Global Dominance: America at the Olympics* (New York: Routledge, 2013).

12. John Nauright, *Long Run to Freedom: Sport, Cultures and Identities in South Africa* (Morgantown, WV: Fitness Information Technology, 2010); Saskia Irene Welschen, "Making Sense of Being South African: The Analysis of National Identity Construction in Talk (paper presented at the ISA World Congress of Sociology, Gothenburg, Sweden, July 11–17, 2010).

13. Alan Bairner, *Sports, Nationalism, and Globalization: European and North American Perspectives* (Stony Brook: State University of New York Press, 2001); Neil Blain, Raymond Boyle, and Hugh O'Donnell, *Sport and National Identity in the European Media* (Leicester, UK: Leicester University Press, 1993); Robertson R. Giulianotti, "Recovering the Social: Globalization, Football and Transnationalism," *Global Networks* 7 (2007): 166–86; Barrie Houlihan, "Sport, National Identity and Public Policy," *Nations and Nationalism* 3 (1997): 113–37; Joseph Maguire and Emma K. Poulton, "European Identity Politics in Euro 96: Invented Traditions and National Habitus Codes," *International Review for the Sociology of Sport* 34 (1999): 17–29; Lloyd L. Wong and Richard Trumper, "Global Celebrity Athletes and Nationalism Fútbol, Hockey, and the Representation of Nation," *Journal of Sport & Social Issues* 26 (2002): 168–94.

14. Jane Mower, "London 2012: Olympic Success Is Key to National Pride," *BBC News World*, last modified January 1, 2012, http://www.bbc.com/news/world-16245075.

15. Lincoln Allison and Terry Monnington, "Sport, Prestige and International Relations," *Government and Opposition* 37 (2002): 106–34.

16. Pravin K. Trivedi and David M. Zimmer, "Success at the Summer Olympics: How Much Do Economic Factors Explain?" *Econometrics* 2 (2014): 169–202.

17. Baron Pierre de Coubertin, quoted in Adrianne Blue, *Faster, Higher; Further: Women's Triumphs and Disasters at the Olympics* (New York: Random House, 1988).

18. International Olympic Committee, "Fact Sheet: Women in the Olympic Movement," *International Olympic Committee* (2016): 1–5, last modified January 22, 2016, https://stillmed.olympic.org/Documents/Reference_documents_Factsheets/Women_in_Olympic_Movement.pdf.

19. National Women's History Museum, "Breaking Records," *National Women's History Museum*, retrieved August 16, 2016, http://www.nwhm.org/blog/breaking-records/.

20. Bill Chappell, "Year of the Woman at the London Games? For Americans, It's True," *NPR*, last modified August 10, 2012, http://www.npr.org/sections/thetorch/2012/08/10/158570021/year-of-the-woman-at-the-london-games-for-americans-its-true.

21. Messner, "Sports and Male Domination."

22. Rachel Blount, "For China, Olympics Have Been a Win-Win-Win Situation: The Country's Investment Has Brought Home Gold and Inspired a New Age for Fans, Athletes," *McClatchy-Tribune Business News* (2008).

23. Jomills H. Braddock II, Jan Sokol-Katz, Anthony Greene, and Lorrine Basinger-Fleischman, "Uneven Playing Fields: State Variations in Boys' and Girls' Access to and Participation in High School Interscholastic Sports," *Sociological Spectrum* 25 (2005): 231–50.

24. Jessica B. Weiss and Paul M. Sommers, "Does Team Racial Composition Affect Team Performance in the NBA?" *Atlantic Economic Journal* 37 (2009): 119–20.

25. Craig T. Bogar, "The Relationship Between Racial Diversity and Winning Percentage: A Study of Men's and Women's Basketball Teams and Coaching Staffs in the Atlantic Coast Conference from 2005," *The Sports Journal* 17 (2014).

26. Andrew B. Bernard and Meghan R. Busse, "Who Wins the Olympic Games: Economic Resources and Medal Totals," *Review of Economics and Statistics* 86 (2004): 413–17; Johnson and Ali, "Coming to Play"; Daniel Johnson and Ayfer Ali, "A Tale of Two Seasons: Participation and Medal Counts at the Summer and Winter Olympic Games," *Social Science Quarterly* 85 (2004): 974–93; Mark Baimbridge, "Outcome Uncertainty in Sporting Competition: The Olympic Games 1896–1996," *Applied Economics Letters* 5 (1998): 161–64; George Vagenas and Eleni Vlachokyriakou, "Olympic Medals and Demo-Economic Factors: Novel Predictors, the Ex-host Effect, the Exact Role of Team Size, and the 'Population-GDP' Model Revisited," *Sport Management Review* 15 (2012): 211–17; Gerald Kuper and Elmer Sterken, "Olympic Participation and Performance Since 1896," *SSRN* 274295 (2001).

27. Trivedi and Zimmer, "Success at Summer Olympics."

28. Ibid., 169–202.

29. "NBC Olympics: Athletes," *NBC Universal* (2012), retrieved August–December 2012, http://www.nbcolympics.com/athletes/index.html; London 2012 Olympics, "London 2012 Olympics: Athletes," *The Official of London 2012 Olympics and Paralympic* (2012) *Games*, retrieved August–December 2012, http://www.london2012.com/athletes/; Team USA, "Team USA: Athletes," *2012 United States Olympic Committee* (2012), retrieved August–December 2012, http://www.teamusa.org/Athletes.aspx.

30. U.S. Commission on Civil Rights, *Social Indicators of Equality for Minorities and Women* (Washington, DC: U.S. Government Printing Office, 1978).

31. Suzanne M. Donovan and Christopher T. Cross, *Minority Students in Special and Gifted Education* (Washington, DC: National Academy Press, 2002).

32. Bogar, "Relationship Between Racial Diversity and Winning"; Weiss and Sommers, "Team Racial Composition."

33. Trivedi and Zimmer, "Success at Summer Olympics."

About the Editors and Contributors

EDITORS

ADRIENNE N. MILNER, PhD, is Lecturer of Global Public Health at Barts and the London School of Medicine and Dentistry, Queen Mary University of London. She is coauthor of *Sex Segregation in Sports: Why Separate Is Not Equal* (Praeger, 2016). Milner has served as principal investigator on two grants that assess how sex and racial differences affect physical activity and health outcomes and is recipient of an American Heart Association Worksite Innovation Award for this research. Her published works on sport, sex, gender, and equality include numerous teaching materials.

JOMILLS HENRY BRADDOCK II, PhD, is a professor at the University of Miami in the Department of Sociology. Dr. Braddock has been researching and teaching about sport and social issues for over 35 years at top sociology institutions. His research focuses on sport and race/ethnicity, gender equity, and results and reactions to social policy. For over 10 years, Professor Braddock served as the director of the Center for Research on Sport in Society at the University of Miami. Dr. Braddock has published more than 20 papers on sport in top sociology journals and served as principal investigator on grants focusing on sport research that totaled more than $5.25 million. He was awarded the honor of serving as the outside representative to the NFL Players Association and is the recipient of the James E. Blackwell Founders Award for distinguished service and lifetime achievement from the Association of Black Sociologists. Dr. Braddock has organized, presented, and served as a panelist and discussant at over 50 professional conferences and also served as an expert witness at the Congressional Oversight Hearing on Equal Employment Opportunity in the National Football League.

CONTRIBUTORS

JACQUELYN ALLEN-COLLINSON is a professor of sociology and physical culture at the University of Lincoln (United Kingdom).

SCOTT NORMAN BROOKS is the associate dean of undergraduate education, an associate professor of education, society, and culture and education policy and leadership, and the special assistant to intercollegiate athletics at the University of California–Riverside.

J. A. CARTER is a visiting assistant professor of sociology at Miami University Regionals.

ROXANE COCHE is an assistant professor in journalism at the University of Memphis.

DIANA TRACY COHEN is an associate professor of political science at Central Connecticut State University.

MARVIN P. DAWKINS is a professor of sociology at the University of Miami.

JONATHON ROBERT JAMES EDWARDS is an assistant professor of kinesiology at the University of New Brunswick (Canada).

ANGIE HENDERSON is an associate professor of sociology at the University of Northern Colorado.

CHRISTINE NANCY INGOLDSBY is pursuing a PhD in sociology at the University of Northern Colorado.

CHERYL MACDONALD is a postdoctoral fellow in the Institute for Sexual Minority Studies and Services at the University of Alberta (Canada).

ASHLEY BETH MIKULYUK earned her PhD in sociology at the University of Miami.

RACHEL LAWS MYERS earned her PhD in Africana American and African studies from Michigan State University and is a teacher and coach at The Hotchkiss School.

HELEN OWTON is a chartered psychologist and a lecturer in sport and fitness at the Open University (United Kingdom).

KENNETH NATHANIEL ROBINSON is a lecturer in sociology at Buffalo State, State University of New York.

CHRISTINA SANCHEZ-VOLATIER earned her PhD in sociology at the University of Miami.

MEREDITH MARIE SCHERTZINGER is an undergraduate student in psychology at the University of Alabama at Birmingham.

MARK SHUEY is pursuing a PhD in sociology at the University of Northern Colorado.

COURTNEY SZTO is pursuing a PhD in communications at Simon Fraser University (Canada).

ANDREW J. YOUNG is a PhD candidate in sociology at Temple University.

Index